Library of
Davidson College

PERGAMON INTERNATIONAL LIBRARY
of Science, Technology, Engineering and Social Studies
*The 1000-volume original paperback library in aid of education,
industrial training and the enjoyment of leisure*
Publisher: Robert Maxwell, M.C.

THE EUROPEAN PARLIAMENT
What it is · What it does ·
How it works

THE PERGAMON TEXTBOOK
INSPECTION COPY SERVICE

An inspection copy of any book published in the Pergamon International Library
will gladly be sent to academic staff without obligation for their consideration for
course adoption or recommendation. Copies may be retained for a period of 60
days from receipt and returned if not suitable. When a particular title is adopted or
recommended for adoption for class use and the recommendation results in a sale
of 12 or more copies, the inspection copy may be retained with our compliments.
The Publishers will be pleased to receive suggestions for revised editions and new
titles to be published in this important International Library.

Other titles of interest

CLOSE
Europe Without Defense?

DE ROUGEMONT
The State of the Union of Europe

FELD
Western Europe's Global Reach
Regional Cooperation and Worldwide Interests

GOLDSMITH
Strategies for Europe
Proposals for Science and Technology Policies

KERR
The Common Market and How it Works

LONG
The Political Economy of EEC Relations with African, Caribbean and Pacific States
Contributions to the Understanding of the Lomé Convention on North-South Relations

A related Pergamon Journal

HISTORY OF EUROPEAN IDEAS

Free specimen copy gladly sent on request

Photograph courtesy of the European Parliament

THE EUROPEAN PARLIAMENT
What it is · What it does · How it works

by

MICHAEL PALMER
Deputy Director General, European Parliament

PERGAMON PRESS
Oxford · New York · Toronto · Sydney · Paris · Frankfurt

U.K.	Pergamon Press Ltd., Headington Hill Hall, Oxford OX3 0BW, England
U.S.A.	Pergamon Press Inc., Maxwell House, Fairview Park, Elmsford, New York 10523, U.S.A.
CANADA	Pergamon Press Canada Ltd., Suite 104, 150 Consumers Road, Willowdale, Ontario M2J 1P9, Canada
AUSTRALIA	Pergamon Press (Aust.) Pty. Ltd., P.O. Box 544, Potts Point, N.S.W. 2011, Australia
FRANCE	Pergamon Press SARL, 24 rue des Ecoles, 75240 Paris, Cedex 05, France
FEDERAL REPUBLIC OF GERMANY	Pergamon Press GmbH, 6242 Kronberg-Taunus, Hammerweg 6, Federal Republic of Germany

Copyright © 1981 Pergamon Press Ltd.

All Rights Reserved. No part of this publication may be reproduced, stored in a retrieval system or transmitted in any form or by any means: electronic, electrostatic, magnetic tape, mechanical, photocopying, recording or otherwise, without permission in writing from the publishers

First edition 1981

British Library Cataloguing in Publication Data

Palmer, Michael
The European Parliament
1. European Parliament
I. Title
341.24′22   JN36   80-41837

ISBN 0–08–024536–6 Hard cover
ISBN 0–08–024535–8 Flexicover

The views expressed in this book are the personal ones of the author and do not necessarily represent those of the European Parliament as an institution.

Printed in Great Britain by A. Wheaton & Co., Ltd., Exeter

This book is dedicated to the memory of

PETER KIRK

whose work for Europe was cut off by his early death

Preface

When Geoffrey Rippon suggested that I should write this book we thought at first in terms of a defence theme, but the imminence of the first direct elections to the European Parliament, and the pressing need for the British public to be informed adequately and simply about what the European Parliament is, what it does, and how it works, led us to decide that the directly elected European Parliament should be the subject.

Between Britain's entry into the Community, in January 1973, until his untimely death in April 1977, I was privileged to work closely with Peter Kirk, to whose memory this book is dedicated, in his capacity as rapporteur of the European Parliament's Political Committee concerning the powers of the Parliament and institutional problems[1]. Peter Kirk's illness and death prevented him from finishing the major report on which he worked devotedly over a period of years, and which Lord Reay eventually completed. But in making proposals concerning the future of the European Parliament I have drawn freely on some of the ideas which were developed by Peter Kirk and myself during the time we worked together.

I wish to acknowledge the valuable help given to me by those colleagues and friends who so kindly and patiently read the first draft of the book and whose many suggestions have greatly improved its accuracy, substance and style. Particular thanks are due to: Zafar Ahmad, Tim Bainbridge, Tony Barrett, William Beare, Hugh Beesley, Roland Bieber, Dunstan Curtis, David Dewar, Stavros Gavril, Jean-Guy Giraud, Paul Heim, The Earl of

---

1. Sir Peter Kirk was also, from 1973 to 1977, Chairman of the European Conservative Group and, until the arrival of British Labour members in the Parliament in 1975, Leader of the British Delegation in the European Parliament.

Listowel, Fiona MacLeod, David Millar, Eoghan O'Hannrachain, Julian Priestley and James Spence.

A number of ladies in the secretariat of the European Parliament have most generously helped to type the text, but a special debt of gratitude is owed to Vera Reckinger who was responsible for the bulk of the typing.

The main body of the text takes account of changes and developments in the Community and the European Parliament up to 1 October 1980. More recent developments of importance, up to 1 February 1981, are either mentioned in footnotes or discussed in Appendix III, including the effects of Greek accession to the Community on the operation of the Parliament. The three Appendices are up to date as of 1 February 1981. The conversion of European Units of Account and foreign currencies into £ sterling has, in all cases, been calculated at the rate obtaining on 21 April 1980.

Luxembourg,   MICHAEL PALMER
February 1981.

Contents

1.	Direct Elections	1
2.	Historical Background	19
3.	The Functions and Institutional Role of the European Parliament	25
4.	Structure and Operation	64
5.	A Member's Life	100
6.	The Future	113
7.	Conclusions	132

Appendix I:	(a) Officers and Members of the European Parliament: Essential Facts	141
	(b) Essential Facts concerning Greek Members	226
Appendix II:	Further Reading	231
Appendix III:	Recent Developments	233

1

Direct Elections

Between 7 and 10 June 1979, 111 million voters in the nine member countries of the European Community elected 410 members of the European Parliament.

The June 1979 election was not merely a long awaited event[1] in the building of the European Community, but also a revolutionary event. Revolutionary? Yes. In electing the 410 members of the new European Parliament the peoples of the Nine[2] replaced, in a single gesture of political faith, historic rivalries and struggles by a demonstration of their shared will to work together, across national frontiers, as part of a joint political system. Mainly in the European Community, but also in the Atlantic Alliance, the Council of Europe and elsewhere, governments have already sought to replace war and tensions between Western Europeans by lasting peace and economic and social stability. To a large extent they have succeeded. But the holding of direct elections went far beyond governmental action, involving as it did the direct democratic participation of the peoples of the Community in the process of European integration for the first time, and providing them with the means to influence the policies and decisions of the European Community.

Significance

What is the significance of the European election? This question is

1. The Treaty obligations concerning the holding of direct elections are set out in Chapter 2.
2. The Ten since Greek accession on 1 January 1981. For all activities of the member states since the beginning of 1981 read "The Ten" for "The Nine" throughout the book.

usually answered in terms of the effects direct elections might have on Parliament's role within the institutional structure of the Community—for instance, the possible increase of its influence on policy-making. This answer is fine as far as it goes. Indeed, much of this book is concerned with the impact of direct elections on the competences of Parliament and the institutional balance within the Community. But the real purpose of direct elections was not to inject new life into one Community institution or to make it more influential *vis-à-vis* the other European institutions. It was to give the peoples of the Community a voice and influence of their own —as expressed through their elected representatives—in the shaping and execution of Community policy. This is not explicit in the 1976 Convention on direct elections but it is implied in Article 1 of the Convention which speaks of the directly elected members as: "the representatives in the Assembly of the peoples".

Direct or village oak-tree democracy as envisaged by Rousseau cannot exist in the modern world even at the national level, let alone at the transnational level. But for the Community voter to have one or more members of the European Parliament, elected by himself, able to voice his economic or social concerns on his behalf is clearly a major advance on the previous situation in which the nominated members of the Parliament were only indirectly related to the peoples of their home countries. In Britain, with a first past the post constituency system, the voter in a European constituency will be represented by a specific member, responsible to him. In France, on the other hand, with a list system covering the whole country, an individual voter will have helped to elect all those French members of the Parliament for whose political party he voted. Even where the Community voter feels little concern with the problems dealt with by the member or members he has elected, he at least has the reassurance, except in the case of certain minority parties (of which the British Liberal Party is the largest with 1.7 million voters), of knowing that the political party for which he voted will represent and defend his broad political approach whenever Parliament plays its part in influencing EEC decisions.

It has been suggested that the Commission will derive a new degree of "legitimacy" from direct elections because of its responsibility to the European Parliament. It is difficult to verify the truth of this argument, but it seems sensible to suggest that it would be more convincing if the members of the Commission were appointed by the European Parliament as opposed to merely being capable—and so far in theory only—of being sacked by Parliament.

It has also been argued that direct elections are necessary to "legitimise" the European Community. Before direct elections, the Community was no less "legitimate", in legal terms, than other international organisations of which Britain is a member, such as NATO or the Council of Europe, since the terms of entry and membership and the degree to which concessions of national sovereignty are involved had, in each case, been negotiated and agreed by all the governments concerned and had been, to a large extent, ratified by national parliaments. On the other hand, the European Parliament itself will certainly be more "legitimate" after direct elections than before, since the direct election of its members by universal suffrage is the most characteristic and essential feature of a parliament—though not of all parliamentary chambers, such as the House of Lords, where membership is either hereditary or by appointment, or the upper houses of some national parliaments where membership can be *ex officio* or due to indirect election or royal or governmental appointment. Further, the Parliament will also be more "legitimate" now, in a second, political sense, because of the direct and continuing involvement of millions of voters in its work. Thus an informal kind of "legitimacy" is provided by contacts between electors and members of the Parliament and a more formal one by the new mandate given to members every five years.

But the key to the significance of direct elections is quite simply that it has provided for the democratic representation of the peoples in the decisions of the Community which affect their basic welfare and daily life. It is comparatively unimportant that the peoples of the member countries of NATO or the Council of Europe should be democratically represented in the decisions taken by these two bodies. Although the decisions taken by NATO and the Council of Europe can be of great importance, the interests of the peoples of the member states are adequately represented and safeguarded by national ministers in the North Atlantic Council and the Committee of Ministers of the Council of Europe and, at parliamentary level, by the MPs who are delegated by their national parliaments to sit in the North Atlantic Assembly or the Parliamentary Assembly of the Council of Europe.

The European Community is different from these inter-governmental organisations both in nature and degree. At the lowest common denominator

4 The European Parliament

level of economic and commercial life the EEC has become the arena in which most of the major decisions, and many of the minor ones, concerning the economy and trade of the member states are taken. At the less easily defined political level, the Community, even though it is not yet a federation and might never become one, is the forum in which its member governments choose to take a great proportion of their most significant decisions, with the notable exception of those in the defence and security fields which continue to be taken within the Atlantic Alliance. The priority given by the member governments to the Community in this respect is seen at its most spectacular in the "club" of heads of government of the Nine formed by the European Council, which has come into existence to meet a real need, not to satisfy any Treaty requirement. This priority is also seen in the scale of the financial commitment made by the member states to the Community, whose budget of some £10 thousand million (for 1979) represents both a major investment on the part of the governments of the Nine and a politically significant transfer of resources.

In short, the Community is the forum to which its member governments are most committed and in which they are most involved. Much of even their domestic business is a direct outcome of Community decisions. It is for these reasons that it is important that the Community peoples should be able to express their views, through a parliamentary body, concerning the whole range of subjects dealt with by the Nine.

For the European voter the effect of direct elections is to give him an additional political right. He now not only has the right to vote in local and national elections, but the right to vote and be politically represented in the Community as well. In a national context the voter can make or break governments. This he cannot do in a European Parliament election since there is no European government. But, in view of the growing importance of Community decisions on questions as diverse as agricultural prices, energy, or the entry of Greece, Portugal and Spain into the Community, this new political right to share in the election of members of the European Parliament, and through them to be able to influence Community decisions, has a significance that is directly related to the increasing proportion of major decisions which are taken by the Community rather than by individual national governments. The large size of the Community's budgetary dimension also gives the European voter an interest in indicating, through his elected representatives in the Parliament, how he wants the Community funds he provides as a Community taxpayer to be spent, and also in influencing, through Parliament, Community decisions on spending in that sense.

For the Community citizen to be able to benefit from "his" member or members of the European Parliament, he needs to know who his member is and how he can get hold of him. In Britain, which is a single-member constituency country, although there is a problem about a voter knowing who his European Parliament member is it is less grave than elsewhere. This problem is more difficult in countries like Italy, where there is a list system and in France, where theoretically at least, all 81 French members represent France as one single constituency—though in fact the party lists were established in France with due regard to regional representation and most, if not all, French members are sensitive to public opinion in their region. It is, therefore, highly desirable that constituency, regional or, at least, national headquarters are set up from which directly elected members can operate when they are in their home countries and where they can be reached either by constituents or, in countries where there are no constituencies, by those industries, trades unions, farmers' groups or individuals who wish them to defend or promote their interests at the Community level.

The problem of being able to identify and contact an appropriate member of the European Parliament is a symptom of the change in emphasis within the Community from its being an organisation geared towards elite groups and opinion leaders, as it was in the 'sixties and 'seventies, to being one appealing directly to the public for its legitimacy. As yet, it is still far from clear what facilities members of the Parliament will have in their home countries, but there is a strong case for the provision of Community financed offices and staff along the lines of, though less lavish than, the facilities provided for U.S. Congressmen.

Meanwhile, the directly elected members already receive—see Chapter 5—allowances for some research and secretarial assistance and they continue to receive the professional assistance of their political group secretariat, that of the staff of the committees of which they are members, and that of the Parliament's research service.

The need for efficient assistance for members in their home countries is underlined by the fact that they are likely to spend between 100 and 150 days a year at one or other European Parliament meeting, which means that there will be very great pressure on the limited time that they will be able to spend in their national capitals or in their constituencies. Most will

6 The European Parliament

also be deprived of the facilities provided for their predecessors by their national parliaments.

Although the go-ahead for direct elections was given by the European Council, and the governments themselves agreed on the final details included in the Convention, some governments have already made it clear that they are opposed to any significant growth in Parliament's powers. The British and French governments have both declared that treaty amendments and national parliamentary ratification are required to enable Parliament to enlarge its competences. In France, particularly, the European election campaign served as an alert to anti-integrationist political forces both of the left and of the right.

There could be one unexpected result of direct elections. In the past much of Parliament's influence was based on the close contacts that members of Parliament had, due to the fact that they were all also members of national parliaments, with their home governments. This meant that national governments could not totally ignore the views of members of the European Parliament who were colleagues of theirs and who could lobby them in their national capitals. With the great majority of directly elected members of the new Parliament having one mandate only there is a risk that the political influence that members could previously exert on their home governments, and through them on the Council, will disappear. But whereas most members of the old nominated Parliament were backbenchers in national parliamentary terms, a number of major national party leaders sit in the elected Parliament and they are likely to be concerned that their national party viewpoint should be adequately expressed in the Parliament and in Community policies.

One possible result of direct elections on the character of the Parliament could be to make it a focus for the aspirations of those regions of the Community which, like Brittany, Corsica and Scotland, have tried to obtain a greater degree of autonomy over recent years. Members from the ethnic regions might not remain satisfied with trying to obtain Regional Fund money for local projects but might also try to use Parliament and the Community's regional policy as instruments to advance their political ends.

Then there is the impact of direct elections on the political groups. This and the possibility of the development of transnational parties is examined in Chapter 4.

Following direct elections the Commission will certainly be more sensitive than ever before both to Parliament as a whole and to individual members. It is interesting to speculate as to whether the Commission will become "coloured" politically in view of the political majority in the new Parliament. Will the centre-right majority of Christian Democrats, Conservatives and Liberals insist, for instance, that Commission proposals should reflect the views of the political majority? If the centre-right majority in Parliament considers that the Commission's proposals, on major areas of policy, are too "left" or "socialist" will this lead to confrontation and the use by Parliament of its power to censure the Commission or attempts to sack Commissioners whose political views do not correspond with those of the majority in Parliament? Any development of this kind would fundamentally change the character of the Commission, which until now has always acted as the "honest broker" of the Community, putting forward proposals that are neutral in a party political sense, in the interests of the Community as a whole. Will this continue to be the case?

Only time will tell whether direct elections will have a major impact on Parliament's relations with the member governments in the Council. In particular, will direct elections lead the Council to pay greater attention to Parliament's resolutions and give greater weight to Parliament's opinions on Commission legislative proposals? *Prima facie* it is unlikely that the Council will feel obliged to change its attitude towards Parliament simply because Parliament's members now sit as directly elected representatives of the peoples. But, looking at this problem from another angle it seems that European elections have already given the directly elected members additional confidence, both in themselves and in Parliament as an institution, in their attempts to obtain a more cooperative response from the governments and a greater degree of political accountability from them.

The Vote

Voting participation averaged 62.8% throughout the Community but it varied greatly from country to country. In Belgium, over 91% of the electorate went to the polls. In Luxembourg the proportion of those voting was nearly as high. But the most impressive demonstration of interest in the election was in Italy, where in one of the largest member states, and only one week after national elections, the turnout was over 85%. In

8 The European Parliament

Britain there was a poor showing of under 33% of registered voters. In Britain, as in Italy, the European election had been shortly preceded by a national election. The policy of the British Labour Party concerning the preparation of the election campaign, the selection of candidates, and the encouragement of party supporters to actually turn out to vote, showed an ambiguity towards the election which did much to account for the record of Labour voters. Whereas in Italy the success or failure of the different parties in the national election of the previous week did not discourage the Italian people from massive voting in the European Parliament election, the victory of the Conservatives in the British national election seems to have discouraged Labour voters from polling a second time.

In comparing national figures it is only fair to remember that voters in Belgium, Italy and Luxembourg were obliged, under national law, to vote, whereas in Britain, as in the remaining Community member states, there was neither a legal obligation to vote nor a financial penalty if electors did not have a good reason for failing to vote.

A number of fascinating questions could be discussed in a full-length study of the first European election. Regrettably the present brief general guide does not provide the appropriate framework for examination of questions of this kind. Some of them can be raised but not answered here. Why were there differences between member states in levels of turn-out? Could these differences have been due to different public attitudes towards the European Community, different levels of media coverage, different electoral systems, different types of candidates or different electoral organisations? How did the European election results compare with the most recent previous national election results or polls? Was there a "European dimension" in voting patterns? Did the three "new" member states—Britain, Denmark and Ireland—vote differently from the old?

The Results

In the directly elected Parliament Britain, France, Germany and Italy have 81 seats each, the Netherlands having 25, Belgium 24, Denmark 16, Ireland 15 and Luxembourg 6.

Direct Elections

The Socialists won[1] 112 seats in the European Parliament, with 26.6% of votes cast throughout the Community, making them the largest group in the Parliament. The Group of the European People's Party (formerly the Christian Democratic Group) gained 108 seats with 29.5% of the total vote. The European Democratic Group (formerly the European Conservative Group) won 63 seats, with a vote of 6.2%. The Communist and Allies Group obtained 44 seats, with 13.5% of the vote. The Liberal and Democratic Group obtained 40 seats, with a vote of 10.6%. The Group of European Progressive Democrats won 22 seats, with 3.5% of the vote. The Group for the Technical Coordination and Defence of Independent Groups and Members won 11 seats, with roughly 3.0% of the vote. Finally, 9 non-attached members who represent a 2.0% "cocktail" of the vote were also elected. Although the Socialist Group is the largest single group in the Parliament, the rough and ready voting alliances between the Group of the European People's Party (EPP) and the European Democratic Group, and to some extent, the Liberals, which operate concerning many of the questions debated in Parliament, provide these parties of the "centre-right" with an effective working majority.

In order to fight the European election campaign many of the political parties of the member states formed transnational federations to work out joint electoral platforms which could be advocated and defended by their candidates[2]. This was true for the Socialists, the Christian Democrats and the Liberals of the Nine. Despite the continuing friction between the French and Italian Communists, the Italian Communist leader, Mr Enrico Berlinguer, campaigned for the French Communist Party in south-eastern France.

National Round-up

In Belgium the electoral system used was to divide the country into a Flemish constituency of 13 seats, and a French-speaking Walloon constituency of 11 seats, with voters in Brussels, the bilingual capital city, being

1. The present composition of the political groups, which has changed since the elections, is analysed, in national and party terms, in Chapter 4. The figures given here for the electoral results represent the situation on 17 July 1979, the first day's sitting of the new Parliament.
2. Relations between the political groups in the Parliament and the transnational federations are outlined in Chapter 4.

able to vote for candidates on either the French or Flemish lists. The Christian Democrats won 10 seats, the Socialists 7 seats, the Liberals 4, and the smaller parties 3. The former Prime Minister, Mr Leo Tindemans, a Fleming, was elected in Brussels, which is predominantly French-speaking, with a large personal vote. Other prominent personalities elected included Baron Charles-Ferdinand Nothomb, President of the Chamber of Deputies, and Mr Jean Rey, former President of the EEC Commission[1].

For direct elections, the whole of Denmark was a single electoral area, with a method of proportional representation. The most successful party was the "Anti-Common Market Party", which won 4 of the 16 seats, with the Social Democrats winning 3, the Conservatives 2, the Socialist People's Party 1 and the Centre Democrats 1. The Greenland seat was won by a local candidate, Mr Lynge, who advocated a referendum on Greenland's withdrawal from the Community. The 4 Anti-Common Market members sit, in the European Parliament, in the very diverse Group for the Technical Coordination and Defence of Independent Groups and Members. As the name of their party indicates, they are opposed to Danish membership of the Community and wish to secure Denmark's withdrawal. Niels Jørgen Haagerup, a leading foreign affairs commentator, is one of the most prominent Danish members of the Parliament.

For the European elections the whole of France was considered to be one constituency, for which all 81 members were elected. The voting system used was that of party lists on a nation-wide scale with proportional representation. Parties obtaining less than 5% of the vote are not represented in the Parliament. An alliance of centre-right groupings, led by Mrs Simone Veil, Minister of Public Health and Family Affairs in the French Government immediately before direct elections, who was elected as first President of the new Parliament in July 1979, was the big winner, taking 26 seats (moving up from 25 after a recount, with the Socialists dropping down, after the recount, from 22 to 21). The Socialists won 21, the Communists 19, and the Gaullists 15. The Socialists lodged an appeal concerning the election results in view of the acceptance by the returning officers of a number of "spoiled" ballot papers. They have since obtained an additional member of the Parliament, following the resignation of a

---

1. Baron Nothomb and Mr Rey have both subsequently left the Parliament, Baron Northomb to become Foreign Minister of Belgium and Mr Rey to retire from political life.

French member of the Group of the European People's Party. Those elected included a number of leading politicians such as Jacques Chirac, former Prime Minister and Mayor of Paris, Michel Debré, former Prime Minister, Edgar Faure, former Prime Minister and former President of the National Assembly, Maurice Faure, signatory of the Rome Treaties and former minister, Jean Lecanuet, President of the *Union pour la démocratie française* and of the *Centre des Démocrates Sociaux*, Georges Marchais, Secretary General of the French Communist Party, Pierre Messmer, former Prime Minister, François Mitterand, Leader of the French Socialist Party, Pierre Pflimlin, former Prime Minister and Mayor of Strasbourg, and Michel Poniatowski, former Minister of the Interior and honorary President of the *Parti républicain*.[1]

In Germany, where the parties had the choice of a regional *Land* list or a national list, with proportional representation, parties not obtaining 5% of the vote were not entitled to be represented in the Parliament. The Berlin members were nominated under the terms of the Four-Power agreements on Berlin. Although the former Chancellor of the Federal Republic, Willy Brandt, was elected at the head of the SPD list, the Socialists did less well than they had hoped, winning only 35 seats compared with the CDU/CSU alliance which won 42 seats. The Liberal Party, the FDP, won 4 seats. Prominent German members of the former Parliament who were elected included Martin Bangemann, Leader of the Liberal Group in the nominated and the elected Parliament, Ludwig Fellermaier, Chairman of the Socialist Group in the former Parliament, and Egon Klepsch, Chairman of the Christian Democratic Group in the nominated Parliament and Chairman of its successor Group, the Group of the European People's Party in the elected Parliament. Prominent newcomers include Katharina Focke, former Minister for Youth, Family and Health Affairs in the Federal Government, Bruno Friedrich, Vice-Chairman of the SPD in the Bundestag, Alfons Goppel, former Prime Minister of Bavaria, Otto Habsburg, commentator on the international scene, Kai-Uwe von Hassel, former Federal Defence Minister, former President of both the Bundestag and Bundesrat, and former Prime Minister of Schleswig-Holstein, Johann Katzer, former Federal Minister for Labour and Social Affairs, Heinz Kühn, former Prime Minister of Nordrhein-Westphalen, and Heinz

1. Mr Chirac, Mr Debré, Mr Messmer and Mr Mitterand have resigned from the Parliament.

Oskar Vetter, President of the German federation of trades unions and former Chairman of the International Confederation of Free Trade Unions.

In Ireland the single transferable vote system (STV) applied in 3, 4 or 5-member seats based on 4 constituencies. The government party, Fianna Fail, won 5 seats, with Fine Gael and Labour each winning 4. The other 2 seats were won by independents. Amongst those elected were Mark Clinton, former Minister for Agriculture, Jeremiah Cronin, former Minister for Defence, Michael O'Leary, deputy leader of the Irish Labour Party, Richie Ryan, former Finance Minister, and Sile de Valera, granddaughter of Eamon de Valera, first Prime Minister of the Irish Republic.

For direct elections Italy used a form of proportional representation with regional lists operating in 5 constituencies. The Christian Democrats, headed by the President of the outgoing European Parliament, former Prime Minister of Italy, Emilio Colombo, won 29 seats, the Communists 24, the Socialists 9, the Social Democrats and the Neo-Fascists (MSI) 4 each, the Liberals and the Radicals 3 each, with the 5 remaining seats being divided between smaller parties—the South Tyrol *Volkspartei* member sitting alongside the 29 Italian Christian Democrats in the Group of the European People's Party. The list of candidates included many outstanding personalities, and amongst those elected were Susanna Agnelli, a member of one of Italy's best known industrialist families, Giorgio Amendola, leader of the right wing of the Italian Communist Party, Maria Baduel Gloriosa, former President of the European Community's Economic and Social Committee, Enrico Berlinguer, Secretary General of the Italian Communist Party, Vincenzo Bettiza, a prominent journalist, Bettino Craxi, Secretary of the Italian Socialist Party, Marco Pannella, Chairman of the Radical Party, Mariano Rumor, former Prime Minister, and Altiero Spinelli, former member of the EEC Commission.[1]

The whole of Luxembourg formed one constituency for direct elections with a proportional representation list system, operating under a *"panachage"* method by which voters could vote for candidates from different political parties. The Christian Socialist People's Party won 3 seats, the Democratic Party 2, and the Socialist Workers Party 1. Although two former Prime Ministers, Pierre Werner and Gaston Thorn, were amongst the 6 Luxembourg members elected both of them resigned in order to

1. Mr Colombo resigned from the Parliament in the spring of 1980 in order to become Foreign Minister of Italy. Mr Amendola died in the summer of 1980.

become Prime Minister and Deputy Prime Minister, respectively, in the new government. Colette Flesch, Mayor of Luxembourg town, is prominent amongst those members who took up their places.[1]

The Netherlands formed one national constituency for the June 1979 election. Of the 25 Dutch members elected 10 were Christian Democrats, 9 Socialists, 4 Liberals and 2 from the Democrats '66 Party. Amongst those elected were the Socialists Pieter Dankert, a veteran of the outgoing Parliament and of other international assemblies, and Anne Vondeling, former leader of the Labour Party and Speaker of the Second Chamber (killed in a car accident in November 1979), whereas the Liberals included a former President of the Parliament, Cornelis Berkhouwer, and Hans Nord, Secretary General of the outgoing Parliament.

Finally, in Britain, the Conservatives, with six and a half million voters, representing 50.6% of the British poll, won 60 seats. Labour, with four and a quarter million voters, representing 33% of the poll, took 17 seats. Although polling nearly 1.7 million votes and over 13% of the total vote, the Liberals won no seats at all. The SNP returned their one member of the old Parliament, Mrs Winifred Ewing on 1.9% of the vote. As opposed to the other eight member states of the Community which all made use of some form of proportional representation for direct elections, Britain used the first past the post system in the 78 single-member constituencies in England (66), Wales (4) and Scotland (8). In the one three-seat constituency in Northern Ireland the single transferable vote (STV) method was used. The Ulster Unionists won 1 seat in Ulster, the Social Democratic and Labour Party 1 seat, and the Reverend Ian Paisley took the third seat for his Democratic Union Party.

Those elected to the new Parliament included on the Conservative side, James Scott-Hopkins, leader of the European Conservative Group in the nominated Parliament and now leader of the European Democratic Group, a few members of the outgoing Parliament, and a high proportion of newcomers including Sir Fred Catherwood, former Chief Economic Advisor at the Department of Economic Affairs, and formerly both Director-General of the National Economic Development Council and Chairman of the British Overseas Trade Board, Basil de Ferranti, former President of the European Community's Economic and Social Committee, Baroness

1. Miss Flesch has become Foreign Minister of Luxembourg and Mr Thorn has since become President of the Commission.

14 The European Parliament

Elles, Chairman of the European Union of Women and former Opposition Spokesman on Commonwealth and foreign affairs in the House of Lords, Edward and Elaine Kellett-Bowman, a husband and wife team, Sir Henry Plumb, formerly President of the National Farmers' Union and of COPA (the EEC farmers' association) and Chairman of the British Agricultural Council, and Sir Fred Warner, former ambassador to Laos, the UN and Japan. If the result of the election was a disappointment to Labour supporters, the Labour members elected included the best known British member of the Parliament, Barbara Castle, formerly Minister for Overseas Development, Minister of Transport, Secretary of State for Employment, Secretary of State for the Social Services, member of the National Executive and former Chairman of the Labour Party. Otherwise the Labour members elected include a smaller number of well known names than the Conservatives, though Janey Buchan is Chairman of the Labour Party in Scotland. A feature of the election in Britain was the disqualification of Miss Shelagh Roberts, a Conservative, for "holding an office of profit under the crown"—membership of the Occupational Pensions Board, the "profit" being £355 for the financial year 1978–79 before tax! At the ensuing by-election Miss Roberts won in a very low poll against lively opposition from the Liberal candidate, Mr Christopher Mayhew.

Electoral Anomalies

Many of the anomalies between the different electoral systems used by the member states, notably that distinguishing the British single-member constituency system from the continental method of proportional representation, are due to be eliminated if member governments accept the proposals for a uniform electoral method that Parliament is obliged to make during its first five-year term under Article 7 of the Convention on direct elections agreed by the member governments in September 1976. But, as indicated in Chapter 3, it is by no means certain that all governments will be prepared to accept a uniform electoral system for the second European elections due to be held in 1984. The most obvious of these anomalies—the lack of proportionality in the British system—led to the Conservatives, who had a 17% greater share of the poll than Labour, returning more than three times as many members, and to the Liberals not having even one member to represent their 1.7 million voters. Another anomaly is that of the ratio of voters to members in different countries and regions. Thus, whereas the 5 million population of Scotland elects only 8 members, the same number of Danes are represented by 16 members and 380,000 Luxembourgers by 6. There is, however, a reason for this anomaly. Whereas Scotland is not an independent country, Denmark and Luxembourg are states, and the member governments, in fixing the number of members of the Parliament, recognised that the adequate representation of national interests was essential in the new Parliament. Thus the larger member states are under-represented in the Parliament compared with the smaller ones.

Some results of these anomalies come to light in the way that members behave in Parliament. For instance, in a speech made in one of the first debates held in the directly elected Parliament, Mr Pflimlin stated that he was "speaking for the electors of France", whereas in the same debate some British Conservative members who took part made it clear that they were speaking on behalf of specific and identified industrial firms in their own constituencies. One of the many paradoxes of the directly elected Parliament is that the 60 British Conservatives, who, together with 3 Danish members, form the European Democratic Group, constitute the third largest political group in the Parliament. The British Conservatives secured 50.6% of the very low United Kingdom total poll, of 12,874,000 voters, which in turn represented a mere 31.8% of the potential British electorate—by far the lowest national percentage turn-out in the Community.[1] But the British Conservative members have not yet been accused in Parliament's chamber of being less "representative" than any other members on that score. One minor, but interesting, feature of the European election in Britain was that it gave peers, for the first time, the right to seek and win electoral office at the national level.

The Members

The membership of the directly elected Parliament is extremely varied. First, there are a number of "big names" from the current European political scene or from recent history, such as those mentioned in the national round-up above.

1. These figures exclude Northern Ireland, in view of its different electoral system.

16 The European Parliament

Second, 77 of the directly elected members were already members of the old nominated European Parliament—of whom 67 sat in the last nominated Parliament. These members can play a particularly valuable role in handing on to the new members the political and procedural traditions established in the former Parliament. They included at the beginning of the new Parliament Ernest Glinne, the Belgian chairman of the Socialist Group, Egon Klepsch, the German chairman of the Group of the European People's Party (EPP), James Scott-Hopkins, the British chairman of the European Democrats, Giorgio Amendola, the Italian chairman of the Communist Group, Martin Bangemann, the German chairman of the Liberal and Democratic Group and Christian de la Malène, the French chairman of the Group of European Progressive Democrats.

It is no coincidence that the chairmen of all the larger political groups were members of the old nominated Parliament. They provide continuity and a considerable collective knowledge of the operation of all aspects of Parliament's work.

Third, there are a number of members who have already achieved distinction in their own professions and careers, without ever having sat in national Parliaments, and who can bring their knowledge and experience to bear on "their" subjects. These include, for instance, on the British side, Sir Fred Catherwood, former Chief Economic Adviser at the Department of Economic Affairs, and Sir Henry Plumb, former President of the National Farmers' Union.

Fourth, a high proportion of new members are parliamentary novices who still have most of their political career ahead of them. In the near future it is perhaps in the hands of these "unknowns" that the development of the European Parliament mainly lies, since most of them share the aim of making their name in and through the Parliament. Many of these "new boys" have a refreshing degree of political enthusiasm and conviction.

A striking feature of the directly elected Parliament is the high proportion of women members. 66 women members out of 410 give the Parliament a higher proportion of women parliamentarians than any other Western parliament, except the Danish. This compares with the 17 women who sit in the House of Commons out of 635 members.

125 members of the Parliament hold a dual mandate, being also members of their national Parliaments. This important nucleus of national parliamentarians provides the European Parliament with the personal links with

national parliaments which are so necessary in the period of transition during which the members of the new Parliament have to learn how to stand on their own political feet without, in most cases, being able to call on the political resources and parliamentary facilities which were available to them in the old Parliament. The switch from the dual mandate system which was universal in the nominated Parliament to what is now essentially a single mandate system will mean that three-quarters of the new members will be able to give their work as European parliamentarians the full-time attention it needs. This should enable Parliament and its committees to work in greater depth than in the past with regard to both Parliament's legislative and budgetary roles, and, also, its supervision of the Commission.

What can the Member do for his Voters?

One of the most useful techniques available to members of the European Parliament is the right to table questions to the Commission, the Council and the Foreign Ministers, the purpose of these questions being either to obtain information or to raise issues of Community policy. The instrument of the parliamentary question can easily be adapted to respond to the needs of constituents, pressure groups and lobbyists, as in national parliaments.

Directly elected members are also likely to try to influence the member governments and the institutions with regard to Community expenditure so that their constituencies, regions, countries or the industries or types of farming in which they are interested can profit from Commission grants for research, modernisation or reconversion. When it comes to deciding how the major Community funds are to be spent, particularly the Regional and Social funds, members will be under pressure from their fellow countrymen or their constituents to influence governmental and Community decisions so as to channel Community money in their direction. There is likely to be competition between members from different countries and regions to obtain Community finance for projects in their areas. This could have a bearing on their success in being re-elected.

Directly elected members of the Parliament will enjoy greater status and prestige than their predecessors in the non-elected parliament. Instead of being sent to Luxembourg and Strasbourg by their parties for a variety of reasons—some of them very strange reasons indeed—the new members can point, with some pride, to the massive numbers of voters whom they represent. In itself, the election is bound to add greater weight and greater significance to Parliament's activities simply because the new member is a different political animal from the old one. It is clear, also, that most of the directly elected members feel frustrated by the modest role played by Parliament within the Community at present and that they will try to increase Parliament's competences and its political influence. The prospects of their being able to do so are examined in Chapter 6.

2

Historical Background

The European Parliament was a product of the confused but dynamic movement to achieve European unity that marked the late 1940s and early 1950s. When it became clear to the six states which were to create the European Coal and Steel Community (ECSC) that the Council of Europe would not succeed in achieving European unity, because of the refusal of Britain and the Scandinavian countries to go beyond limited measures of intergovernmental cooperation and to accept European federation as a goal, the frustrated President of the Council of Europe's Assembly, Mr Paul-Henri Spaak, resigned in December 1951. From then on the idea of a distinct supranational Community of the Six gained momentum.

The proposal put forward by Mr Robert Schuman on behalf of the French Government in May 1950, by which the resources of the French and German coal and steel industries were to be placed under a common authority in an organisation open to other European countries, met with immediate support from the Six who signed the ECSC Treaty in April 1951. In signing the Treaty of Paris, the Six made it clear that the ECSC was only a beginning and their next aim was the establishment of a full economic community which was to lead in turn to political integration. Britain refused to join the ECSC since it was not prepared to accept the transfer of control over its coal and steel industries, nor was it prepared to accept economic, let alone political integration. This decision was to cut off Britain from the mainstream of European integration until January 1973, when it finally joined the Common Market.

The ECSC began work in 1952. In marked contrast to the Council of Europe the ECSC had limited but real powers in that it was entrusted with supervising the coal and steel industries of its member states. As opposed to the Consultative Assembly of the Council of Europe which, from the beginning, has been primarily a forum for debate, the parliamentary assembly of the ECSC, the Common Assembly, had real political responsibilities deriving from its power to supervise the activities of the executive of the ECSC, the High Authority. The Assembly consisted of 78 members of Parliament designated by their national parliaments. A significant phrase of Article 20 of the ECSC Treaty stated that they were "representatives of the peoples of the Member States brought together in the Community"—a first hint of a direct democratic mandate. A second hint was contained in the original wording of Article 21 which held out the possibility of members—if they were not appointed by their national parliaments —being "elected by direct universal suffrage".

The main power conferred upon the Common Assembly by the Treaty of Paris was that of being able to force the High Authority to resign by vote of censure. This gave the Common Assembly a comparatively greater role within the ECSC than the European Parliament enjoys, constitutionally, within the present merged Community of the Nine, since the High Authority was responsible for taking most of the decisions governing the work of the ECSC whereas in today's Community it is the Council—which is responsible not to the European Parliament but to national governments and parliaments—which takes decisions. The main single task given to the Common Assembly was that of debating the High Authority's annual report. Members of the Common Assembly were able to put questions to the High Authority. Finally, it was able to make proposals concerning its own budget and to appoint its own independent secretariat. The members of the Common Assembly soon showed their dissatisfaction with the limits of the role given to them under the Treaty and made it clear that political supervision of the High Authority rather than technical control was their aim. In his study *The Parliament of the European Communities*,[1] Murray Forsyth comments: "The main objective of the Assembly in furthering this aim was to extend its powers from those of *a posteriori* criticism of the actions of the High Authority and the Council, into those of *a priori* initiative and guidance. In this it achieved no small measure of success. In the matter of the Community budget . . . it was able to extend its supervisory powers. And in several other fields—but most strikingly in those of

1. PEP, London, 1964.

social and transport policy—the Assembly succeeded in pushing the High Authority and Council along the path which it had previously mapped out."

As opposed to the parliamentary assemblies of the classical intergovernmental organisations, such as the Council of Europe and Western European Union, where members sit and operate primarily in national delegations, the Common Assembly pioneered a new approach that was to be significant for the future. Political groups were first recognised in the Assembly in June 1953 and three groups were set up—the Christian Democrats, the Liberals and the Socialists. From then on members sat, worked and voted by party groups rather than by national delegations.

Early in the history of the Common Assembly a major but abortive episode occurred in the development of European integration in which the Assembly played a fascinating role. Following the outbreak of the war in Korea in June 1950, the U.S. Government demanded a German contribution to the defence of the Central European front. France refused to agree to German rearmament and to Germany becoming a member of NATO. Public opinion in Britain was uneasy. On their side, the Germans refused to rearm unless they were given full equality of rights. In this tense situation Mr René Pleven proposed, in October 1950, on behalf of the French Government, the creation of a European army to which each participating state would contribute its European military resources and which would be jointly controlled. A conference was held in Paris on the "Pleven plan" in February 1951 and by November of that year the six members of the ECSC had agreed to take part in a European army. In December, the Foreign Ministers of the Six declared their intention of establishing a European Defence Community (EDC) under the control of a Joint Defence Commission and a Council of Ministers, with an Assembly and a Court of Justice parallel to the institutions of the ECSC.

Although Churchill had, in his Zurich speech of 19 September 1946, been the first to propose the idea of "a European army in which we all will play a full and honourable part", and although the British Government hoped that the EDC would come into being and offered to cooperate closely with it, it refused to join the proposed Community. The EDC Treaty was signed in May 1952 and was ratified by five of the six national parliaments. But in August 1954 the French National Assembly refused ratification and the EDC collapsed. Before the EDC Treaty was submitted to the national parliaments for ratification the Foreign Ministers of the Six had already begun to explore the possibility of creating a European Political Community (EPC). They requested the Common Assembly, together with nine co-opted members from the Consultative Assembly of the Council of Europe, to study the creation of a European political authority. This joint group became the *Ad Hoc* Assembly.

In March 1953, the *Ad Hoc* Assembly made detailed proposals to the Foreign Ministers of the Six, including the establishment of a European Political Community which would incorporate both the ECSC and the EDC. The institutions would include a directly elected Parliament and the supreme executive authority was to be vested in a European Executive Council and a Council of National Ministers. These proposals were set out in a "Draft Treaty embodying the statute of the European Community". This remarkable attempt to extend the sphere of European integration to include the sensitive areas of defence and foreign policy could only succeed if the EDC were set up, so when the French Parliament failed to ratify the EDC Treaty the EPC project failed as well. In view of more recent suggestions concerning the institutional form of a possible "European Union" and the proposals that are sometimes made for transforming the European Parliament into a bicameral Parliament,[1] it is interesting to recall that the Parliament proposed in the *Ad Hoc* Assembly's draft was to consist of two chambers. There was to have been a People's Chamber of 286 directly elected members and a Senate of 87 members chosen by national parliaments. The legislative initiative in EPC was to have been shared between the Parliament and the European Executive Council. In 1952 Mr Michel Debré, as a member of the *Ad Hoc* Assembly, drafted a Pact for the Union of European States as an alternative to the draft EPC Treaty with which he disagreed. In this Union a Political Council, composed of Heads of Government, was to define policy and take binding decisions by majority vote. Mr Debré's scheme clearly influenced subsequent French Government proposals including the Confederation of States proposed by General de Gaulle and the proposals to create a Political Secretariat which were discussed in the early 1960s.

The problem of how to rearm Germany in a manner acceptable to France was soon solved by the creation of Western European Union (WEU).

1. See, for instance, Valentine Herman and Juliet Lodge *The European Parliament and the European Community*, Macmillan, London, 1978.

The Six were not deterred by the failure of their plans to create supranational defence and political communities and they returned to the attack on the economic front. At Messina, in June 1955, the Foreign Ministers of the Six proposed the establishment of an industrial common market and an atomic energy pool. Mr Paul-Henri Spaak, then Belgian Foreign Minister, was made Chairman of a special group to consider how these proposals could be achieved. The report of the Spaak group was the basis of the intergovernmental negotiations which followed and which led to the signature of the EEC and Euratom Treaties in Rome in March 1957.

At first the EEC and Euratom existed separately alongside the ECSC, each possessing its own Commission and Council of Ministers though sharing a single Court of Justice. Largely due to the efforts of members of the Common Assembly it was decided not to have a separate parliamentary assembly for each of the three communities but for the Common Assembly to be transformed into a new single assembly for the three Communities— the European Parliamentary Assembly. In March 1962, the European Parliamentary Assembly decided to take the name "European Parliament".

The new Parliament's membership was enlarged to 142, which was further enlarged to 198 in January 1973 when Britain, Denmark and Ireland became members of the Community.

For the Parliament the most significant feature of the EEC Treaty was the inclusion in it of a paragraph in Article 138 which stated: "The Assembly shall draw up proposals for elections by direct universal suffrage in accordance with a uniform procedure in all Member States".

From its establishment in its new form as the Assembly of the three Communities, the European Parliament showed a keen interest in acting on these instructions given to it by the Treaty. In October 1958 its Political Committee set up a working party under Mr Fernand Dehousse to make specific proposals. Parliament adopted a Convention on direct elections based on the Dehousse draft in May 1960. But the Parliament's Convention had to be approved, under Article 138, by all the governments.

Following initial resistance by the French Government, the Council consistently refused, in the following years, even to discuss the Convention. But at the meeting held by the European Council in Brussels in July 1976, the governments decided that direct elections should be held to the Parliament in May or June of 1978 and that the directly elected Parliament should consist of 410 members. The Convention that was approved by the

Council of Ministers in September 1976 (technically in the form of a "decision" to adopt an "Act") was largely founded on a new set of proposals adopted by the European Parliament on the basis of a report written by Mr Schelto Patijn. Because of delays in ratification and enabling legislation direct elections were not held until June 1979.

3

The Functions and Institutional Role of the European Parliament

The three institutions of the Community which are mainly responsible for Community legislation and which are most closely involved in the Community decision-making process are the European Parliament, the Commission and the Council of Ministers. Before discussing the part played by the European Parliament in the work of the European Community it might be useful to outline the main tasks of the other Community bodies which include the Court of Justice, the Economic and Social Committee, the European Investment Bank and the Court of Auditors.[1]

The Commission

The Commission, whose main headquarters are in Brussels, with an outpost in Luxembourg, consists of thirteen members[2] (two from each of the larger member states and one from each of the smaller countries) appointed by the member governments, but theoretically independent of them. The Commission performs three main functions. First, it initiates

---

1. Of the Community's total staff of 15,000 some 10,000 work for the Commission, with the Council and the Parliament having a secretariat of 2,000 each and the Court of Justice and the Court of Auditors 250 each.
2. Fourteen, including the Greek Commissioner, since 1 January 1981.

26 The European Parliament

Community legislation, playing the honest broker in promoting compromises between the different interests involved. Second, it administers, on a day to day basis, the decisions taken by the Council of Ministers. Third, it is the watchdog or guardian of the Treaties, ensuring that the Treaties and all subsequent Community laws are fully observed.

The Council

The Council of Ministers consists of one member of each government. In its "normal" form this is the Minister for Foreign Affairs. But in practice, there is a wide range of different specialist Councils of Ministers, each covering a major area of Community activity such as agriculture, finance or transport. The Foreign Ministers try to coordinate and supervise the work of the specialised Councils. The Council of Ministers has developed in two significant ways not foreseen by the Treaties. Above the ordinary Council the Prime Ministers of the member states—its President in the case of France—meeting three times a year, have formed the "European Council". This, although not formally part of the Community, acts as a "Super-Council" deciding on the reactions of the Nine to important problems and launching major Community initiatives, such as the creation of the European Monetary System.

Below the ordinary Council a Committee of Permanent Representatives, known as COREPER, the acronym for the French title of this body, has developed—officially recognised for the first time in the Merger Treaty[1] —which helps the Council in the preparation of its decisions and itself effectively takes decisions on many technical points known as "A-points", where these are judged, in agreement with the Council, to be uncontroversial. The Council of Ministers has a dual nature, since its members defend national interests as well as taking decisions on behalf of the Community as a whole.

The most supranational element in the Treaties is the obligation that the Council should take almost half its decisions by majority. But since the "Luxembourg Agreement" or "Compromise" of January 1966 which ended the struggle between the French Government under President de

1. The Treaty of April 1965 under which a single Council and a single Commission were created common to all three Communities—EEC, EURATOM and ECSC.

The Functions and Institutional Role of the European Parliament 27

Gaulle, and the Commission under Professor Hallstein, overtly concerning regulations financing the Common Agricultural Policy, but in reality concerning the political and institutional character of the Community and its future, most decisions have been taken by unanimity, it being agreed that the "vital interests" of a member state cannot be overruled. General de Gaulle described majority decisions as "pretentious, founded on abusive myths and opposed to common sense and reality". But, on another occasion, the former Belgian Prime Minister, Mr Paul-Henri Spaak defended the majority principle for the following reasons: "I have always opposed what people call *"l'Europe des patries"*. I consider this idea to be inadequate and insufficient. The unanimity rule leads us finally into the situation in which the stubborn nature of one country's attitude makes the majority accept the policy of the minority. I am against the veto in the United Nations and against the unanimity rule in NATO. I cannot see how there can be any progress in European unification unless we move on to qualified majority voting in economic affairs and majority decisions for political matters." Although the Heads of Government agreed in December 1974 that "it is necessary to renounce the practice which consists of making agreement on all questions conditional on the unanimous consent of the member states, whatever their respective positions may be regarding the conclusions reached in Luxembourg on 28 January 1966" unanimity still applies to major decisions in the Council of Ministers.

Since the "Luxembourg Agreement" the balance of power inside the Community has shifted from the Commission to the Council. The political edge of the Commission's right to initiate legislation has been blunted. Whereas formerly a Commission proposal could, in most cases, only be changed by a majority of member states, now the onus is on the Commission to find unanimous backing for its proposals after consulting the governments to ensure that its new proposal is acceptable to them. In short, the governments' power to dispose has become more important than the Commission's power to propose. Britain, Denmark and France, which have in recent years viewed the more supranational or federal strands within the Community with scarcely concealed hostility, have taken advantage of the "Luxembourg Agreement" to underline the significance of national sovereignty.

The Commission's role has been further undermined by major policy proposals introduced by the European Council. It has been proposals of the European Council which have led to the decisions to establish the European Monetary System and to hold direct elections to the European Parliament. Thus the Commission no longer monopolises the right to make policy proposals even if it continues to hold the sole formal right of legislative initiative, that is to say under the Treaties legislative proposals must be formulated by the Commission, even if another body has already put forward the original ideas.

The Court of Justice

The Court of Justice, which is based at Luxembourg, has to ensure that the law is observed "in the interpretation and the application" of the Treaties under which the Community was established. The Court consists of nine Judges,[1] appointed by agreement between the member states, assisted by four Advocates-General. It is competent to judge cases resulting from non-observance or infringement of the Treaties. These may be brought before it by the Commission, Council, member states or firms and individuals, including Community staff. The Court's rulings are binding and are not subject to appeal. Despite the many difficulties in relating national to Community law, in general decisions of the Court have been accepted. However, there have been occasions when British and French national courts have not consulted the Court of Justice, concerning competence, in cases where that might have been appropriate. In other cases governments, notably the British in the tachometer ("black box in the cabin") affair and the Italian, in an art treasures export tax case, have taken as long as two years to implement rulings of the Court. The French Government has not yet implemented fully a ruling of the Court of September 1979 concerning imports of British lamb and mutton. But in the great majority of cases the Court's decisions are applied without question, and if the Treaties are the basis of Community law a new dimension of Community law has been added by the corpus of case-law and precedents built up by the Court's decisions.

The Economic and Social Committee

The Economic and Social Committee which is composed of "repre-

1. Ten, including the Greek judge, since 1 January 1981.

sentatives of the various categories of economic and social life" includes representatives of employers' organisations, trades unions and consumer groups. Although not strictly speaking a Community institution, the Committee's opinions concerning Commission proposals are generally taken seriously by the Commission, since they reflect the views of highly qualified experts.

The European Investment Bank

The European Investment Bank, which operates on a non-profit basis, grants loans and provides financial guarantees for the financing of projects in less developed regions of the Community, in cases where these cannot be financed by national means, and finances projects in the African, Caribbean and Pacific countries which are associated with the Community under the Lomé Convention, and other developing countries.

The Court of Auditors

The Court of Auditors, which started work in 1977, is charged with examining "the accounts of all revenue and expenditure of the Community" and with examining "whether all revenue has been received and all expenditure incurred in a lawful and regular manner and whether the financial management has been sound". The Treaties specifically oblige the Court "to assist the Assembly and the Council in exercising their powers of control over the implementation of the budget".

The European Parliament

The role of the European Parliament in the operation of the Community is outlined in the most general way in Article 137 of the EEC Treaty which states that "the Assembly shall exercise the advisory and supervisory powers which are conferred upon it by this Treaty". In itself this phrase poses a problem. Whereas the Treaties refer to "the Assembly" the Parliament decided in 1962 that its title should be "the European Parliament"—though French Gaullist members of the Parliament continue to use the word "Assembly". Since then a favourite pastime of political scientists has been to discuss, with great sophistication, whether the European Parliament is a mere assembly or a real parliament or more nearly one than the other. In doing so parallels are drawn with national Parliaments which, for obvious historical and political reasons, have very different functions and tasks from those of the European Parliament which is the unique parliamentary body of a unique transnational political structure. Thus comparisons between the European Parliament and national parliaments risk being at least as misleading as they are helpful. Most of the analogies are wrong. When it is remembered that the parliamentary chambers of the countries of the Community are not called the "French Parliament" or the "British Parliament", but the "National Assembly", the "Senate" or the "House of Commons", it might be sensible to conclude that there is little point in exaggerating the importance of a linguistic conundrum. This said, Parliament's decision to call itself the "European Parliament" symbolises its wish to play a part within the European Community comparable in significance to that of national parliaments in national states. For our purpose it is enough to conclude that the European Parliament is trying to transform itself from a consultative assembly into a body capable of exerting real influence on Community decision-making and whose supervisory activities are respected by the other institutions.

Traditionally, the main function of the European Parliament has been its consultative role in legislation. Although views differ as to how far the Commission is the "executive" of the Community as compared to the Council, there is little doubt that as regards legislation the task of the Commission is to initiate proposals in the interest of the Community as a whole, whilst it is the Council that takes the decisions. But whereas Article 148 of the EEC Treaty lays down that the Council shall decide by majority and Article 149 provides that the Council can only amend a Commission proposal by unanimity, which, taken together, theoretically makes the Commission the dominant partner in decision-making, the effects of the "Luxembourg Agreement", under which all major decisions are taken by consensus or unanimity, have been to reverse the Treaty and to make the governmental body, the Council, the significant institution when decisions are taken.

The Treaties indicate areas where the Council must consult the European Parliament before it decides, consultation of Parliament being theoretically optional in other cases. In practice the Council requests the European

The Functions and Institutional Role of the European Parliament 31

Parliament to give its opinion on most Commission proposals for regulations and directives. Regulations apply directly as law in the member states. Directives bind member states concerning "the results to be achieved", but do not lay down the means by which the results are to be achieved. In practice, however, directives have in some cases become more like regulations in the way in which they are drafted with the result that the member states have to adopt and enact them virtually word for word. The Council also adopts decisions, recommendations, and opinions and has, in recent years, started to make use of declarations and resolutions, which are not defined in the Treaties, and concerning which the European Parliament does not have to be consulted.

Article 149 of the EEC Treaty permits the Commission to alter its original proposal on the basis of the European Parliament's opinion, if the Council has not yet decided. This provision has given Parliament the opportunity to propose amendments to Commission legislative proposals. Although the Commission has often made changes in accordance with Parliament's suggestions[1] it is very often the case that the Council does not accept these amendments.

But the Treaties do not oblige the Commission to amend draft legislation in the sense indicated by the European Parliament, and amendments made by the Commission to its original proposals in the light of its consultation with the Council do not have to be submitted to the Parliament, though they often are if they involve substantial changes.

The most important weakness in the European Parliament's consultative function is that there is no obligation on the Council to amend legislation in conformity with Parliament's opinion. The Council does not even explain why it has not taken account of Parliament's suggested amendments. Only too often members of the European Parliament have had the impression that the Council has hardly even bothered to open the envelope and read the text of Parliament's opinion when it arrives at the Council's mail registry before announcing a decision prepared by the Permanent Representatives and the expert committees well in advance. The biggest

1. In *Parliament for Europe*, Cape, London, 1979, David Marquand shows that in 1976 Parliament gave opinions on 246 Commission proposals, suggesting modifications in 61 cases. The Commission accepted 32 of these modifications (52%). In the first eleven months of 1977 Parliament gave 273 opinions on Commission proposals. It suggested modifications in 44 cases. The Commission accepted 30 of its modifications (68%).

flaw in Parliament's legislative function—which amounts to no more than a consultative role—is the fact that its opinion is not binding on the Council, except for the establishment of certain parts of the Community budget.

Parliament's committees do however have an opportunity to influence Commission legislative proposals both before they are formally presented at the "pre-legislative" stage and, through discussions with the relevant members of the Council of Ministers, under the conciliation procedure—described later in the present chapter. The part played by committees in helping to shape Community legislation is examined in Chapter 4.

The European Parliament and the Budget[1]

The European Parliament has exploited its budgetary powers more effectively than the other powers in its limited armoury. Although the Community budget amounts to only 2.5% of the total national budgets—amounting to about £10 thousand million for 1979—its size and balance are crucial to the shaping and character of Community policy. The Common Agricultural Policy (CAP) accounts for over three-quarters of the Community budget. The remainder of the budget covers Commission expenditure and all other policies, together with the repayment to member states of the costs of collection of tariffs and levies on imports from non-Community countries, and the administrative expenditure of the Commission and the other institutions. The expenditure of the European Investment Bank, the European Development Fund and the European Coal and Steel Community (ECSC) are budgeted separately. The Commission's budget accounts for almost 98% of the Community's budget. The two parts of the Budgetary Authority, Council and Parliament, have a tacit agreement under which neither institution will interfere with the budget of the other. This agreement was broken by the Council in 1979—when it rejected supplementary budget proposals put forward by Parliament to enlarge its staff in view of direct elections—possibly in revenge for Parliament's victory in the struggle over the 1979 budget of the Community.

1. See also *Purse Strings of Europe* written by the secretariat of Parliament's Committee on Budgets, and published by the Information Office of the European Parliament, London, 1979.

The Functions and Institutional Role of the European Parliament 33

The system of financing Community expenditure by national contributions has been replaced progressively since 1970 by a system of self-financing from resources belonging to the Community itself, known as "own resources". These are composed of the customs duties provided by the common external tariff and from levies on agricultural imports together with a percentage slice (maximum 1%) of Value Added Tax (VAT) on a uniform basis of assessment. It is hoped that the move to the new system of own resources will be completed in 1980. To simplify the calculation of the Community budget, a European unit of account (EUA), whose value is calculated and published daily by the Commission, has been introduced. Special rates of exchange are used for agricultural trade—hence the "green pound"—in order to take account of fluctuating rates of exchange between the currencies of the member states.

The Community's budgetary procedure is governed by Article 203 of the EEC Treaty which has been significantly changed by the Budget Treaties of April 1970 and July 1975. Since 1975, the European Parliament has been, together with the Council, the budgetary authority of the Community.

In the first months of the calendar year the Commission draws up a preliminary draft budget for the next year on the basis of estimates made by the different institutions. At this stage the national Finance and Foreign Ministers meet in the Council to establish priorities and examine technical problems. The President of the Council will then normally attend a meeting of Parliament's Committee on Budgets to inform it of the Council's plans. In March the Committee on Budgets names its rapporteur on the budget, one of Parliament's top jobs. He is responsible for initiating and coordinating Parliament's work on the budget. The rapporteur drafts a report on this text which is debated by Parliament in April or May. The Commission also establishes the "maximum rate" during the spring and informs the other institutions. This is the rate at which "non-compulsory" expenditure can be increased. It is worked out in light of a number of considerations including increases in national budgets and in the cost of living, and trends in the gross product of the Community. "Compulsory" expenditure, which accounts for about three-quarters of the Community budget, is expenditure resulting directly from the Treaties or from decisions implementing policies outlined in the Treaties, such as expenditure on the CAP. "Non-compulsory" expenditure consists of expenditure on subjects not covered in the Treaties such as the Regional Fund, together with administrative costs, including salaries. The preliminary draft budget is sent by the Commission to Parliament in June, and Parliament holds a debate on guidelines for the budget in July.

Also in June the Commission sends the same draft to the Council which starts to draw up the draft budget itself. The Council works out the draft budget in view of a report of the Budgetary Committee of the Council which is then examined by COREPER. The Budget Council then resolves remaining problems. The Commission takes part in these meetings. Before the Budget Council finalises the draft budget it holds a meeting with a delegation of Parliament, led by its President and composed of members of its Committee on Budgets. The Council then sends (usually before the end of August) the draft budget to Parliament whose rapporteur and Committee on Budgets start work on the preparation of draft amendments. After several meetings of the committee, during which its views on the draft budget take shape, the rapporteur tables "preliminary draft amendments". Parliament's other committees examine "their" part of the draft budget at this stage—for instance, the Regional Policy Committee studies the budgetary proposals relating to the Regional Fund—and they table their own amendments. In October the Committee on Budgets meets, for several days, to consider amendments tabled by the committees, the political groups or any five members of the Parliament—in 1978, 350 amendments were examined by the committee at this meeting. The Budget Minister of the country holding the chair of the Council and the Budget Commissioner attend this meeting. In October, Parliament holds the "first reading" of the budget. After a major two-day debate on the report of the Committee on Budgets Parliament votes on amendments and modifications on the third day. For amendments to items of compulsory expenditure to be adopted a majority of those voting is required. For non-compulsory items, an amendment needs a majority of all Parliament's members for adoption.

In November the Budget Council starts its second examination of the Budget. Council's Budgetary Committee and then COREPER study Parliament's amendments. Around 20 November the Budget Council meets Parliament's delegation for an exchange of views and then the Council takes its final decision on the budget. Where Parliament's modification of a compulsory item suggests a decrease or no increase in expenditure the Council can only reject or alter the change by a qualified majority

The Functions and Institutional Role of the European Parliament 35

vote.[1] Where Parliament's amendments to compulsory expenditure aim at increasing expenditure the Council can only agree to them by a qualified majority vote. Where Parliament has amended non-compulsory expenditure (upwards or downwards) the Council requires a qualified majority to reject or change these amendments. After taking its decisions on Parliament's amendments the Council sends the amended budget back to Parliament.

At the end of November and in early December the Committee on Budgets and other committees of Parliament meet to consider Council's decisions and to decide whether to retable amendments to non-compulsory expenditure. The Committee on Budgets is likely, at this stage, to adopt provisionally its resolution and report for Parliament's December session. Parliament's delegation and the Budget Council are likely to meet now to try to reach agreement on as many of the remaining problems as possible, particularly on any proposals to exceed the maximum rate which require the agreement of both parts of the budgetary authority—Parliament and the Council.

Parliament's "second reading" of the budget takes place in the December session. After the Committee on Budgets has adopted its final report including its amendments to non-compulsory items a major debate is held in which the President-in-Office of the Council and Parliament's rapporteur on the budget explain and defend their respective positions. The Committee on Budgets examines any final amendments on the report of the Committee on Budgets and on the budget itself. The vote on the amendments concerns non-compulsory expenditure only. Parliament cannot make further changes to compulsory expenditure. For non-compulsory items Parliament can amend the changes made by Council by a vote of a majority of all its members and three-fifths of the votes cast.

The final moment of the budgetary procedure is the adoption of the budget by Parliament, which gives it the "last word" on the whole of the Community budget.

The adoption by Parliament of the Community budget for 1979 was

---

1. For qualified majority votes in the Council, the votes of member states are weighted as follows: Belgium 5, Denmark 3, Germany 10, France 10, Ireland 3, Italy 10, Luxembourg 2, the Netherlands 5, and the United Kingdom 10. To take a decision under this procedure, the Council requires at least 41 votes in favour when decisions are taken on a proposal by the Commission, and 41 votes in favour, cast by at least six member states, in other cases (Article 148 of the EEC Treaty).

the climax of a controversy between Council and Parliament over non-compulsory expenditure. Parliament was accused of exceeding its powers in amending upwards the Regional Fund, and at first, the British, Danish and French governments contested the legality of that part of the budget. Parliament's case, which, despite grumbles from these three governments, won the day, was not that it had exceeded its powers of amending non-compulsory expenditure, but that the Council had failed to reject Parliament's amendment concerning the Regional Fund at the appropriate procedural stage—Council's second reading of the budget.

Parliament has the power to reject the budget as a whole by veot of a majority of all its members. Parliament must state a reason for rejecting the budget, which excludes the possibility of the budget being rejected because different interests vote against it for different reasons.

If neither of these provisions are fulfilled, the budget is declared adopted even if only a handful of members take part in the vote or if the majority of those voting are against. On 13 December 1979 Parliament rejected the Community's draft budget for 1980 and the Community was plunged into a crisis. Parliament's rejection of the first budget submitted to it following direct elections was due to the refusal of the Council to accept the amendments proposed by Parliament, which were basically aimed at reducing expenditure in the agricultural sector and increasing Regional Fund spending. The sums of money involved, under Parliament's amendments, were not great (in effect Parliament's amendments proposed increases of about £500 million in regional and other structural expenditure, and reductions of approximately £180 million in the agricultural sector), but both the Parliament and the Governments dug in over the fundamental issue of Parliament's right to have a say over agricultural spending.

In February 1980, the Commission submitted new budgetary proposals which, in general, corresponded to the line expressed by Parliament during the budgetary debates it held during the course of 1979. In particular, the Commission's proposals aimed at restoring the cuts made by the Council to expenditure in the regional and social sectors. In March 1980, Parliament debated the proposals on agricultural prices made by the Commission. Because of the significance of the CAP in the overall budgetary situation the size of the price increases in agricultural prices proposed by the Commission was of great significance. In effect, the Commission suggested comparatively restrained increases averaging 2.4%. In the debate it held in

The Functions and Institutional Role of the European Parliament 37

March, Parliament indicated that any agricultural price increases—even of the modest nature proposed by the Commission—would have to be balanced by comparable increases in other sectors of the Community budget, notably in the Regional and Social Funds.

During the months of May and June, the Committee on Budgets considered the situation further and meetings with the Council were held in the framework of the budgetary concertation procedure. On 26/27 June 1980, at the sitting in Luxembourg, Parliament debated the new draft 1980 budget and adopted amendments totalling some £6.7 million, which were accepted by the Council the following week.

At the July 1980 session in Strasbourg, the President of Parliament declared that the 1980 budget was finally adopted, since two new motions for rejection of the budget had not been endorsed by the House. When the long and difficult 1980 budget procedure was being brought to a close, the rapporteur for the Commission budget, Mr Dankert, and the Chairman of the Committee on Budgets, Mr Lange, indicated certain positive aspects. The use of the rejection weapon had led to a shift within the budget. The Commission had sought out economies in the management of the dairy sector and had brought forward reform proposals. Also, Parliament's action had caused the Council to agree to certain of Parliament's proposals. Moreover, Parliament's action in rejecting the budget heightened the Council's awareness of the need to reform the balance within the budget.[1]

Parliament's decision of December 1979 to reject the budget did not paralyse the operation of the Community since, until the new Community budget was introduced and adopted, a twelfth of the previous year's budget was available to the Community institutions each month. However, members of the Parliament received only 60% of their daily allowance and their travel expenses, and payment of their office expenses was suspended. Some newspapers hailed the rejection of the 1980 budget by Parliament in December 1979 as proof that Parliament had developed efficient teeth since direct elections and was seen to be using them but Parliament's teeth proved, in the event, to be rather less sharp than hoped for since the budget that was finally agreed was not only very much a compromise but a compromise tilted in favour of the Council. Nonetheless, it is clear that the directly elected Parliament acted with greater courage and determination

1. The adoption of the 1981 budget is examined in Appendix III.

than the former designated Parliament could have done in the same situation. In future budgetary procedures, its stance will be taken far more seriously by the Council.

The Council and Parliament might agree that the maximum rate itself should be increased. This can be done by a three-fifths' majority vote by Parliament and a qualified majority vote by the Council.

Parliament's right to increase the budget through the maximum rate is more complex in the case where the Council does not wish to increase the budget for a non-compulsory item at all, or by less than "its" half of the maximum rate. The legal situation under Article 203 of the EEC Treaty is not explicit, but Parliament takes the view that over and above "its" half of the maximum rate it has the right to use any unused part of the Council's half. Parliament also considers this to be the case concerning non-compulsory items where the Council might propose a reduction in the budget.

It seems, by now, to be generally accepted that Parliament has the right to increase non-compulsory expenditure by half the maximum rate, irrespective of action by the Council. If the maximum rate is 20%, and Parliament decides to increase expenditure on a non-compulsory item by "its" half of the maximum rate, that is by £100 million, the Council is not limited merely to the other half, which means that in reality, the "maximum rate" is not limited to the theoretical 20%, but is one-and-a-half times that amount, in this instance £300 million.

Parliament's powers to increase the Community budget are often derided as being minimal. But although it is true that some 70% of the Community budget still falls under compulsory expenditure, concerning which Parliament's rights to force amendments remain extremely limited, the non-compulsory part of the budget rose from about 3% to about 30% during the 1970s. Depending on the precise level of the maximum rate, amongst other factors, Parliament can now increase the Community budget by between £200–£400 million a year. This may seem to be a small proportion of the total Community budget which amounted, in 1979, to about £10,000 million, but it represents a significant and constantly growing proportion of the non-compulsory part of the budget. Looking ahead, increases in Community expenditure are almost inevitable, as new policies are decided upon by the Council, in the non-compulsory part of the budget. This means that Parliament's effective power to increase

The Functions and Institutional Role of the European Parliament

Community spending will grow automatically in direct proportion to the growth of the non-compulsory part of the budget.

The problem of how to enable the Community to raise money to finance loans for specific purposes has been solved by the approval given by the Council in 1977 to the Commission's proposal that it should be authorised to float loans on the international money markets. This right is known as the "Ortoli facility"—after Mr Francois-Xavier Ortoli, Vice-President of the Commission. Each of these loans corresponds to a specific goal: the building of nuclear plants; aid to British Petroleum, or aid to productive investments. The financial management of these loans has been entrusted to the expert hands of the European Investment Bank. Whereas the Community's operational budget covers one financial year only, "Ortoli facility" loans are raised on a longer-term basis.

One of the major problems facing the Community is that its expenditure is approaching the ceiling imposed by its total revenue. It has been suggested that the next move to increase the Community's revenue should be to raise the ceiling of the percentage slice of VAT paid to the Community from 1% to 2%. Another approach could be for the Commission to be authorised by a unanimous decision of the Council to apply the "Ortoli facility" technique to the raising of major and more general loans to finance Community operations, which would be possible under Article 201 of the EEC Treaty.

One of the things that must be done if the future of the Community budget is to make sense is for the Council to be brought to reason concerning the budgetary consequences of its decisions. Whereas the Council and the European Council are happy enough to take decisions agreeing on new fields of activity by the Community, when it comes to financing the administration of these policies they are often reluctant to provide the Commission with sufficient funds to recruit the additional staff required. Replying to a question put to him in an interview with *The Economist*, London, (of 29 September 1979) the German Chancellor, Helmut Schmidt, stated: "I think it's good that for the time being the budget is being limited because the value added tax component of the Community's revenues is being limited to 1%. I think it's a good limitation and it should be kept and not be violated." At the same time little discipline is exercised by the normal Council (the Foreign Ministers) over the Council of agricultural ministers, so that agricultural expenditure continues to outpace disproportionately other and new sectors of the Community budget. In the same interview Helmut Schmidt commented: "I think that agricultural policies as a whole have run out of control, and ought to be brought back under control. They are consuming, now, I think, over two thirds of the finances of the EEC. This is ridiculous." However, when the European Parliament tried to change, during 1979, the balance of the 1980 budget towards less spending on agriculture and more on other sectors the member governments resolutely refused to accept such a shift, as proposed by Parliament, and their refusal led to Parliament's rejection of the draft budget.

Whether Parliament succeeds or not in gaining, through concessions made in a new budget treaty, an equivalent degree of influence over compulsory spending, notably on agriculture, the future growth of the non-compulsory part of the Community budget will give it real influence on the allocation of limited Community funds as between competing policies. In short, through the power of the purse, Parliament will be able to have a major say in determining Community policy priorities.

In considering the development of Parliament's influence on the shaping of the Community budget attention is usually focused on the success that Parliament increasingly enjoys in influencing non-compulsory expenditure. But this success has tended to distract attention from a serious problem which Parliament has not yet tackled successfully.

Lord Bruce of Donington, writing in the summer of 1979, as Parliament's rapporteur on the Community accounts for 1977, drew attention to the nature of this problem which is twofold. First, the Commission consistently underspends the amounts made available to it in the budget for any one year. Second, the Commission frequently indulges in the custom of transferring money that should be spent under one heading of the budget to another, introducing considerable distortions into the Community's budget and thus into its policies.

Lord Bruce has commented that after the budget procedure has been concluded "the Commission and the Council proceed to do as they please. On the basis of spurious legal arguments and as a result of inertia, Parliament's amendments are almost systematically *not* implemented. Vast movements of funds within the budget knock it out of recognition as regards to budget as originally adopted. *Sums are added, subtracted and transferred with the barest Parliamentary involvement* and the sums

The Functions and Institutional Role of the European Parliament 41

concerned are far greater than the minute amounts over which Parliament went into battle during the original procedure."

Taking the twenty-nine amendments adopted by Parliament concerning the 1977 budget, Lord Bruce stressed that twenty-one of these were not implemented at all and that the amount of payment appropriations actually spent by the Commission in 1977 totalled approximately a mere 3% of the amendments voted by Parliament. The nature of the problem that is posed to Parliament in trying to supervise Commission expenditure is pinpointed in a further telling passage in Lord Bruce's report. Referring, again, to the 1977 budget he comments "Parliament's amendments, after a bargaining process which could be described as bitter, totalled a meagre 154 million u.a.[1] An essential item of this was 5 million u.a. for hydrocarbon development (and in the end nothing was spent) which Council made Parliament believe was the 'breaking point'. And yet this same Council which streams into Luxembourg to berate Parliament over 5 million u.a. sanctions the management of the budget which permits uncontrolled transfers within it of 376 million u.a., supplements to it of 2,278 million u.a. (from carryovers) and 778 million u.a. (from supplementary budgets) and cancellations at the end of the day of 1,900 million u.a. These are the real problems of budgetary management. *They show more clearly than anything else that Parliament is left to fight for control of the petty cash while the Commission and Council are free to determine without any democratic control the use or misuse of thousands of millions of units of account.*"[2]

In these circumstances it is clear that Parliament's new Committee on Financial Control, even with the full support of the Court of Auditors, has a long and uphill struggle to ensure that the real expenditure of the

1. u.a.=units of account.
2. Replying to Lord Bruce's arguments Christopher Tugendhat, the Budget Commissioner, has commented that in many cases the Commission can only *start* to spend funds voted by Parliament's amendments in the budget year in question, with further expenditure following later, on account of the inevitable delays involved in recruiting staff or tendering for contracts. He has also argued that in some cases the Commission considers that a separate legal basis, apart from the budget, is required to justify the disbursement of money.

The numerous Management and Legislation Committees, composed of national experts, which advise the Commission concerning the use of the powers delegated to it by the Council to implement the day-to-day running of agricultural markets and other sectors of Community activity play an important role in authorising the Commission to proceed to the expenditure of the Community budget. Their role and powers in these respects have been questioned by Parliament.

Commission in one year corresponds to the budget for that year fought out and adopted by Parliament and the Council.

Perhaps the single most interesting development in Parliament's powers in recent years has been the introduction of the conciliation procedure, following a joint declaration of Parliament, the Commission and the Council in March 1975. Although the conciliation procedure is *related* to the budgetary procedure it is not formally *linked* to it. Indeed, the interest of Parliament, for which the conciliation procedure represents a foot in the door of legislative powers, is that there should be no formal link.

Under the conciliation mechanism wherever there is a conflict between Parliament and the Commission on one side, and the Council on the other, concerning a Commission proposal of general application which has "appreciable financial consequences", the procedure can be activated by either side. It takes place between nine ministers from the appropriate specialist council and a delegation of nine members of the Parliament, led by its President and including the relevant committee chairman and rapporteur. A maximum of three months is set for agreement. Although any final decision must follow the rules of the Treaty, the working of the conciliation procedure gives Parliament an opportunity to arrive at a compromise with the Council and, in effect, provides Parliament with a "suspensive veto" for the length of the procedure. If agreement is reached between the two sides during the three-month period, its substance is included in a new report from the committee of the Parliament directly concerned, which is then adopted as a new resolution by Parliament as a whole. Parliament's new opinion is then accepted by the Council.

Although there is no guarantee that agreement can be reached through the conciliation procedure,[1] it provides Parliament with an opportunity to plead its case and to persuade or convince ministerial doubters about the merits of its arguments. Since Parliament is not able to force the governments to agree to its views, a procedure of this kind provides some means of reducing the number of deadlocks between Parliament and the Council concerning Community legislation even though the results of the conciliation procedure have, in general, proved disappointing for Parliament.

1. Although the system of consultation between Parliament's delegation and the Budget Council concerning the development of the budgetary procedure, described earlier in this chapter, resembles the conciliation procedure in some respects, it is nonetheless separate and should not be confused with it.

Parliamentary Supervision of the Executive

Although political scientists often refer to Parliament's role in "controlling" the Commission, the use of the word "control" is perhaps misleading. It is used in this sense as a translation of the French "*contrôler*", which is more appropriately translated by "supervise" or by "inspect", "verify" or "check". It is important to use a more accurate word here since "control" implies a greater degree of supervision by Parliament over the Commission than is justified by political reality. Parliament itself has fallen into this trap, calling its new audit committee the "Committee on Financial Control".

Parliament's supervision of the Commission is based on Articles 143 and 144 of the EEC Treaty, under which the Commission is obliged to submit an annual general report to Parliament and, more significantly, to "resign as a body" in the event of Parliament adopting a motion of censure against it. Although the four attempts Parliament has made to adopt a motion of censure against the Commission have failed, the threat of such a motion being carried is the main basis of the Commission's accountability to Parliament. A further basis is Article 140 of the EEC Treaty which obliges the Commission to "reply orally or in writing to questions put to it by the Assembly or its Members".

Parliament's power to sack the Commission is so far-reaching, that it is extremely difficult to use. Experience has shown that governments will go to great lengths to persuade members of the Parliament not to censure Commissioners. Even if Parliament were to succeed in passing a censure motion, Article 158 of the EEC Treaty enables the governments to replace the sacked Commission by exactly the same individuals. So this power is one that some members of Parliament believe must be refined so that Parliament can censure and sack an individual Commissioner—and ensure that he is not reappointed.

On the basis of Article 140 a question time was introduced in 1973 and now questions are put to the Commission for one and a half hours, on Monday afternoon during each of Parliament's sessions, as are questions to the Council and the Foreign Ministers, which are taken on Wednesday. Questions for oral reply are submitted to the President who decides whether they are in order and how they are to be grouped.

As a form of parliamentary scrutiny questions certainly make Community procedures more "open" and make the activities of the institutions more "visible", thus providing some degree of accountability. It is largely through Parliament's question time that some degree of openness has been introduced into the Community. But much of the working of the Community is still insufficiently open and one task of directly elected members will be to refine and develop the present use of questions. They will also need to press the Commission and the Council to give franker and fuller replies to questions, and will need to ensure that the Ministers do not shift their responsibility for replying to questions away from the European Parliament to national parliaments.

Another way in which Parliament used, in the past, to supervise the work of the Commission was through its debate on the Commission's Annual General Report. But since the debate on this report merely related to past activities of the Commission, of which Parliament was already informed, this became an increasingly sterile operation and has been replaced by a debate on an annual programme of future Community activity introduced by the President of the Commission.

Parliament also supervises the work of the Commission through its committees. Each committee maintains close contacts with the Commissioner responsible for its area of activity and with the appropriate members of the Commission staff. Commissioners and their staff appear frequently before committees at their meetings and are questioned on both the aims and administration of Community policy. The President of the Commission regularly briefs Parliament's Political Committee on current Commission thinking, and it would be a bold Commissioner who consistently refused invitations to attend committee meetings.

One of the top priorities of directly elected members is likely to be the strengthening of the Parliament's scrutiny of Commission expenditure. Before direct elections this was effected through the Sub-committee on Control of Parliament's Committee on Budgets which consisted of only nine members. This Sub-committee was too small to do more than scratch the surface of the many problems involved in the auditing of Community expenditure. One of the decisions taken by the directly elected Parliament at its first session in July 1979 was to transform the Sub-committee into a full Committee. The Court of Auditors, which was set up during 1977, will be available to carry out investigations concerning Commission expenditure at the Committee's request. Working closely together the Committee and the Court should be able to cut down frauds and abuses, especially in the agricultural sector. Although in the past the Commission has sometimes been reluctant to transmit to Parliament "confidential" documents relating to expenditure, following direct elections it will be increasingly difficult for the Commission to refuse to hand over internal documents when so requested by Parliament.

Although Parliament needs to secure better and more rapid replies to oral and written questions put to the Commission by its members, and although it needs to improve its existing methods of scrutinising Commission expenditure, there is already a considerable degree of accountability from the Commission to Parliament.

Accountability of the Council

The real problem of accountability lies elsewhere. It is the problem of obtaining an adequate degree of accountability from the Council to Parliament. With the growing importance of the Council this key problem has become increasingly difficult to solve. The founding fathers considered the Commission to be the central and most significant of the institutions and therefore thought it enough to provide—through the motion of censure, the Annual Report and question time—means of accountability from the Commission to the Parliament, which, had their assessment of the Commission's role been justified over the years, would have allowed for adequate accountability. But the Treaties do not provide for direct accountability from the Council to Parliament. As a Community body the Council is not accountable to either the Commission or the Parliament. Indeed, the only effective method of ensuring that the Council tows the line in Community matters is through recourse to the Court of Justice. So in the final resort, it is only individual ministerial members of the Council who are responsible to their national governments and national parliaments for Council decisions. In a Community context the Council is technically "irresponsible".

As Sir Peter Kirk pointed out in his report on Inter-institutional Relations[1] Parliament has lacked both the foresight and the courage to give the closing of the "accountability gap" with the Council the requisite

1. Which was completed by Lord Reay, following Sir Peter's death, and submitted by him to the Political Committee. Luxembourg, 1978 (Document 148/78).

priority. In concentrating the use of its weapons of parliamentary supervision on the Commission, Parliament has not done enough to obtain an adequate degree of political accountability from the Council.

The creation of the European Council and of COREPER has converted the Council into a triple-layer heads of government/ministerial/ambassadorial sandwich. This has made it even harder for Parliament to obtain political accountability. Although the European Council sometimes acts as the Council of the European Communities at the highest level, it is not a normal form of the Council, and since there is no reference to it in the Treaties there is no provision for accountability from it to any of the Community institutions, or indeed to any national institutions.

Major initiatives taken by the European Council—such as the creation of the Regional Fund, the decision to hold direct elections to Parliament and the launching of the European Monetary System—have injected much-needed political impetus into the Community in recent years, but there is no doubt that the "normal" Council has lost much of its influence to this new extra-Treaty and institutionally irresponsible Super-Council.

COREPER not only prepares decisions taken by the Council but in effect takes many decisions for the Council under the special procedure (known as "A–points") which allows the Permanent Representatives, if they reach agreement with the Commission, to propose that the Council should take a decision without discussion. The extent to which Council decisions have fallen into the hands of COREPER is shown by the Paris summit communiqué of December 1974 which stated: "Greater latitude will be given to the Permanent Representatives so that only the most important political problems need to be discussed in the Council". Since the Permanent Representatives are national officials they are not accountable to either the European Parliament or even their national Parliaments for their decisions, despite the fact that in meeting together in COREPER they are taking Community decisions and are acting collectively as a Community body.

As a result of these changes it is only the thin central slice of the Council sandwich which is accountable to Parliament; the European Council and COREPER escaping parliamentary supervision completely.

But Parliament has managed to obtain some precarious footholds on the vast crags of the political mountain-range formed by the Council. Although there is no Treaty obligation on the Council to reply to parliamentary questions, the practice has developed of the Council answering questions

The Functions and Institutional Role of the European Parliament   47

put to it by members of the Parliament in a similar way to the Commission. Since 1975, the Chairman of the Conference of Foreign Ministers has replied to questions put by members of the Parliament concerning political cooperation[1]. Questions to the Council and the Foreign Ministers are traditionally dealt with during a period of an hour and a half on the Wednesday of each session of Parliament, which is primarily reserved for "Council business". Replies given by the Council to parliamentary questions are usually less informative than those given by the Commission, since they represent the common position of the nine governments. But some Presidents of the Council have made a point of adding their own personal comments at the end of the prepared replies to questions.

Apart from replying to questions the President of the Council, or an appropriate specialist Minister representing him, will often take part in the debates organised on "Council day". This enables members of Parliament to hold an exchange of views with the Council concerning broad policy issues and to press the Council for explanations.

From time to time members of the Council also attend meetings of Parliament's committees to explain the Council's thinking on questions of concern to members. In the energy and transport sectors Parliament's relevant committees have developed links of this kind with the Council. Parliament's Political Committee has developed a particularly close relationship with the Foreign Ministers within the framework of EPC. Shortly following each quarterly meeting of the Foreign Ministers a closed "colloquy" is held between Parliament's Political Committee and the Foreign Minister chairing the Conference, at which the results of the most recent foreign policy discussions are analysed in a closed question-and-answer session.

But the most significant foothold gained by Parliament on the ministerial glacis is the conciliation procedure. This procedure gives Parliament no guarantee of success in its attempts to swing the Council to the viewpoint with which, together with the Commission, it confronts the ministers. But at the present stage of the Community's development (where governments are still reluctant to think even in terms of "co-decision" between Parliament and the Council let alone in terms of Parliament having "the

---

1. European Political Cooperation (EPC) is an extra-Treaty form of cooperation between the Nine concerning the coordination of some aspects of foreign policy, conducted by the Foreign Ministers.

last word"),[1] the conciliation procedure provides members of the Parliament with an opportunity to plead, argue and persuade—in negotiating or diplomatic style—and it seems to open up the most practical way for Parliament to increase its influence over the Council in the decision-making process. If the members of the European Parliament who are involved in the conciliation meetings with the Ministers have mastered their brief and are effective in presenting their case it is difficult for the Council to be entirely negative or unresponsive to parliamentary pleas. A drawback, for members of the Parliament, in frequent recourse to the conciliation procedure, is that the three-month delay in decision-taking adds to, rather than subtracts from, the cumbersome rhythm of Community decision-making, which has so often been criticised by Parliament itself.

Parliament and the Community's External Relations

The procedure governing the accession of new member states to the Community is laid down in Article 237 of the EEC Treaty, which states that an applicant country "should address its application to the Council which shall act unanimously after obtaining the opinion of the Commission". There is no mention of Parliament in Article 237. It is true that Parliament has debated initiative reports of its appropriate committees concerning, for instance, problems posed by the accession of Greece, Portugal and Spain to the Community and that the Council and the Commission have been involved in these parliamentary discussions. But the absence of the minimal right to be consulted by the Council is an extraordinary gap in the EEC Treaty, which seems all the more strange when the very next Article, 238, states that the Council shall conclude association agreements with third countries "acting unanimously after consulting the Assembly". A suggestion as to how this situation might be rectified is made in Chapter 6.[2]

Although Article 238 speaks of the "consultation" of Parliament by the

1. Except concerning non-compulsory expenditure.
2. There is a comparable gap in the Euratom Treaty, which does not provide for consultation of Parliament by the Council concerning either agreements under which member states receive fissile material from third countries or those under which nuclear technology is provided by Community members to third countries.

The Functions and Institutional Role of the European Parliament 49

Council in the conclusion of an association agreement, the role that Parliament has played in this consultation process has tended to be passive rather than active. The way in which Parliament takes part in the negotiation of association and trade agreements is known as the "Luns-Westerterp procedure". Under the original "Luns procedure", named after the former Dutch Foreign Minister, Parliament has been informed, through its responsible committees,[1] by the Commission concerning the development of negotiations, and by the Council, when negotiations have ended but before an association Treaty is signed. The information given to Parliament's committees is confidential. This procedure supplements and does not replace the official consultation of Parliament by Council which takes place after signature of the association treaty. This procedure has come under fire from members of Parliament on the grounds that the timing of the information given to Parliament's committees is usually too late to allow Parliament's opinion to have any effect on the substance of an association agreement. Subsequently the Council extended the "Luns procedure" to permit Parliament's committees to be informed, in a similar way, concerning the evolution of negotiations between the Community and third states concerning trade agreements. This new procedure is called the "Westerterp procedure"[2] and taken together the two procedures are known as the "Luns-Westerterp procedure".

The second aspect of Parliament's involvement in the Community's external relations does not derive from the Treaties but from Parliament's own initiatives. This is the establishment of delegations of Parliament which hold meetings with parliamentary delegations from countries with which the Community has significant trade relations. The Community's major trade partner is the United States and the primacy of the trans-Atlantic relationship has led to the holding of an annual meeting between a delegation of Parliament and members of the U.S. House of Representatives. The meetings are held alternately in Washington and in Europe. A meeting is organised every two years between a delegation of Parliament and members of the Canadian Parliament. But Parliament also arranges similar meetings with parliamentarians from other countries, such as Australia, Israel, Japan, New Zealand and Yugoslavia and, also, meetings

1. Normally the Political Committee, the Committee on External Economic Relations and the Committee on Agriculture.
2. Named after the former Dutch Minister of State for Foreign Affairs.

with parliamentary bodies of regional groupings, such as the Latin American Parliament and a delegation from ASEAN.

Four salient features of the work of these delegations, of which there are at present 23, are of interest. First, through its delegations the European Parliament has a very wide range of contacts with the countries of the outside world. As opposed to the Council and the Commission the meetings held with parliamentarians of non-Community countries emphasise the political and democratic nature of the Community and demonstrate to the politicians, the media and the peoples of those countries that Parliament supports and will work to defend democracy, the rule of law and human rights in all friendly countries. It is often the case that the countries with which the Community develops close trade and parliamentary links regard the significance of the Community as being far greater than that of its individual member states—a view that could well surprise many Community citizens who have a tendency to under-estimate the impact of the EEC on the outside world.

Second, the information acquired by members of Parliament concerning the government policies of the countries with whose parliaments they organise meetings allows Parliament to play an informed role in Community relations with the outside world. When a European Parliament delegation visits Washington or Ottawa its working programme is not limited to discussions with American Congressmen and Canadian MPs but includes briefing sessions with members of the United States Administration and the Canadian Government, together with trade union leaders and others. As a result of contacts of this kind, Parliament maintains an up-to-date and in-depth view of national policy-making at all levels in these countries.

Third, the scale and intensity of the activities of Parliament's delegations have created a situation in which the Community's external relations can no longer be described as being solely in the hands of the Council, as initiator, and the Commission, as executive. In effect, the European Parliament's external relations now form part of the Community's overall external relations. Indeed, especially because of the emphasis placed by Parliament on the defence of democratic values and human rights, the parliamentary aspects of the Community's external relations are of particular significance. An instance of the value placed by the United States Congress on its relations with the European Parliament is the series of joint hearings held between Parliament's delegation and members of the

House of Representatives on a code of conduct for multinational corporations.

Fourth, these inter-parliamentary meetings allow parliamentary review of international agreements. For instance the meetings with the Canadian Parliament have featured detailed discussions, in the presence of the Commission, on the work of the Joint Cooperation Committee set up under the Canada–EEC Framework Agreement of 1975. Both Parliaments are able to scrutinise the work of this Committee and to propose changes or extensions to its activities. This type of parliamentary supervision of an international agreement is unusual. Delegations from the Federal Assembly of Yugoslavia and the European Parliament met in 1978 to discuss the course of negotiations on the EEC–Yugoslavia agreement. After meetings at provincial and federal level the Yugoslav delegation presented a report commenting on the agreement under negotiation which was transmitted to the Council of the European Community, though it had no visible effect on the negotiations.

Council of Europe

Almost every year a joint meeting is held between the Parliamentary Assembly of the Council of Europe and the European Parliament. This meeting was due, originally, to the provisions of a Protocol to the ECSC Treaty, which was rather faintly echoed in Article 230 of the EEC Treaty. In the beginning the purpose of these meetings was to provide a forum in which Western European states which did not take part in the work of the original Six could discuss problems of common concern with the parliamentary representatives of the Community. But few practical benefits have flowed from these discussions and over the years the joint meetings became broader and vaguer in character, with general themes such as inflation or human rights being the subject of debate.

Parliamentary Links with Greece and Turkey

Quite apart from meetings of the kind described above which do not have a Treaty basis, there are important Treaty-based links between the

European Parliament and two parliaments of European states which are associate members of the Community one of which will shortly become a full member of the EEC. The Joint Parliamentary Committees with Greece and Turkey were set up within the framework of the Association Agreements between the Community and these two countries in 1961 and 1963 respectively. In each Committee the European Parliament is represented by 18 members, as are the Greek and Turkish Parliaments. The purpose of the Joint Committees is to monitor their respective Association Agreements though they have interpreted their responsibilities very broadly and discussed the problems that have arisen in the negotiations conducted by Greece and Turkey with the Commission concerning the accession of these two countries to the Community, and even such questions as the maintenance of peace in the Eastern Mediterranean. The special nature of Greek and Turkish Association with the Community is, indeed, due to their intention to become full members of the Community.

When the Colonels came to power in Greece in April 1967 the European Parliament was the first of the Community institutions to react. In its resolution of May 1967 it urged the freezing of the Association Agreement until "democratic structures, political freedom and freedom for trade unions are restored in Greece". Following continuing pressure by the European Parliament the Association Agreement was frozen in 1971, and shortly following the restoration of democracy in Greece, in July 1974, the Parliament voted a resolution demanding the immediate "defreezing" of the economic aspects of the Association, and confirming that the Association could be fully resumed following parliamentary elections.

Following elections in Greece, the Joint Parliamentary Committee began to operate once more and, like the Turkish Joint Committee, normally meets twice a year. The "freezing" of the EEC–Greece Association Agreement was largely due to the pressures applied on the Commission and the Council by Parliament. To date it remains the high-water mark of Parliament's success in its forays into external relations. As a result of the "freezing" of the Association Agreement by the Community, in protest against the Colonels' regime, the new Greece has turned towards the Community rather than to NATO or to the United States to symbolise its attachment to Western democracy. In this context Greece's application for membership of the Community is a moral imperative which cannot be assessed only in trade figures and statistics.

The Functions and Institutional Role of the European Parliament 53

In the light of Spain's application in 1977 to become a member of the EEC, the Spanish Cortes and the European Parliament decided to set up a Joint Committee to meet every six months with the aim of involving the European Parliament and the Spanish Parliament directly in the negotiations concerning Spain's membership of the Community. Contacts between the European Parliament and the Portuguese Parliament should lead to meetings of a similar Joint Committee between members of the European Parliament and Portuguese parliamentarians, again with the aim of ensuring regular parliamentary links during the negotiations concerning Portuguese membership.

The Convention of Lomé/Yaoundé

Article 131 of the EEC Treaty sets out the Community's aim of establishing an association with those non-European countries which already enjoyed special relations with the member states before the Community was created.

After an initial period in which free trade arrangements were set up between the Community and member states' colonies, the newly independent African and Malagasy states negotiated the Yaoundé Convention with the Community in 1963 which, after a period of renewal, expired at the end of 1975.

The Yaoundé Convention provided for trade and aid advantages to the associated states. Under the Convention a Parliamentary Conference of the association was created, which was to meet once a year, with an equal number of members of the European Parliament and of members from the Yaoundé countries. The Conference, which had 57 members from each side, met alternately in Africa and in Europe. The main function of the Conference was to examine the annual report of the Ministerial Council of the Association concerning the working of the Association.

In February 1975 the Community of the Nine signed the new Lomé Convention with 46 African, Caribbean and Pacific countries (often known as the ACP countries). There are now 60 ACP countries. The new Convention set up a scheme to enable the associated countries to stabilise their export earnings (STABEX) and incorporated the European Development

Fund, which was set up under the Yaoundé Convention[1]. The Consultative Assembly of the Lomé Convention, which replaced the Yaoundé Conference, meets annually. The associated countries are each represented by two parliamentarians and the European Parliament is represented by an equal number of its own members, at present 118. The main business of the Consultative Assembly is, once again, to examine the annual report submitted to it by the ACP–EEC Council of Ministers. A Joint Committee composed of one parliamentarian from each ACP country and an equal number of members of the European Parliament prepares the work of the Assembly, meeting twice a year.

Apart from its concern with the operation of the Lomé Convention the Consultative Assembly has taken a stand on apartheid in South Africa and has dealt with human rights questions.

A number of difficulties beset the working of the Consultative Assembly. First, there is the problem of getting parliamentarians to these meetings, many of the ACP states being represented by their ambassadors in Brussels. In the case of the forty or so ACP states which do have parliaments, it has to be asked whether the appointment of ambassadors to represent them in the Consultative Assembly is useful and whether an adequate dialogue can be held under these circumstances. It is difficult to assess the impact of the work carried out by the Consultative Assembly in the ACP countries but it has had little impact on public consciousness in Europe. By the nature of its meetings the Consultative Assembly has not been able to respond flexibly or quickly to questions arising concerning the operation of the Lomé Convention, and thus has not been able to exert very much influence over the ACP/EEC Council of Ministers.

European Political Cooperation (EPC)

The Foreign Ministers of the original Six adopted a first report on political cooperation in 1970. Subsequently the Foreign Ministers of the Nine have approved a second report on EPC which improved the

---

1. The total amount envisaged for the European Development Fund for the five years duration of the initial Lomé Convention is roughly £1,800 million. This includes the STABEX fund of some £200 million available for loans to the Lomé countries from the European Investment Bank.

procedures for coordinating the foreign policy moves of the Nine. European Political Cooperation does not operate within the Treaties. It is an extra-Treaty activity conducted on an almost informal basis between the Foreign Ministers of the Nine with the help of national Foreign Office officials. There is no centralised secretariat for EPC, and administrative responsibility for keeping things running smoothly lies with the Chairman of the Conference of Foreign Ministers who is the same Foreign Minister who chairs the Council of Ministers of the European Community. As yet there has been little attempt by the Nine to develop "a Community foreign policy" since the British, Danish and French Governments have made it clear that although they have found it extremely useful to coordinate or harmonise certain selected aspects of foreign policy they have not been prepared to "integrate" their foreign policies with the loss of national sovereignty entailed.

Although EPC is not a Community activity as such, but a separate operation of the governments, it is closely related to the Community and there are links and overlapping between EPC, EEC and European Council activities.

The Foreign Ministers hold quarterly EPC meetings at which foreign policy decisions are taken. The quarterly meetings are prepared by monthly meetings of the Political Committee—sometimes known as the "Davignon Committee"[1]—which is composed of the political directors of the national Foreign Ministries. There are also frequent meetings of expert working parties which discuss both topical and long-term foreign policy problems —including *détente*, Southern Africa and the Middle East—and report to the Foreign Ministers.

COREUNET, a complex telex system, provides for instant and simultaneous communication of political information between the Foreign Ministers. The Commission, which is present at almost all parts of all EPC meetings, and which also takes part in some of the working parties, receives most of the COREUNET telegrams.

Over the years, links have developed between EPC and the U.S. Government concerning issues of mutual concern such as the Cyprus and Rhodesian problems.

It is through its contacts with the European Parliament that EPC is most

1. After Viscount Davignon, formerly Political Director of the Belgian Foreign Ministry and now Commissioner responsible for industry.

nearly linked to the Community. Under the first report of the Foreign Ministers of the Six ("the Davignon Report") the system of colloquies, or closed discussions, between the Foreign Ministers and the Political Committee of the Parliament was instituted "to discuss questions which are the subject of consultation, of foreign policy and cooperation". The Davignon report also provided for an annual progress report to Parliament on EPC. Under the second report of 1973, four colloquies were to be held each year and the political directors were invited to draw the attention of the Foreign Ministers to "proposals adopted by the European Parliament on foreign policy questions".

At their meeting in Paris in December 1974 the Heads of Government agreed that the Presidency of the Council would reply to questions put by members of the European Parliament on political cooperation. In October 1973, the Danish President of the Council, Mr K. B. Andersen, agreed that a debate on EPC should be held following his statement on political cooperation. An annual debate of this kind has been held since.

EPC was seen at its best in the preparation of the western approach to the Conference on Security and Cooperation in Europe (CSCE). This was a subject of importance to the Nine, which, because of the long time span of the different stages of the Conference, gave them sufficient time to work out, in detail, a joint approach to each individual agenda item and which was not controversial in the sense that different members of the Nine adopted radically different attitudes to it. Above all, since CSCE dealt mostly with abstract notions and principles, there were no splits between the Nine over major economic or financial interests. With the careful preparation that the Nine were able to give to CSCE it was they who dominated both the ministerial and expert phases of the talks held at Helsinki and Geneva. Not even the Soviet Union, the United States or NATO—with which the Nine maintained extremely close liaison during the preparation of the Conference—made a greater input into CSCE than the Nine and none of them were more successful than the Nine in achieving what they wanted.

But there have been many occasions when the Nine have been unable to react jointly either to an unforeseen crisis or to issues where overriding national interests divided them. Thus the Nine's record in voting together at the UN has been disappointing, reactions to political disturbances in Africa have been confused and, above all, the fragile network of EPC was

The Functions and Institutional Role of the European Parliament 57

almost ripped to pieces by the conflicting national reactions to the Yom Kippur War and the ensuing oil crisis.

It is not surprising that Mr Erik Blumenfeld, in a report for Parliament's Political Committee, has criticised the many evident weaknesses in the operation of EPC and has proposed, as a minimal step forward, the creation of a permanent administrative infrastructure for EPC in the form of a "political cooperation office" which would "coordinate and plan the foreign policy of the Community and its member states in the short-, medium-, and long-term".

The colloquies between Parliament's Political Committee and the Foreign Ministers, the annual debate on EPC and the replies given by the Council to questions concerning political cooperation have provided Parliament with a legitimate starting-point for a growing involvement in foreign policy. Parliament's questions and debates on EPC have enabled members of Parliament to go beyond strict Treaty subject-matter and to explore and help to develop a broad new area of activity by the Nine concerning a particularly significant area. This widening of the field of Community activity has not resulted from a struggle between Parliament and the other institutions but has grown, organically, in a pragmatic way from cooperation between the Foreign Ministers, the Commission and Parliament itself.

It is sometimes argued that the European Parliament is not competent to discuss foreign policy and above all defence. But over the years Parliament has developed an active interest in both these subjects. With foreign policy there is no longer any problem of formal competence. Parliament has been associated with EPC since the Foreign Ministers first started to coordinate selected foreign policy issues. The annual report of the Foreign Ministers to Parliament, the colloquies between the Foreign Ministers and Parliament's Political Committee together with questions tabled to the Conference of Foreign Ministers provide Parliament with a recognised basis for its discussions of foreign policy.

In its debates and resolutions Parliament has made its own impact on the external relations of the Nine by insisting on the need to defend, with other like-minded countries, human rights throughout the world, and on the need to oppose racism and apartheid, and on the need to promote forces working for democracy wherever this is feasible. Parliament has, indeed, been seen at its best in its repudiation of the Colonels' dictatorship in Greece and in the political encouragement it gave to the democratic political parties which replaced the Franco and Salazar régimes in Spain and Portugal.

Parliament has also started to debate security problems. Its right to do so is still questioned by those, such as the French Gaullists or the British Labour Left who regard defence, for different reasons, as being outside Parliament's competence. Those members of Parliament who are convinced that foreign policy cannot be seen in isolation from related defence problems have always claimed that the Bonn Declaration of July 1961 justifies Parliament's debating not only foreign policy but also defence.[1]

Thus, although any discussion of defence still remains controversial, a number of precedents have been established. It seems likely that security problems—or at least the security aspects of foreign policy—will be a subject of growing concern to Parliament in the future. In December 1975 the Parliament adopted a resolution submitted by Lord Gladwyn on the effects of a European foreign policy on defence questions, and in June 1978 it adopted a report drafted by Dr Egon Klepsch on European arms procurement cooperation.

Any discussion of the development of "European Union" on the basis of the proposals made by Mr Tindemans, the former Belgian Prime Minister, in his report to the European Council, is likely to consider the security aspects of European Union on which Mr Tindemans laid great stress in his report.

Parliamentary Initiatives

Whereas the Council and the Commission are very closely circumscribed in the subject-matter of their work by the strict limits imposed by the Treaties, Parliament enjoys a considerable degree of independence in organising its work. The main legal basis of this independence is Article 142 of the EEC Treaty which proclaims: "The Assembly shall adopt its rules of procedure". This independence is constrained by two provisions of the EEC Treaty. Article 4(1) states that: "Each institution shall act within

1. The Heads of State or Government meeting in Bonn in July 1961 stated that they had decided to "associate public opinion more closely with the efforts already undertaken, by inviting the European Parliament to extend the range of its debates to new fields, with the cooperation of the Governments".

The Functions and Institutional Role of the European Parliament 59

the limits of the powers conferred upon it by this Treaty"; and Article 137 lays down that "The Assembly shall exercise the advisory and supervisory powers which are conferred upon it by this Treaty". On the basis of Articles 4 and 137 of the EEC Treaty it could be argued that Parliament's subject-matter should be limited to (a) Treaty-based questions or (b) matters which the member governments had invited Parliament to examine—such as European Political Cooperation. But this is offset by the licence provided under Article 142, and in practice, Parliament, under its rules, is very much the master of its own agenda, both as concerns subject-matter and the timing of its business. There are obviously many subjects, such as Council consultations on Commission proposals, and the different parliamentary stages of the budget procedure, that Parliament must place on its agenda. But the decision to do so is its own and nobody else's. As compared to national Parliaments where both the subject-matter and timing of the parliamentary programme of work are largely determined by the government, the European Parliament is remarkably independent. The degree of this independence has been criticised on ideological grounds. Mr Michel Debré, before being elected as a member of the European Parliament, suggested that it should be the member governments of the Community which should fix the dates of Parliament's sessions and the subjects of its debates. The price paid for Parliament's freedom is the uncertainty that surrounds the order of business of each session until Parliament itself decides on the agenda for the week on the Monday evening of the session. It is extremely annoying for members of the Parliament, the media and those interested in following a particular debate, to find that the draft agenda for a session, as proposed by Parliament's Bureau, can bear little relation to the real order of business as decided by Parliament itself. Television crews and journalists have all too often arrived in Luxembourg or Strasbourg to cover a particular point only to find that it has already been dealt with on the previous day or has been put off to another time. Whilst the wrangling over the agenda that occurs in the chamber on the Monday of each part-session is certainly democratic, it is not very efficient.

Parliament's freedom to decide its programme of work takes its most interesting form in "own initiative reports". As opposed to the great majority of reports debated by Parliament in plenary, which set out Parliament's opinion on a legislative proposal of the Commission on which it has been consulted by the Council, initiative reports originate from within Parliament itself. A single member, or a number of members, can table a motion for a resolution on a subject dear to his or their collective heart and if the Bureau judges the subject to be sensible and not too far removed from the preoccupations of the Community or of the Nine as a whole it will instruct the appropriate committee to report to Parliament on it. Similarly one of Parliament's committees can request the Bureau for permission to carry out an initiative report. More often than not the Bureau gives the go-ahead.

Generally the initiative reports produced by Parliament's committees are aimed at focusing attention on some subject of general concern, such as road safety or aspects of fisheries policy, in order to draw the Commission's attention to an area where harmonisation measures or legislative proposals are desirable. These reports are aimed at stimulating the Commission into legislation but do not attempt to replace or supplant the Commission's right of initiative.

But in a few cases, and these have been the most interesting, Parliament's initiative reports have themselves either taken the form of draft legislation, with a request to the Commission to take over this legislation and submit it to the Council, or, whilst setting out the aims to be achieved by the Community in a new field, have called on the Commission to submit legislative proposals or an action programme to attain these aims.

An instance of detailed draft legislation being incorporated in an initiative report was that of a regulation concerning the protection of migrant birds. One of the most significant of Parliament's initiative reports was that submitted by Dr. Egon Klepsch, the German Chairman of the then Christian Democrat Group, which was adopted by Parliament in June 1978. The report concerned European armaments procurement cooperation,[1] and the resolution voted by Parliament called on the Commission "to submit to the Council in the near future a European action programme for the development and production of conventional armaments within the framework of a common industrial policy". Speaking on behalf of the Commission, in Parliament's debate, Viscount Davignon, the Commissioner responsible for industrial policy, promised that the Commission would act in the sense of the resolution. In institutional terms the Commission's response to Parliament's resolution marked a major change in

1. Published by Brassey's, London, 1979, under the title of *Two-Way Street: USA-Europe Arms Procurement.*

relations between the Parliament and the Commission since the Commission accepted Parliament's right to instruct it to initiate an action programme in an important field of Community activity. Although the justification, in Community terms, of the Klepsch proposal was that it pinpointed the need to move towards a common industrial policy in a specific sector, the fact that the sector concerned was armaments made the resolution a critical one since, although it primarily concerned industrial policy, it touched on the boundaries of the domains of security and defence which have been traditionally regarded as lying outside the competence of the Community. The adoption of the Klepsch report by Parliament, therefore, represented a courageous act of will and the Commission's promise that it would enact the resolution was even more courageous. The Commission's proposals for an action programme are still awaited but meanwhile members of the French Government and the French National Assembly have denounced both the resolution and the Commission's response to it on the grounds that they dealt with matters outside the competence of the Community.

Since, under the Treaties, it is the Commission which has the basic right of initiative within the Community, Parliament could only develop a major right to legislative initiative at the expense of the Commission. Most of those in Community circles would probably oppose such a development, considering that major legislation should originate, more properly, with an executive body rather than a parliamentary one. But migrant birds and armaments do open up the possibility of something like British private members' bills and there seems no reason why the directly elected Parliament should not complement the major legislative initiatives taken by the Commission with occasional proposals of its own.

Openness

One of the most useful functions of the European Parliament is, quite simply, that it sits in public. The meetings of the Commission at which new Community policy proposals are worked out are held in secret. The arguments between the Commissioners about the advantages and snags of policy proposals are not known, neither are the votes by which the Commission takes its decisions. When the Commission comes to present its proposals to the world it does so collectively as a collegiate body.

The Council of Ministers, too, holds all its meetings in secret and takes its decisions in secret. The cryptic press communiqués published by the Council reveal nothing of the bargaining and horsetrading that lead up to its decisions. Leaks to the press and study of the daily bulletin *Europe*[1] provide the only clues as to the nature of even the most important discussions in the Council.

In contrast to these secret conclaves of ministers and bureaucrats the European Parliament holds all its sessions in public. Whether one day's debate is more "interesting" or "duller" than another's is unimportant compared with the fact that it is held in public. This means that every significant piece of Community business comes to light when the European Parliament examines it. Thus it is the European Parliament that provides the natural focus for all those who wish to know what is happening in the Community. For the media, academic commentators, trades unions, trade associations and pressure groups, as well as the interested public, it is the Parliament which provides the essential elements of accessibility and openness in the Community—known as "transparency" in "Eurospeak".

This openness could certainly be improved. The many problems that the European Parliament still has to overcome in order to achieve effective supervision over Commission expenditure have already been discussed. Also, the need to obtain franker and fuller replies to questions from the Council and the Commission, and thus to bring their activities into the light of day has also been stressed. But these problems only accentuate the value of Parliament's role as the "open" institution of the Community.

Normally the European Parliament's committees meet in private, though representatives of the Commission are present and, on some occasions, representatives of the Council. An obvious way of increasing both the openness and the accessibility of Parliament would be for its committees to open up some selected meetings, or at least parts of them, to the public. There is nothing in the present rules of procedure to prevent this. Well organised discussions of topical problems held in public could do much to increase interest in Parliament's work and to attract coverage by the media. Following direct elections the Committee on Social Affairs and Employment has decided that all its meetings shall, normally, be open to the public.

One of the committees of the nominated European Parliament organised,

1. An extremely well informed news sheet concentrating on the Community's work in all its aspects, privately published in Brussels.

The Functions and Institutional Role of the European Parliament 63

as trial runs, three public hearings. The Transport Committee of the old Parliament held one hearing in Brussels on future methods of inter-city transport followed by two in Paris on the prevention of accidents at sea and air traffic control. Although the exchanges between members of the Committee and the expert witnesses were informative and useful in themselves, the main point of these three hearings was to permit the staff of Parliament's committees to develop the art of organising and mounting successful public hearings with an eye to the future. A number of members of the old Parliament, particularly Sir Peter Kirk and Mr John Prescott on the British side, already suggested that the exploitation of the public hearing technique by Parliament could be one of the most practical ways in which it could enlarge its influence and prestige.

Uniform Electoral System

An important responsibility given to the Parliament by Article 7 of the Convention on direct elections agreed by the member governments in September 1976 is that it "shall draw up a proposal for a uniform electoral procedure". Parliament is planning to make proposals for a uniform electoral system within the first five years of its life and is hoping that this system will be accepted by the national governments and parliaments in time to be used for the second European election campaign of 1984. But some governments will probably not wish to apply this system in the near future, and there is a danger that the use of different national systems of election might well continue for the second and even subsequent elections.

4

Structure and Operation

This chapter describes Parliament's structure and the nuts and bolts of its work. It deals, in turn, with the responsibilities of the President, the Bureau and the Quaestors, and then explains the role of the political groups, the committees in action, the working of the plenary session, and, finally, describes the structure and duties of the secretariat.

The President

The main duty of the President, under Rule 8 of the Rules of Procedure, is to "direct all the activities of Parliament and of its organs". The principal single function of the President, in this respect, is to preside over Parliament's sittings. Rule 8 lays down that: "The duties of the President shall be to open, adjourn and close sittings; to ensure observance of these Rules, maintain order, call upon speakers, close debates, put questions to the vote and announce the results of votes; and to refer to committees any communications that concern them." More generally, the President enjoys wide discretionary powers under Rule 8.

In practice the President's many obligations to chair other meetings, receive visitors and discuss urgent problems concerning Parliament's work result in him being able to preside over sittings of the Parliament for only part of the time that Parliament is in session. When the President himself is unable to take the chair for a sitting of Parliament, he requests one of the twelve Vice-Presidents to replace him.

Theoretically it is the President who chairs the delegations of Parliament which hold meetings with parliamentary delegations from friendly third countries. In practice the President has delegated this responsibility to other members, formerly a Vice-President, now members proposed by the political groups, to chair the 23 delegations that the directly elected Parliament has set up.

A particularly important and delicate task that is undertaken by the President is to chair Parliament's delegation, which is otherwise composed of members of the Committee on Budgets, at the meetings held with the Budget Council under the budgetary procedure. On these occasions the President, who has sometimes been replaced by the Chairman of the Committee on Budgets, has the heavy responsibility of leading Parliament's team in the complex and sometimes controversial negotiations with the Budget Ministers. Quite apart from leading the budget delegation, which involves the President chairing every second meeting between the delegation and the Budget Ministers—the Chairman of the Budget Council chairing the other meetings—the President plays a significant role in the budgetary procedure as a whole.

The President also leads Parliament's delegation, composed of members of the appropriate committee, at meetings held with the Council under the "conciliation procedure."[1]

The President of the Parliament has a demanding triple role. First, politically, he speaks for Parliament as a whole when dealing with the other Community institutions[2] and with national Parliaments and Governments. Second, he has an important ceremonial and protocol role in representing Parliament at conferences and functions and in making official visits. Finally, he has considerable administrative responsibility concerning the organisation of Parliament's work both at the level of plenary sittings and at that of committee meetings. The President's administrative responsibility also involves certain aspects of Parliament's internal administration, such as the appointment of administrative grade officials in the secretariat.[3]

1. The operation of the conciliation procedure is described in Chapter 3.
2. Informal private meetings are held three or four times a year between the President of the Council and the Presidents of Parliament and the Commission, with a small number of officials. These meetings permit the discussion of problems affecting relations between the three institutions.
3. The Presidents of the Parliament have been: Robert Schuman (1958–60), Hans Furler (1960–62), Gaetano Martino (1962–64), Jean Duvieusart (1964–65), Victor Leemans (1965–66), Alain Poher (1966–69), Mario Scelba (1969–71), Walter Behrendt (1971–73), Cornelis Berkhouwer (1973–75), Georges Spénale (1975–77), Emilio Colombo (1977–79) and Simone Veil who was elected in 1979.

Before direct elections the President was elected for an initial term of one year at Parliament's constituent session in March. It was customary for the President to be re-elected for a second year. In view of the prestige attaching to the post, the presidential election has often been preceded by intensive manoeuvring by the political groups. The directly elected Parliament has decided that the term of the presidency shall be two and a half years, half the life of an elected Parliament.

The Bureau

The Bureau consists of the President and the twelve Vice-Presidents of the Parliament. Before direct elections it was customary for each member state to be represented in the Bureau by at least one Vice-President. Following direct elections this has no longer been the case, since no Irish or Luxembourg Vice-Presidents were elected by Parliament in July 1979.[1]

The Bureau meets frequently in another and wider form known as the Enlarged Bureau, which includes the Chairmen of the political groups or their deputies as well as the Vice-Presidents. Different parts of the Rules of Procedure refer sometimes to the Bureau and sometimes to the Enlarged Bureau.

The Bureau, as such, has responsibilities concerning the place of meetings of committees, the verification of the credentials of members, reference of texts or documents to Parliament's committees, studies or fact-finding missions carried out by delegations or committees, the organisation of the secretariat and the establishment of the preliminary estimates of Parliament's draft budget.

The Enlarged Bureau, on the other hand, has responsibilities concerning changes in the dates of sessions, the draft agenda of plenary sessions, oral questions with or without debate, question time in general, decisions about the draft estimates of Parliament's budget and the interpretation of the Rules of Procedure.

Meetings of the Bureau and the Enlarged Bureau, which are held in private, are convened and chaired by the President and are normally held twice a month, once during and once between each session.

1. Though Irish and Luxembourg members were subsequently elected as members of the College of Quaestors in compensation.

In effect, the Bureau and the Enlarged Bureau are the supreme executive bodies of the European Parliament and their views and decisions are all-important in shaping the organisation and administration of Parliament's work. They replace to a large extent not only the "usual channels" in the United Kingdom Parliament but also the "leadership of the House" role which, in conjunction with the Whips' Offices, play so vital a part in the organisation of business at Westminster.

One major reform could be suggested concerning the composition of the Enlarged Bureau. Whereas the two main forces that dominate the substantive work of Parliament are the political groups and the committees, only one of these two forces, the political groups, are represented in the Enlarged Bureau—the permanent members of the Bureau, who are also the permanent core of the Enlarged Bureau, being the Vice-Presidents, representing national interests. But since national interests are not comparable in weight, in Parliament's work, to the weight of the groups or the committees, and are of less importance in the elected Parliament, it would seem logical for the committee chairmen either to sit in the Enlarged Bureau as full members alongside the chairmen of the groups, or to meet together with the group chairmen in a new joint body.

The Quaestors

In 1977, Parliament established a College of Quaestors whose task is to deal with administrative matters concerning members. There are five quaestors. In effect, the quaestors, who report to the Bureau, relieve the Bureau and the Enlarged Bureau of the burden of having to devote much of the limited time available to them to administrative matters. The problems dealt with by the quaestors include members' travel and other allowances, members' insurance rights, the working conditions of members, and the facilities available to members.

Political Groups

Rule 36 of the Rules of Procedure states that "Representatives may form themselves into groups according to their political affinity". The first political groups developed within the Common Assembly of the ECSC, with the Socialists, Christian Democrats and Liberals each establishing a party group in 1952 (although the groups were not recognised in the Assembly's Rules of Procedure until the following year). The European Democrats, the Communists and the European Progressive Democrats set up their groups later, and, following direct elections, the Group for the Technical Coordination and Defence of Individual Groups and Members came into being. In *Political Parties in the European Community*[1] Geoffrey and Pippa Pridham state: "The ultimate aim of the groups individually, and of the Parliament as a whole, is to influence Community legislation emanating from the Council of Ministers and the Commission. Within the Parliament, the main aim of the groups is to present a common political view on all matters arising in the committees and Parliament." To these two aims a third could be added: to act—to a greater or lesser degree depending on the precise political breakdown of each group—as a projection of the philosophies and policies, both national and "European", of the domestic political parties from which the groups are constituted.

The basic number of members required to form a political group, as laid down by Rule 36, is twenty-one in the event of its members all being of the same nationality. Fifteen members are required when two nationalities are involved, and ten is the minimum figure when at least three nationalities are concerned. During the first months of the life of the directly elected Parliament, attempts were made to raise the minimum number of members required to form a political group to take account of the increase in the number of members from 198 to 410, but the members of the newly formed Group for the Technical Coordination and Defence of Independent Groups and Members, who had formed their group, under the old Rules, with eleven members, conducted a spirited battle for survival and in consequence the new Rules agreed by Parliament concerning this point now permit a political group to consist of as few as ten members if these are drawn from at least three member states. There are, currently, seven political groups.

The political groups play a dominant role in the organisation of Parliament's business and have a major role in influencing Parliament's policies, in the form of its opinions on Community draft legislation and of other resolutions and reports, as they develop both in committee and on the

1. PSI, London, 1979.

floor of the house in plenary session. The chairmen of the groups are members of the Enlarged Bureau (see above) and as such they are largely responsible for establishing the draft agenda of plenary sessions and for taking other major decisions concerning Parliament's work. As the late Sir Peter Kirk, as leader of the then European Conservative Group, said in January 1973: "One of the things I've discovered here this week is that this place is virtually run by five men—the leaders of the five main political groups. We must constantly decide how business should be handled."[1] The groups also decide, in effect, on the allocation of each committee chairmanship to a specific group, and on the distribution between the groups of the vice-chairmen of the committees and the major rapporteurs, as explained later in this chapter. In debates group spokesmen are given priority over individual members.

Each group has a chairman and a bureau, which tends to be broadly representative of the national composition of the group. The administration of each group is carried out by its secretary general and secretariat under the responsiblity of its bureau. The policy of the group is decided by meetings of the group as a whole, which are normally held on the Monday, Tuesday, Wednesday and Thursday of each session and on two or more days during the week preceding each session, usually known as "group week". The meetings during the session are held in Luxembourg or Strasbourg, whilst the "group weeks" are normally held in Brussels[2]. The "group weeks" permit the political groups to adopt a group policy concerning the draft resolutions and reports which have already been adopted by Parliament's committees and which are due to be discussed during the following week's plenary session, and thus to lay down guidelines for the spokesmen appointed to speak on behalf of the groups in the relevant debates. The group meetings held during the session allow the groups to continue this process and to deal with or initiate new business, such as resolutions tabled under the urgent procedure, during the session. Apart from these meetings each political group is entitled, twice a year, to hold additional meetings concerned with longer term policy thinking. These are known as "study days".

1. *The Observer*, 21 January 1973. Quoted in *Towards Transnational Parties in the European Community*, Geoffrey and Pippa Pridham, PSI, London, 1979.
2. Though the European Democrats usually meet in London or, occasionally, in Copenhagen and the European Progressive Democrats sometimes meet in Paris or Dublin.

A number of the groups have working parties dealing with major topics of concern, such as agriculture, energy, regional and economic and social policy. These working parties usually meet *en marge* of full group meetings in Brussels or, during sessions, at Luxembourg and Strasbourg.

The costs of the operation of the political groups, including the salaries of their staff, are paid from Parliament's budget on the basis of the number of members of each group and the number of official Community languages represented in each group. Each group is responsible for ensuring that its expenditure does not exceed the budget to which it is entitled, and normally appoints a treasurer to supervise and check its finances. The groups are accountable to Parliament's financial controller and to the Court of Auditors concerning their expenditure. The funds the groups receive to pay the salaries of their staff are provided from Parliament's budget, but the political groups themselves have the sole right to recruit and dismiss their staff members who are not therefore established officials.

Since there are no "government" or "opposition" groups in the Parliament, and since there are seven distinct political groups, with representatives of over 50 national political parties, ranging through a wide political spectrum from the Communists on the left to the Liberals on the right, the political style with which Parliament conducts its business is very different from that of Westminster. Instead of confrontation between two directly opposed parties, Parliament's seven groups tend to look for coalitions when votes are taken in committee and in plenary session, whenever possible. Since, more often than not, Parliament is divided in its reactions to an issue any political group which wishes to assemble a majority in a vote must seek support from other groups. This requires compromises and "horse-trading" and leads to a "coalition" style of inter-group relations characteristic of continental parliamentary practice. This style is reflected in the seating arrangements of members in the chambers at Luxembourg and Strasbourg, which are described later in this chapter.

Although each political group tries to work out and express a common policy or attitude to every major issue arising in the work of Parliament and its committees, the degree of cohesion, in whipping and voting terms, is not comparable to that of political parties in national parliaments. Thus members quite often dissent from the majority view of their group colleagues in votes in committee and in plenary. The group whips would normally expect dissenters to inform them, before a vote, of their intention to take a different line from the group as a whole. The comparative independence of individual members, particularly British members, has increased since nominated members have been replaced by elected ones. The eagerness of some writers to establish that the political groups in the Parliament have already become transnational political parties—when, in effect, they still remain, as their official title of "political groups" indicates, broad coalitions and alliances of parliamentarians with similar, but not necessarily totally shared philosophies and objectives—has tended to create confusion about the character of the groups.

It is unrealistic to expect a very high degree of cohesion from members of a political group who, individually, have been elected to the Parliament as members not of a European political party but of a national one. There is a possibility that transnational European political parties may develop in the coming years. But whilst a dichotomy continues to exist between the separate national parties of which members of the Parliament are members in their home countries, on the one hand, and the political groups on the other, it is unlikely that "European political parties" will be any more cohesive or have any greater substance than the present political groups. As David Coombes has concluded in his book *The Future of the European Parliament*[1]: "It cannot be said . . . that anything resembling a European party system has emerged."

In the present circumstances it is not surprising that national or local interests or, more rarely, economic and social considerations will sometimes prove more important than the thinking of the political groups in determining members' attitudes to subjects considered by the Parliament. A Belgian member of the Group of the European People's Party might easily differ from his German colleagues on policies concerning trades unions, and an Irish Labour member could differ from the great majority of the Socialist Group concerning the level of agricultural prices. A brief study of the political composition of the groups in the Parliament will go far in explaining the differences that must first be resolved if the party groups in the European Parliament are to become transnational European political parties. A political group will have become a transnational party on the day when it presents candidates for election to the European Parliament in a number of member states, under the label of one single

1. PSI, London, 1979.

European party, be it Socialist, Christian Democrat or whatever. This would not necessarily imply the fusion of the different national Socialist or Christian Democratic parties, but it would imply the subordination of their separate identity to a common identity in the context of the European Parliament.

Three political groups are currently linked, at the European level, with transnational federations representing their constituent national parties—the Socialists, the Group of the European People's Party, which is closer to being a transnational party than the other two federations, and the Liberals. The formation of these three federations began with the Socialists in 1974 and gathered significance in view of moves taken by the European Parliament and the governments of the Nine to hold direct elections. The federations worked out policies for the guidance of the candidates of their national parties for the European elections of June 1979 and agreed, also, on forms of coordination between the national parties for the first European election campaign. The federations have also been useful in maintaining links between the three political groups concerned in the European Parliament and the corresponding political parties in the national parliaments of the Nine. The personal identity of the staff working for the political groups and for the federations, and the considerable degree of overlapping between parliamentary members of the political groups and of the federations has also been important in helping to develop a harmonious relationship between the political groups in the European Parliament and their corresponding national parties.

It might now be useful to examine, briefly, the present composition and characteristics of each of the political groups in turn.

The Socialist Group

The Socialists are the largest group in the directly elected Parliament, with 113 members[1]. The group is the most broadly based of all the political groups, with parliamentarians from each of the nine member states, as follows, 35 Germans, 22 French, 18 British[2], 13 Italians, 9 Dutch, 7 Belgians, 4 Danes, 4 Irish and 1 Luxembourger. The tradition of inter-

1. 120 as of 1 February 1981, including 7 Greek members.
2. Including one member from Northern Ireland.

national cooperation between Socialists has been a major factor in enabling the group to develop a considerable degree of political cohesion in its activities in the Parliament. Indeed, before the enlargement of the Community in January 1973 the Socialist Group was the best whipped and most consistently united of the groups with regard to both voting and the expression of political attitudes. The degree of unity achieved by the group also reflected the common ideology shared by Socialists in the member states of the Community. Until July 1975 the Socialist Group was also the most highly organised and disciplined of the groups, internally. Since then the European Democrats have proved to be a more cohesive and more strictly disciplined group than the Socialists, but this has largely been due to the obvious reason that the overwhelming majority of its members come from one party in one country. Thus the Socialists' record remains impressive, particularly in view of the fact that every Community state is represented in the Socialist Group.

However, the ideological solidarity of the group has been weakened both as a result of the very different political approach to the Community and European integration brought into the group by some British members (who first joined the Socialist Group in July 1975 after boycotting the Parliament since January 1973) and by the separate political stance often adopted by French Socialists. Whereas the continental members of the group share a belief in a mixed economy, with cooperation between management and workers as a normal practice, a number of British Labour members of the Parliament do not share the "social democratic" philosophy of their continental colleagues and are also opposed to integration at the European level. The addition of Danish members to the group since January 1973 has also increased the group's problems in trying to achieve common attitudes, since Danish Socialist members have shared the fears of the Danish Parliament concerning the growth of the Community's powers and further moves towards European integration. At present, however, the problems of getting the French to go along with the rest of the group is the major difficulty, due mainly to the tendency of the French Socialists to put the views of the French Socialist Party before those of the group.

If any one national group of members within the Socialist Group has been dominant, it has been the German Socialists (SPD). In a way this is a natural reflection of the major role played by Germany in the Community as a whole. Although the group contains exponents of a "left wing" approach in the form of some British, French and Italian members, the overall tone of the Socialist Group's policies has been "moderate".

It was interesting, in the former designated Parliament, to observe how many of the British Labour members who came to the Parliament as "anti-marketeers" not only became deeply involved in Parliament's work, but ended up as vigorous advocates of at least some Community sectoral policies.

The Socialist Group maintains close links with Socialist members of the national parliaments of the Nine through the Confederation of the Socialist Parties of the Community which was set up in 1974.

Group of the European People's Party

The Christian Democrats sit in the Parliament as members of the Group of the "European People's Party", which is the name of the federation[1] of the Christian Democratic parties in the Community, which was founded in 1976 in view of the forthcoming direct elections[2]. The group has 107[3] members and is the second largest of the political groups. Its members are drawn from seven member states, excluding Britain and Denmark, as follows, 42 Germans (34 CDU and 8 CSU), 30 Italians (including one member of the South Tyrol *Volkspartei*), 10 Belgians, 10 Dutch, 8 French, 4 Irish (all Fine Gael) and 3 Luxembourgers. Traditionally, the Christian Democrats have been the nucleus of the "centre-right" in the Parliament, and have thus acted as the main political balance to the "centre-left" Socialist Group, and a high proportion of Parliament's policy debates have been polarised between the Christian-Democratic and Socialist approaches. Whereas the Socialist Group has been the main spokesman of the "European left", the Christian Democrats have been the leading force of a rough coalition of the "European centre-right" which has often included the

---

1. Although named "Party" it remains, as yet, in the author's view, a transnational federation, albeit more ambitious in its character than the other European party federations.
2. The Christian Democratic parties of the Community and *other* European countries belong to a wider and looser federation, the European Union of Christian Democrats.
3. 108 as of 1 February 1981.

British and Danish Conservatives, and on many occasions, the Liberals. Although the Socialist Group was the largest single group in the period before direct elections and remains the largest group in the new Parliament, pragmatic but consistent voting alliances between the Group of the European People's Party, the European Democrats and the Liberals result in the centre-right holding a basic overall majority in the Parliament,[1] even though French and Italian Communists and some other members will sometimes vote with the Socialists.

Although there is an important Catholic strand in Christian Democracy many Christian Democrats are Protestants, and it is the traditional and overriding devotion of the Group to European federalism that is the ideological hall-mark of Christian Democracy.

If the Socialist Group can be characterised as the Group of the European industrial worker,[2] the Christian Democrats tend to speak for management, business, big and small, and for agriculture—though strong support for the CAP and the farming interest is widespread in the Parliament, cutting across political group divisions.

If, however, the Christian Democrats have found it more difficult than the Socialists to formulate common attitudes concerning some Community sectoral policies, they have been united in consistently stressing, particularly with regard to institutional questions and the long-term aims of the Community, the integrationist nature of their ideology. In their deep commitment to the "European idea" they consider themselves to be the successors of Adenauer, de Gasperi and Schuman.

Since the great majority of the Group (72) are German or Italian it is not surprising that the political attitudes expressed within it very largely reflect the national attitudes of the CDU/CSU in Germany and the Italian Christian Democratic Party. Although many differences of emphasis exist within the Group, for instance between German and Italian and Dutch members, these are not divisive to a significant degree. A pragmatic spirit of compromise informs relations between the different nationalities inside the Group.

1. In the present Parliament this wider coalition, including the Liberals, is known as the "Presidential majority" since it groups together those who supported Simone Veil in her successful bid to become President of the Parliament.
2. Together with the French and Italian Communists and the Belgian Social Christians.

The European Democratic Group

With 64 members[1] the European Democratic Group is the third largest of the political groups. It is composed of 60 British Conservative members, together with 1 Ulster Unionist member from Northern Ireland, 2 Danish Conservatives and 1 Danish Centre Democrat.

The Group was formed as the "European Conservative Group" by British and Danish Conservative members of the Parliament in January 1973, immediately after the enlargement of the Community. Following direct elections the Group changed its name to the European Democratic Group.

Since members of the Group are drawn from two nationalities only, its base is narrow. But the fact that the overwhelming majority of its members are members of a single political party in one member state gives the Group a greater degree of political cohesion than that of any of the other political groups. This makes it comparatively straightforward for the European Democratic Group to work out and present common attitudes concerning Community policy and other questions considered by Parliament. It also makes whipping easy and enables the European Democrats to present a solid and united front in votes both in committee and in plenary. Largely because of this the Group has been able to achieve a greater political impact than its numbers might suggest.

Broadly speaking the British Conservatives in the European Democratic Group tend to represent, politically, management, the professions and agriculture, but, since Britain used a constituency system for European elections of June 1979, each British member of the Parliament, be he Conservative or Labour, represents a distinct geographical area—and the whole complex of employers, labour, industry, commerce and agriculture within that area.

Both in the former designated Parliament and in the directly elected Parliament Conservatives have shown a particular interest in the establishment of an effective system of financial control over Community expenditure. They have also sought to reform the CAP by trying to reduce expenditure on agricultural surpluses and their storage, and, in the present Parliament, Conservative members have been to the fore in leading Parliament towards the discussion of security matters.

1. 63 as of 1 February 1981.

During the first two and a half years following British entry into the Community, in 1973, before the Labour Party decided after the 1975 referendum to send Labour MPs to the Parliament, the Conservative members,[1] by necessity, represented the British national interest in the Parliament, quite apart from representing their party interest.

The European Democratic Group maintains a close relationship with the Group of the European People's Party and often concerts its political strategy and tactics jointly with the Christian Democrats, particularly as regards voting. Within the broader "presidential alliance", grouping the Christian Democrats, Conservatives and Liberals, a special relationship links the Conservatives and the Christian Democrats.

A question that is often asked is why do the Conservatives not join the Christian Democrats within the Group of the European People's Party? Since 1973 there have been contacts between Conservatives and Christian Democrats, Liberals and Gaullists concerning the possible establishment of intimate and permanent political links between the Conservatives and one or other of these other groups. Although British Conservatives would probably find it easier to form a joint political group with the Christian Democrats than with the Liberals or the Gaullists, the present position seems to be that the pragmatic alliance based on mutual interests that already works well between the Conservatives and the Christian Democrats has proved its utility and does not need to be formalised in the immediate future.[2] Under the existing arrangement each of the Groups retains: first, its independence and a considerable degree of flexibility, in the knowledge that its ally is usually to be relied on in supporting it in time of need; second, all the advantages which go with being a separate group.

The British Conservative members of the Group keep in close touch with the Conservative Party leadership at Westminster and the Chairman of the Group has direct access to Mrs Thatcher. However, the Group is in many respects an autonomous entity and on occasion it has adopted policy stands different from those of the Conservative Government, notably on some budgetary issues.

1. Together with two British Liberals and two British Independents.
2. There are also difficulties to be overcome, on both sides, before a joint group could be formed. These include some ideological problems, but at present a major obstacle is that with 61 British members the balance of power within the Group of the European People's Party would be completely overturned.

The Communist and Allies Group

The Communist Group is formed mainly by French and Italian Communists. Besides the 24 Italian Communists and the 19 French Communists there is one Danish member of the Group. Two French and five Italian members of the Group are "allies", who are not members of their national Communist parties but share the Group's overall political approach and were put forward as candidates, at the European elections, on the list of the French and Italian national Communist parties. The Danish member is also an "ally".[1]

Although the French and Italian Communists find it convenient as well as ideologically desirable to belong to a single Communist Group in the Parliament, they are divided by major differences of political philosophy. Also, they often hold disparate views concerning the substantive issues that are debated in Parliament. This situation is reflected in the fact that both French and Italians express a viewpoint on important matters debated by Parliament through separate spokesmen, in place of the single official spokesman speaking for each of the other groups. However, the tensions that continue to exist between the French and Italian members of the Communist Group have made it difficult for the Group to play a political role in Parliament's work commensurate with its size.

Whereas Italian Communists do not hesitate to assert their independence of the Moscow political line, it is clear that French Communist members are often sympathetic to Soviet thinking. Thus while the Italian Communists have consistently supported moves towards European integration, which would, in their view, benefit Italy and Italian workers, French Communists have consistently opposed supranationality and have expressed scepticism about the work and aims of the Community. Occasionally the French and Italian Communists have joined in expressing a common view, in Parliament, concerning world events, particularly in denouncing totalitarian regimes of the extreme right.

The Liberal and Democratic Group

The Liberal Group consists of 40 members,[2] drawn from eight member

1. The Group has 45 members as of 1 February 1981, including one Greek.
2. 39 as of 1 February 1981.

countries. There are 17 French members, 5 Italian, 4 Belgian, 4 Dutch, 4 German, 3 Danish and 2 Luxembourg members, and 1 Irish member.

Although the Liberal Group is no longer one of the largest political groups in the Parliament, it has always played a significant political role in Parliament's work. The national parties which compose the Liberal Group have very differing attitudes concerning major sectoral policies such as agriculture, fisheries and energy.

Whereas the Liberals from Belgium, Luxembourg and the Netherlands tend to support big business, the Danish and French Liberals[1] are reticent in this respect. The diversity of the Liberal Group's philosophy is symbolised by the German Liberal party, the FDP, which includes both right-wing and radical members. If there is an identifiable strand of policy running through all the Liberal parties represented in the Group, it is a concern for the defence of human rights, with a shared dislike of "bureaucracy" as a secondary strand. The Liberals attach great importance to private enterprise.

Partly because of the difficulty that members of the Liberal Group often find in agreeing on joint attitudes concerning major sectoral policies of the Community, they have placed a high priority on theoretical and long-term aims, such as institutional reforms, the development of European Political Cooperation into a common European foreign policy, and the development of a European defence policy, concerning which group cohesion has been easier to achieve.

A specific aim of the Liberal Group is to ensure that the uniform electoral system that Parliament is due to propose to the member governments in view of the 1984 European elections should be based on proportional representation. Under a form of proportional representation Liberals would hope to see several Liberal members elected to the Parliament from Britain.

The Liberal Group in the Parliament works closely with the national Liberal parties of the Community in the Federation of Liberal and Democratic Parties of the European Community, set up in 1976, and it also maintains links with Liberal parties, including parties from non-Community countries, in the Liberal International and the Liberal Movement for a United Europe.

1. Until 1962 the French Gaullists were members of the Liberal Group.

The Group of European Progressive Democrats

The Group of European Progressive Democrats consists of 22 members, with 15 French, and 5 Irish members and one member each from Denmark and Britain (a Scottish SNP member). Whereas a majority of the French members are Gaullists (*Rassemblement pour la République*—RPR), some of them are "allies" of the Gaullists, whose candidates were presented by the RPR on a joint list—list 10, entitled *Défence des intérêts de la France en Europe*—in France for the 1979 European election, the Irish members are all drawn from the Fianna Fail Party.

Politically there is little in common between the French Gaullists and the Irish Fianna Fail members, but both sets of parliamentarians find it useful to share the facilities and enjoy the benefits that membership of a political group confers. Although ideologically their alliance seems a somewhat odd marriage of convenience the Fianna Fail and the Gaullist Party are similar in that each of them draws its inspiration from a single historical figure and in practical terms the alliance would appear to be an arrangement that suits both sides.

Within the Parliament the Gaullists have been—like the French Socialists and the French Communists—vigilant in seeking to maintain and protect the national interests and sovereignty of France. Some Gaullists have inherited the philosophy of General de Gaulle concerning the role and nature of the European Community and of the European Parliament[1] advocating the restriction of the competences of the Community within the limits fixed by the Treaties and trying to ensure that the European Parliament does not encroach on the powers of national parliaments. However, the Gaullists have not always maintained a united front concerning European institutional problems or European policies in general, since the rifts that exist within the RPR at a national level have been reflected within the European Parliament. Gaullist members of the Parliament have—like all French members of the Parliament, regardless of party—consistently supported the CAP in its traditional form and have advocated high farm prices. Like successive French governments, Gaullist members have been prominent in working for close aid and trade links between the Community and developing countries—a process which can be traced back to French concern for France's former colonies in Africa.

1. Which they prefer to call the "Assembly".

Structure and Operation 81

The Fianna Fail electorate is basically Catholic and rural, and, like the Gaullists, Fianna Fail members place a high priority on maintaining both the CAP and high agricultural prices. The Fianna Fail members also share a common approach with the Gaullists concerning regional and social policy.

There is no European Community or international federation of the national political parties which make up the Group of European Progressive Democrats, but the Gaullists belong, together with other Community and non-Community "conservative" parties, including the CDU/CSU and the British and Scandinavian Conservative parties, to the loose European Democratic Union.

The Group for the Technical Coordination and Defence of Independent Groups and Members

The Group, often simply called "the Coordination Group", is the smallest political group, with eleven members. It is composed of 5 Italians (of whom three are members of the Radical Party), 4 Danes, one Belgian and one Irish member.

The Coordination Group has a number of unusual features. First, its chairmanship rotates, every four months, from one to the other of the three members of its Bureau. At secretariat level, the post of secretary general is shared between three co-secretaries general.

The Danish members of the Group are members of the *Folkebevaegelsen*, the anti-common market party which fought direct elections in Denmark on a platform advocating Danish withdrawal from the Community. The three Italian Radicals are members of a new political party which has recently made a considerable impact in Italian politics, first, by increasing its representation in the Italian Parliament from four to sixteen members in the most recent national election and, second, by the colourful means it employs to focus public opinion on its activities.

Because of their fundamental hostility to Danish membership of the Community, the Danish members of the Group have been extremely reticent about committing themselves to an active role in the work of Parliament and its committees. In marked contrast the Italian Radicals have acted with panache and flamboyance in drawing the attention of the

Parliament and the media to their political ideas. Although their unconventional behaviour has been regarded as a nuisance by many members of the Parliament some have seen the activities of the Coordination Group as a refreshing injection of activist democracy in the directly elected Parliament.

The main common interest of members of the Group is the joint protection of the many different minority viewpoints it represents.

The Non-attached Members

There are nine independent or non-attached members of the Parliament, 4 Italian Neo-Fascists, 2 Belgian members of the French-speaking Democratic Front, 2 Dutch Democrats '66 members, and 1 Northern Ireland member of the Democratic Union Party.[1]

The Committees in Action

The European Parliament has fifteen standing committees:
Political Committee, 41 members;
Committee on Agriculture, 39 members;
Committee on Budgets, 37 members;
Committee on Economic and Monetary Affairs, 37 members;
Committee on Energy and Research, 34 members;
Committee on External Economic Relations, 36 members;
Legal Affairs Committee, 25 members;
Committee on Social Affairs and Employment, 27 members;
Committee on Regional Policy and Regional Planning, 29 members;
Committee on Transport, 25 members;
Committee on Youth, Culture, Education, Information and Sport, 25 members;
Committee on Development and Cooperation, 27 members;
Committee on Budgetary Control, 27 members;
Committee on the Rules of Procedure and Petitions, 27 members.[2]

1. As of 1 February 1981 16 Greek members, sitting separately, still have to decide which political group, if any, they will join.
2. For details of changes in the size of Committees following Greek accession see Appendix III.

An *ad hoc* Committee on Women's Rights, with 35 members, was also set up at the end of 1979 to report back to Parliament on the problems and status of women. Its work should have been completed by the summer of 1980.

Membership of Parliament's committees is determined by the political groups. Each group has the effective right, subject to a formal decision by Parliament as a whole, to so many seats in each committee, proportionally, according to its size. The independent members of Parliament, such as Madame Spaak, of the Belgian "French-speaking Democratic Front", who do not belong to any of the party groups, have the effective right to membership of one committee each. The chairmen of the committees, although formally elected by the committees themselves, are, in reality, the nominees of the political groups, as are the vice-chairmen. Each political group has the right to a number of committee chairmanships, and vice-chairmanships, according to its size. Rule 37 of the Rules of Procedure provides that committees shall have a minimum of three vice-chairmen each. The chairman and vice-chairmen of a committee together constitute the committee's *"Bureau"* and will sometimes meet in private to prepare committee business. The political groups choose, in turn, the committee chairmanships they wish to occupy, within the framework of the overall agreement concerning the number of chairmanships each group should have, starting with the largest group and working through to the smaller. Thus the Socialist Group, as the largest political group in Parliament following direct elections, holds five committee chairmanships at present, whereas the Liberals and the European Progressive Democrats have one chairmanship each. The Group for the Technical Coordination and Defence of Independent Groups and Members, which is by far the smallest of the political groups, has no chairmanship. Chairmanship, vice-chairmanship and membership of the committees lasts for a year. The committees are reconstituted each March, when their officers are elected or re-elected. In the directly elected Parliament it is normally the case that a member of the Parliament is a full member of one committee and a substitute member of another. Substitute members may attend and speak at committee meetings but may only vote in the absence of the full member.

The main task of the committees is to prepare Parliament's opinions on the legislative proposals of the Commission. When the Commission transmits a legislative proposal to the Council it sends, unofficially, a copy to Parliament at the same time. This enables Parliament's appropriate committee to start work at secretariat level on the preparation of Parliament's Opinion even before the Council officially requests Parliament to give its opinion on the Commission proposal prior to the Council taking its decision. When Parliament is formally "seized" by the Council, the President of the Parliament formally transmits the Council's request for an opinion to the competent committees, together with the Commission's legislative proposal. One committee will be requested to submit a report to the plenary session on the substance of the Commission proposal, together with a draft resolution, whilst other committees—but not, normally, more than three—which have a direct and legitimate interest in the proposal may submit opinions to the committee responsible for preparing the report, which it can take into account in formulating its report and draft resolution.

The committee responsible for preparing the report appoints a rapporteur. The text of a report (known as the explanatory statement) is the personal text of the rapporteur, who may alter it at the request of members of the committee but often decides to maintain it unchanged. Before the rapporteur drafts his text it is normal for the committee to hold a general exchange of views on the proposal under consideration. This can provide the rapporteur with an idea of the committee's thinking, and, if necessary, guidelines for his work. The rapporteur will prepare the draft report and resolution which, bearing in mind the views expressed by the draftsmen of other committees which wish to submit an opinion on the proposal, will be examined by his committee on one or more occasions before the committee votes on and adopts the draft resolution. The draft resolution may be amended by the committee when its vote takes place before it is sent on to a subsequent plenary session of Parliament.

Although the rapporteur is appointed by the committee, his nomination normally results from an agreement between the political groups. In several of the committees each political group is represented by a "coordinator". The group coordinators of the separate committees concerned meet together on a regular basis and are responsible, within the framework of the instructions given to them by the political groups, for the distribution of rapporteurships. A similar system governs the appointment of the draftsmen of committee opinions.

Once a rapporteur has been appointed it is customary for him to act as the spokesman of his committee as a whole on the subject of his report

Structure and Operation 85

rather than as a national or group spokesman. Expression of a political group or national slant or policy is not excluded but traditionally the rapporteur expresses the consensus or majority viewpoint of his committee.

When the committee's report and draft resolution are debated in plenary session, it is the task of the rapporteur to explain and defend his committee's views and proposals before Parliament as a whole, and when it comes to the consideration of amendments tabled to the committee's resolution it is for the rapporteur to try to guide members of the Parliament by stating whether he finds each amendment acceptable or not.

As soon as Parliament has adopted the resolution—in its original or amended form—it becomes Parliament's Opinion on the Commission's legislative proposal and it is immediately sent, together with the supporting report, to the Council and the Commission in the hope that it will influence their decisions on the Commission proposal it being for the Commission to decide, in the first place, on Parliament's amendments.

Quite apart from their formal role in Community legislation, Parliament's committees have an informal opportunity of influencing Community policy. The Commissioner responsible for the subject-matter covered by one of Parliament's committees will normally make a point of attending meetings of that committee from time to time so as to discuss Community policy in that sector with its members. In addition senior members of his staff will invariably be present when asked to attend. These contacts permit members of the committee to develop an understanding of Commission thinking and provide useful opportunities for members of the committee to make suggestions to the Commissioner. The Commissioner will often find it useful to outline his ideas concerning major new policy proposals that he has in mind before these are formally tabled. In doing so he will hear the views of members of the committee who may be able, in this way, to influence the formulation of Commission policy proposals at the pre-legislative phase.

Committees are also able to influence Community policy-making through initiative reports, known as "own initiative" reports, in which they can explore and suggest new areas of Community activity. But if a committee wishes to draw up an initiative report it must first request the permission of the Bureau, which acts as a filter for unsuitable topics.

In effect the preparation of Parliament's plenary sessions is largely carried out in committee, to the extent that the reports debated in plenary session result directly from the work of the committees. The criticism has sometimes been expressed that the intensive examination of reports and draft resolutions at the committee stage means that the real debate on a Commission proposal has already taken place, with the result that the debate on the floor of the house is often less interesting than the preparatory discussion in committee. There is some truth in this criticism, but there is enormous pressure on the limited amount of time available for debates in plenary session and as this pressure is continually increasing it seems possible that, in the years ahead, a high proportion of the most intensive discussions will continue to take place primarily in committee rather than in plenary session. But plenary debate allows the general perspective to be considered as a counterbalance to the more technical view taken by a committee—and also acts as a democratic check to committee work.

A small number of Parliament's committees, notably its Transport and Energy Committees, have established the practice of holding, from time to time, an exchange of views with the Council of Ministers by inviting to their meetings the President of the appropriate Council of specialist ministers. The Political Committee holds quarterly meetings, in the form of the Colloquy, with the Foreign Minister chairing the Conference of Foreign Ministers[1] to examine progress in European Political Cooperation, as described in Chapter 3. Appropriate committees—often including the Political and Development Committees and the Committees on Agriculture and on External Economic Relations—also hold at least one meeting with the President of the Council during the course of each major negotiation between the Community and a third country concerning an association, cooperation or commercial agreement, in order to be briefed concerning the development of the negotiations. As explained in Chapter 3 this procedure is known as the "Luns-Westerterp procedure". Meetings of the kind described above can provide members of the Parliament with a valuable insight into the thinking of the Council and the Foreign Ministers though they have not yet provided very much parliamentary input into Council policies. The directly elected Parliament might well be able to develop links of this kind with the Council in such a way as to influence the Council's sectoral policies.

1. Formally known as the Foreign Ministers meeting in Political Cooperation.

Members of the secretariat of the Commission normally attend meetings of Parliament's committees, as do members of the Council secretariat. Commission staff are frequently asked to explain the Commission's viewpoint, in the absence of the responsible Commissioner, at the request of members. In the past, Parliament's committees have traditionally met in private, but following direct elections the public has been admitted to some committee meetings, notably those of the Committee on Social Affairs and Employment. Before direct elections at least two of Parliament's committees held public hearings, and in the new directly elected Parliament a number of committees have organised public hearings in order to obtain information from outside experts on subjects concerning which they are preparing reports. These hearings resemble, in some respects, public hearings held by committees of some of the national parliaments of the Nine or by those of the U.S. Senate and House of Representatives. The two essential features of a public hearing are, first, that the public and the media are admitted, and, second, that the verbatim record of the proceedings is published. These hearings, which are still at an experimental stage, could develop in two directions—first, fact-finding, in view of a consequent report and recommendations of the committee concerned, and, possibly leading to Community legislation; second, investigatory, concerning, for instance, expenditure of Community funds in a specific sector. Public hearings should not be confused with open or public meetings of committees, which have also been held since direct elections, which are merely normal committee meetings opened to the public and the media, who may listen to the proceedings without actively taking part.

The work of Parliament's committees is subject to the intricate interplay of political group policies and national interests, but the technical interest of the subject-matter of some of the committees tends to develop a committee "team spirit" which can transcend party and national differences, especially under good chairmanship.

Committees are not normally permitted to meet during plenary session of Parliament except, as in the case of the Committee on Budgets during the budgetary procedure, in urgent circumstances. They normally meet during the first and second weeks following each session of Parliament, either once or twice, with meetings normally spread over two days, starting on the afternoon of the first day and finishing towards lunch-time the next day. Committee meetings are usually held in Parliament's offices at Brussels.

TEP - G

Each committee is entitled to hold one meeting a year outside Parliament's three working places of Brussels, Luxembourg and Strasbourg.

Following direct elections some of the committees have set up sub-committees and working parties which prepare the approach of their parent committees to major problems. Thus the Political Committee has created sub-committees on a uniform electoral system and on institutional questions, and the Committee on Agriculture has set up a sub-committee on fisheries.

The Plenary Session

Under the Treaties the European Parliament holds one "session" a year, but in practice this is divided into "part-sessions" which are normally held for one week each month, with the exception of August, alternately in Luxembourg and Strasbourg.[1] Parliament holds a "constituent session" in Strasbourg each March, when the membership of its committees is decided and when the chairmen and vice-chairmen of the committees are elected or re-elected. In the past Parliament elected or re-elected its President each March also, but, as indicated above, the directly elected Parliament has decided that the President's term of office shall last half an electoral period, that is two and a half years.

A part-session of Parliament (referred to quite simply as "session" for the sake of convenience) normally runs for a week from the Monday afternoon, ending in the early afternoon on Friday.

First and foremost, Parliament makes use of its session to debate the reports of its committees on Commission legislative proposals, and when it adopts the accompanying resolutions these are transmitted to the Commission and the Council as Parliament's opinions on the Commission's proposals. Second, it is during sessions that Parliament's supervision of the work of the Commission is most clearly to be seen, especially in the form of questions which are normally put to the Commission on Mondays. Third, Parliament's sessions provide, on Wednesdays, its main opportunity for contacts with the Council, both through questions to the Council

1. During 1979 and 1980 most sessions of the directly elected Parliament are being held in Strasbourg where a chamber capable of holding 410 members is already available.

and the Foreign Ministers and in the form of debates in which members of the Council can outline the Council's policies and submit them to parliamentary scrutiny. Fourth, Parliament devotes a considerable proportion of its working time to oral questions with debate. Political groups each have the right to place one oral question on the agenda of each session. Oral questions with debate give Parliament the chance to discuss topical matters of public concern.[1] Parliament's committees can also submit initiative reports on subjects they consider to be important and these are debated in plenary session. Finally, the Community budgetary procedure not only passes through Parliament but is largely enacted during Parliament's sessions, especially the crucial final stages and the vote on the adoption or the rejection of the budget as a whole.

It is to Parliament that the incoming Presidents of the Council announce the programme for their country's six-month presidency, and it is to Parliament also that the President of the Commission announces his action programme for the current year in February. Reports are also made to Parliament after European Council meetings by the Prime Minister or Foreign Minister of the country chairing the European Council, and, annually, by the Chairman of the Foreign Ministers concerning their previous year's activities in European Political Cooperation. These are all debated.

A normal session of Parliament is organised broadly as follows: following meetings of the political groups the session will open at 5 o'clock on Monday afternoon with the discussion of the week's agenda. Although Parliament's agenda is previously planned by the Enlarged Bureau, there are usually suggestions or complaints concerning the draft agenda, and this procedural debate can drag on for some time until Parliament agrees its definite programme for the week. The decision on the agenda is followed by a statement by the Commission on the action it has taken on Parliament's opinions and proposals. This is followed, until 8.00, by a period of questions to the Commission lasting for an hour and a half.

On Tuesday and Wednesday Parliament sits from 9.00 until 1.00 and from 3.00 to 7.00, with time for political group meetings being reserved from 7.00 until 8.00 in the evening. On Thursday the political groups meet from 9.00 until 10.00. Parliament then sits from 10.00 until 1.00 and from 3.00 until 8.00, when there is a break for dinner, with the late hours being

1. Though they can have the effect of a major theme being less well prepared for debate than by a committee in the form of a report and draft resolution.

reserved for a night sitting, which may last until midnight. On Wednesday an hour is reserved for question time to the Council concerning Community business, and a half-hour to the Foreign Ministers concerning European Political Cooperation.

On Friday, Parliament meets at 9.00 in the morning until it concludes its week's work early in the afternoon.

The debates on committee reports lie at the heart of Parliament's business, together with Parliament's monthly debate on a theme of major political importance. For a report to be debated in plenary session it must be adopted and tabled by the committee concerned at least twelve days before the session and be made available in the six working languages at least twenty-four hours before the debate. Exceptions are made for debates concerning reports, under the urgent procedure (see below).

The rapporteur of the responsible committee opens the debate. He is followed by the spokesmen of the political groups, who speak in the order of the size of their groups. The group spokesmen are followed by other members of the Parliament. The rapporteur and sometimes the chairman of the committee concerned will reply to the debate, and the Minister speaking for the Council and the competent Commissioner usually speak towards the end of the debate, just before the rapporteur's reply.

Speakers are limited as to the time of their speeches according to a general decision taken at the beginning of each session, unless a different specific decision is taken by the Parliament, as to the time for a particular debate. Generally speaking, the maximum time allotted to rapporteurs and group spokesmen is fifteen minutes, with ten minutes for other speakers though Parliament often reduces this. For many debates Parliament decides that the total speaking time will be divided between the political groups, in accordance with their size, which results in each political group dividing up speaking time between its speakers to fit into the overall time allotted to the group.

Debates on declarations made by the President of the Council or by the Commission are handled in a similar way.

Speakers who raise points of order have priority at all times, if the President considers that the points they are making are genuine points of order.

For oral questions with debate, the spokesman of those members tabling the question is allowed to speak for ten minutes, and other speakers are given five minutes.

Structure and Operation 91

At question time the member tabling the question must be present in the chamber when his question is called, though he may be replaced by a substitute subject to prior notification to the President. If he is not present a reply is given in writing. The Minister or Commissioner then replies on behalf of his institution. Members may then put supplimentary questions to the Minister or the Commissioner. These, and the replies, must be brief. Questions to the Commission must be tabled with at least one week's notice and to the Council with at least five week's notice.

Members may also table questions for written answer to the Council, the Foreign Ministers and the Commission. These questions and their answers are published in the Official Journal; answers are supposed to be provided within two months, but are often delayed for many months.

Debates may be held by Parliament under the urgent procedure. The Rules lay down that a debate may be treated as urgent following a request in that sense by the President, by 21 members or more, or by the Commission or the Council. If such a request is made in writing by one third of the members of the Parliament it is automatically granted. The President informs Parliament concerning other requests for urgent debate and a vote on such a request is held at the beginning of the next sitting. Matters for which urgent debate is agreed take priority on the agenda of that part session. An urgent debate may be held on the basis of a statement made by the appropriate committee or without report.

Parliament takes its decisions by vote. Normally members vote by show of hands. If the result of such a vote is doubtful, a fresh vote is taken by sitting and standing. If the result of this method is also doubtful, the vote is taken by roll call. A roll call vote is also held when a political group or at least twenty-one members request the use of this method. The President may decide that a vote shall be held by using an electronic voting system— which was used by Parliament for the first time in December 1979. The President announces the result of the vote: his decision is final. Members are permitted to make a brief statement explaining their vote immediately before a vote is taken.

With a few exceptions for which special procedures are laid down in the Rules, and which mainly concern votes under the budgetary procedure, motions of censure on the Commission, and the election of Parliament's officers, motions put to the vote are adopted if they secure a simple majority of the votes cast.

92 The European Parliament

Votes concerning the election of Parliament's principal officers are taken by secret ballot.

Parliament is considered as having a quorum for debates or votes unless the President, at the request of 21 or more members, ascertains that a quorum is not present. A quorum is constituted by the presence of a third of the members of Parliament. If there is no quorum the vote in question is held at Parliament's next sitting. If thirty members of the Parliament so request, before voting begins, a vote shall be valid only if a majority of members of Parliament take part in it: in the absence of this participation the vote is postponed until Parliament's next sitting.

In the case of votes on motions for resolutions submitted by Parliament's committees for adoption by Parliament in plenary session, consideration has to be given to any amendments tabled by members. Amendments are tabled in writing and signed by their authors. Normally they are not put to the vote unless they have been printed and distributed in all the languages of the Community. In the vote on a resolution, amendments are voted on before the text to which they refer. If a number of amendments are tabled concerning the same part of a text, the most radical amendment is put to the vote first, and so on. The President decides the order in which amendments shall be taken. Amendments may be referred to committee at the request of one or more members. In the event of this happening, Parliament normally fixes a time limit within which the responsible committee must report back to Parliament stating its conclusions concerning the amendments in question. Unless Parliament decides otherwise, no member may speak for more than three minutes concerning an amendment.

Votes on resolutions submitted by committees are held at the next fixed voting time following the debate on the resolution and report concerned. Votes, whose times are fixed in advance so that members are all aware when they will be held, are usually taken during the afternoon of the following day of the session, and following each debate on Friday, though exceptions are sometimes made.

Some motions for a resolution submitted by Parliament's committees accompanying totally "uncontroversial" and "technical" matters may be voted by Parliament without debate, if the Commission agrees with a proposal in this sense made by the parent committee, and if no member wishes to speak on the text concerned.

Structure and Operation   **93**

The way that Parliament votes during the budgetary procedure is described in detail in Chapter 3.

Compared with national Parliaments debates in the European Parliament are heavy in style, first, because of the impossibility of engaging in cut-and-thrust discussion due to the need for interpretation; and, second, due to the series of formal set speeches by the group spokesmen which open Parliament's debates. Unlike the House of Commons, therefore, it is most unusual for speakers to give way to others who wish to interrupt a speech, although the rules provide for this, except on points of order. The absence of a "government" and "opposition" in the Parliament also tends to rob the debates of the political tension that normally exists in national Parliaments. This point is underlined by the seating arrangements in the hemicycle. Instead of the major rival political parties confronting each other from opposing benches, as at Westminster, there is a semicircular arrangement of members, with a gradual merging of "left" and "right" in the "coalition" or "consensus" style of continental parliamentary practice.

Although party and national differences divide members of the Parliament over issues such as agricultural surpluses and fisheries policy, it is often the case that a large majority of the Parliament, composed of different political groups and nationalities, will simply take a "Parliament" line, in alliance with the Commission, against the Council, or, more rarely, against the Commission itself.

As mentioned above, the technical nature of a high proportion of Parliament's work leads to a situation in which Commission proposals for draft Community legislation often stimulate more intensive and lively discussion in committee than in the subsequent debate in the chamber. In plenary session, Parliament is seen at its liveliest when it is fighting to impose its views on the Council in drawing up the Community budget or in debating those policies, such as agriculture and fisheries, where Community action and decisions are of crucial importance in directly affecting the well-being of a significant proportion of the peoples of the Community. After the debates on the budget, it is usually the annual debate on agricultural price levels that shows Parliament working most intensively.

Members of the Parliament sit both in the Chamber—known as the hemicycle, which is semi-circular in shape—and in committee, not in national delegations or in alphabetical order, but according to their political affiliations. But members sit in alphabetical order within their groups, with the exception of the chairmen and vice-chairmen of the groups. Going round the half-circle, starting from the President's left, is a block of seats reserved for the Socialist Group. Behind the front rows of the Socialist Group, immediately to the President's left, sit the members of the Communist Group. In the centre of the hemicycle, directly opposite the presidential rostrum, sit the members of the Group of the European People's Party, with, behind them, and behind the right-hand benches of the Socialist Group, members of the Group for the Technical Coordination and Defence of Independent Groups and Members. Moving further towards the President's right, the next main segment of the chamber is occupied by the European Democratic Group. Behind the Group of the European People's Party, and slightly further to the right, sit the independent members. Immediately to their right, in a block towards the rear of the chamber, sit members of the Group of European Progressive Democrats, behind the European Democratic Group. The Liberal Group occupies the section to the extreme right of the chamber, as seen from the presidential rostrum. Members of the Council and their advisers sit in a small number of seats reserved for them immediately to the President's left, in front of the Socialist and Communist members. Members of the Commission sit in places reserved for them directly to the right of the President, next to the front rows of the Liberal members.

Apart from the places for the 410 members of the Parliament, the Council, and the Commission, in the hemicycle itself, the chamber contains a gallery with areas reserved for the press, distinguished visitors and the general public. Glass panelled booths for the interpreters are sunk into the walls of the chamber. Documents and messages are taken to members by parliamentary ushers.

The lay-out of the chamber is similar in Luxembourg and Strasbourg, and the seating plan for members identical. In both Luxembourg and Strasbourg each place in the chamber is equipped with a microphone and an electronic voting device.[1]

---

1. All the material arrangements discussed above will have to be altered to provide extra seats for first Greek, and then Spanish and Portuguese members, following the next enlargement of the Community. The interpretation and translation arrangements will also have to be adapted to provide for the use of Greek, Spanish and Portuguese. It is agreed that there will be 24 Greek members and it is proposed that there will be 25 Portuguese and 58 Spanish members of the Parliament.

The Secretariat

The secretariat of the Parliament consists of approximately 2,000 officials. It works under the direction of the Secretary General, who has three main functions.

The Secretary General helps the President, the Bureau and Parliament's other organs to carry out the different tasks and studies for which they are responsible, and assists them in preparing contacts with the other European institutions, parliaments of the member states of the Community, and other outside bodies. Second, he acts as Clerk of the Parliament, and in this capacity assists the Bureau and the Enlarged Bureau and is responsible for carrying out their decisions. Finally, he supervises the work of Parliament's secretariat and administers its budget. As the senior permanent official of the Parliament, the Secretary General is the appointing authority for executive and secretarial staff, the President being the appointing authority for administrative grade officials.[1]

The secretariat is basically divided into five Directorates General.

The Directorate General for Sessional and General Services helps the Secretary General to prepare and organise Parliament's sessions, and its staff are responsible for providing the President with procedural advice on the handling of problems that arise during sessions. They ensure that the agendas, minutes and verbatim reports of Parliament's proceedings are prepared and distributed. They also handle oral and written questions tabled by members and ensure that Parliament's decisions are published and distributed.

The Directorate General provides the secretariat for the Bureau and the Enlarged Bureau, and is responsible for Parliament's translation services. It also has the responsibility of publishing, printing and distributing all Parliament's official documents. Finally, the Directorate General provides assistance, in similar ways, to the Conference of the ACP/EEC Association.

The Directorate General for Committees and Interparliamentary Delegations provides the secretariat of all the parliamentary committees. Its staff helps the chairmen, vice-chairmen, rapporteurs and members of the committees both in the preparation of committee meetings and with the

---

1. The Secretaries General of the Parliament have been: M. F. F. A. de Néree tot Babberich (1958–60), Hans Nord (1961–79) and Hans Joachim Opitz who was appointed in 1979.

96 The European Parliament

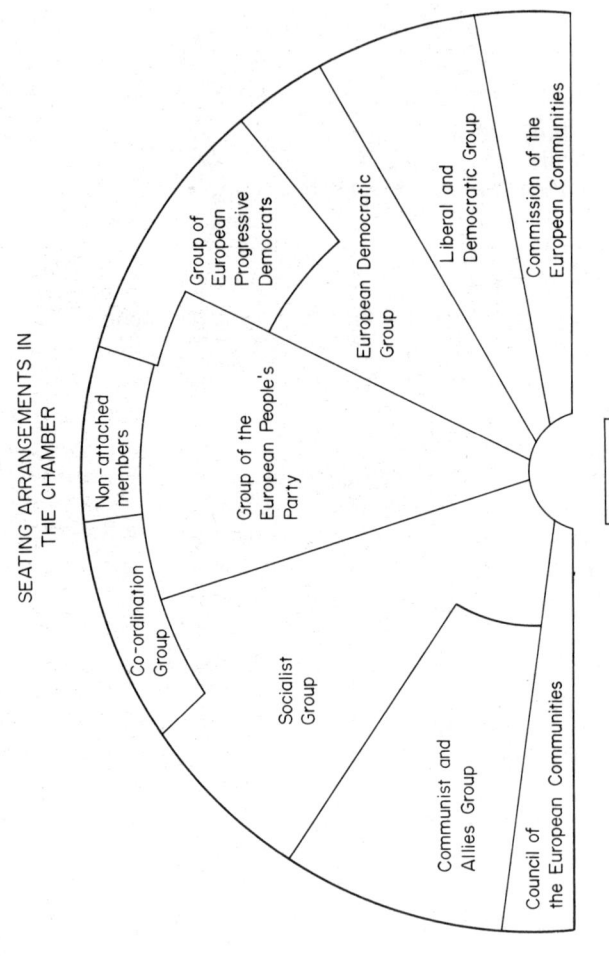

SEATING ARRANGEMENTS IN THE CHAMBER

Essential facts concerning the officers and members of the Parliament are set out in Appendix I.

substantial work of the committees, notably in aiding rapporteurs with the preparation of their reports and draft resolutions.

The other main responsibility of the Directorate General is to prepare and organise the meetings with parliamentary delegations from third countries.

The Directorate General for Information and Public Relations is responsible for providing the public and the media with information concerning Parliament's work. To help it fulfil this task the Directorate General mans Parliament Information Offices in the capitals of each member state.

The Directorate General for Administration, Personnel and Finance is responsible for staff recruitment and management, and for the social welfare of officials. It prepares the secretariat's budget and supervises its expenditure. It is responsible for the maintenance of Parliament's buildings and offices, and for purchasing and providing equipment and supplies.

A specially important responsibility of the Directorate General is the material organisation of plenary sessions, and of group, committee and other meetings. The Directorate General's remaining functions cover the broad range of Parliament's administration, including security and protocol. Finally, the Directorate General is responsible for providing interpretation for plenary sessions and group and committee meetings.

The Directorate General for Research and Documentation provides the President, members of the Parliament and the political groups with studies and documentation concerning Community affairs at their request. It also publishes a series of reference works and, amongst its other functions, staffs Parliament's legal service and runs Parliament's library.

Parliament's secretariat also includes a number of smaller units, such as the private offices of the President and the Secretary General, the secretariat of the Quaestors and the Financial Control Division.

Although the staff of the political groups are recruited directly by the groups themselves, their salaries are paid from Parliament's budget and they are classed as temporary members of Parliament's secretariat.

The interests of Parliament's secretariat are represented and defended by the Staff Committee, whose members are elected by the staff, which works for the improvement of the professional and social conditions of staff members. The Staff Committee has access to the President and the

Secretary General and discusses matters of personnel policy with Parliament's administration in the *Comité de contact*. It is also represented, together with the Administration, in the *Commission paritaire* which is responsible for advising the President and Secretary General on recruitment and promotion matters.

Like members of the Parliament, the secretariat is placed under considerable strain by Parliament's rhythm and conditions of work. Constant travel from Luxembourg to Brussels and Strasbourg, together with journeys accompanying delegations to farflung parts of the globe, the large number of meetings of all kinds, and the need to get out documents in different languages preparatory to parliamentary meetings do not lead to a calm working atmosphere. Many staff members are separated from their families for a considerable part of the year, and, finally, there are the problems of house-buying and children's education which are greatly complicated by the uncertainty concerning Parliament's seat. On the other hand salaries, as is generally the case in international organisations, are high by British standards, and leave is generous.

5

A Member's Life

The Rt. Hon. The Earl of Windermere, G.C.M.G.,
Constable Hall.

Dear Freddy,

You have asked my advice as to whether you should seek nomination as a candidate for the European elections.

I personally very much hope that you decide to stand, and that you are selected by the Euro-constituency Association. It would be splendid to have you in the directly elected Parliament where, I am sure that with your experience as a former Cabinet Minister and as a Committee Chairman in the Assembly of the Council of Europe you could make an extremely constructive contribution to the work of the new Parliament, particularly in the Development Committee where your main interest would probably lie.

But there are a number of snags that I believe I must point out to you.

First, there is the physical strain imposed by the number and length of the meetings and the attendant travel. It is all very different from the Council of Europe. You will remember that the Assembly of the Council of Europe meets some three times a year in Strasbourg, with committee meetings in Paris once or twice between each session. The rhythm of work of the European Parliament is totally different. You will have to count on there being from twelve to fourteen sessions a year, half in Strasbourg and half in Luxembourg[1], most of which last a whole working week from Monday afternoon to Friday afternoon.

In the new Parliament it is likely that you will be a full member of one

---

1. Though in practice the Parliament, during the second half of 1979 and 1980, held almost all its sessions in Strasbourg.

committee and a substitute member of another. Each committee meets at least once a month and sometimes twice and you will not be well viewed if you miss more than a handful of these meetings.

Then your political group will meet for two or three days, in the week immediately preceding each session. Apart from that, the group has a number of working parties on subjects of importance, such as energy and agriculture, which also meet regularly over and above the full group meetings.

I fear that is not all. You will almost certainly find that you are appointed to be a member of one or other of the many delegations of the European Parliament which maintain contacts with parliamentarians from those countries with which the Community has significant trade relations. With your experience of developing countries you may also find that you are appointed to serve as a member of the ACP/EEC Consultative Assembly, which meets annually for a week.

In the nominated Parliament active members have already spent between 110 and 130 days a year on European Parliament business. In the directly elected Parliament the burden is likely to be even greater.

It is also really a job for a young, robust person. Since you are no longer young you may find the sheer amount of work involved extremely taxing, and the travel fatiguing.

Going to meetings in Brussels, Luxembourg or Strasbourg often means catching a plane early in the morning or late at night, very often in disagreeable conditions, with many hours wasted hanging around when there is fog or snow. It is also tiring not to be able to go home at night after a long day of travel and work, but to have to put up with hotel life, during sessions for several days at a time. And although the restaurant food is excellent in the working centres of the Parliament, a diet of cream sauce and fried potatoes is not good for your figure or your health.

If all these meetings were in one city you could have a flat and a single permanent office where you could keep a typewriter and all your documents, but this is not possible with meetings divided between the three towns of Brussels, Strasbourg and Luxembourg.

A particular problem for you, I know, will be the difficulty of combining membership of the Parliament not only with attendance at the House of Lords, but far more important, with any real family life. Most weeks of the year you will be away from home for some if not all of the week, and I know that this would be very difficult for you and the family to accept.

I hope these comments do not dissuade you from standing as a candidate for direct elections. But I think that you ought to know what membership of the Parliament involves in terms of work and travel.

Yours ever,

Michael.

This letter was sent by the author early in 1979 to an old friend who was interested in standing for direct elections. It should make it clear that the life of a member of the European Parliament is an extremely busy and hard-working one.

The Working Month

If you were a member of the European Parliament, your typical working month would be organised in the following way: the first week of the month would be devoted to a plenary session of Parliament held in Luxembourg or in Strasbourg. You would probably arrive at the chamber at around midday on Monday and, normally, following the opening sitting from 5 p.m. to late evening on Monday, you would be in or near to the chamber most of the time from 9 a.m. until 1 p.m. and from 3 p.m. until about 7 p.m. on Tuesday and Wednesday and, in view of the night sitting usually held on Thursday, until midnight that day, with a final sitting on Friday from 9 a.m. until the early afternoon. On Tuesday and Wednesday evening you would be expected to remain behind, following the day's debates, to attend your political group meeting between 7 p.m. and 8 p.m. On Thursday morning Parliament's sitting would not start until 10 a.m. but your group would meet at 9 a.m.

Your timetable could be further complicated by the possibility of having to attend one or more extraordinary committee meetings, slipped into session week because of urgent business, and meetings of working parties of your group. Finally, it is possible that you would spend some additional time during the week meeting, as a member of one of Parliament's delegations, members of a visiting parliamentary group or preparing the delegation's visit to the country concerned.

A Member's Life **103**

Friday evening to Sunday evening might be free for you to see your family, but some of the week-end would probably be eaten into by constituency business, in the case of a British or Irish member, or by meetings with your agent, with members of your national political party or with pressure groups or lobbyists.

During the second and third weeks of the month you would probably attend two or possibly three committee meetings either in your capacity as a full member or one of Parliament's committees or in your capacity as a substitute member of another. From Britain this would involve flying to Brussels, where the great majority of committee meetings are held, on the morning of the day your meeting begins and flying back on the following afternoon, since committee meetings are normally held in the afternoon of one day and the morning of the next.

In the fourth week of the month you would be expected to spend two or three days at a meeting of your political group which would be concerned chiefly with the preparation of the group's approach to the business coming up at the following week's plenary session, or, twice a year, at the group's "study days" which are devoted to the examination of major policy issues. As a British Labour member of the Parliament your group meeting would probably be held in Brussels, whereas the Conservative members of the European Democratic Group normally hold their group meetings in London.

Any remaining time in weeks two, three and four that was free from committee or group meetings would be available to you for other business or for your family. But if you were one of the 125 members of the European Parliament with a dual mandate, practically all the time left over from European Parliament business would be swallowed up in dealing with your work as a national parliamentarian. In some cases there would be even greater demands on your time since it is normal, for instance for a member of the French Parliament to be mayor of his local town and, also, in many cases, a member of the regional *Conseil général*,[1] just as you might be involved in local government.

So, dual mandate or not, your month's programme would be a full one!

1. At present Mr Christian de la Malène, who is Chairman of the Group of the European Progressive Democrats, is not only a member of the European Parliament but also member of the French Senate for Paris, First Assistant Mayor of Paris, member of the *Conseil général* of Paris and member of the *Conseil municipal* of Paris.

But although life as a member of the European Parliament involves constant strains and tensions, it is balanced by the incentives and the rewards.

The main incentive for members of the new directly elected Parliament is the challenge of the job itself. Now that members of the Parliament can speak and act with the mandate conferred upon them by millions of European voters, they each have a personal responsibility to make the Parliament an effective political instrument in achieving the aims of the voters who sent them to Luxembourg and Strasbourg. For individual members the Parliament also provides the arena in which they can carve out a political career for themselves at a European level and achieve a Europe-wide reputation.

It has sometimes been suggested that members of the EEC Commission should be chosen exclusively from the ranks of the members of the Parliament which would provide a major career inducement for members of the Parliament. But are the qualities of a good parliamentarian necessarily those of an effective Commissioner? Further, a decision in this sense would unduly limit the area of choice from within which members of the Commission are selected. But within the structure of the Parliament itself there are many openings for "promotion". There are important rapporteurships, sub-committee and committee chairmanships and there is the possibility of becoming Vice-president or even President of the Parliament. The political groups also provide for political advancement through the chairmanship of group working parties and the chairmanship of the groups themselves. For members with an interest in one or other non-Community country or region of the world with which the Community maintains significant trade relations there is also the possibility of places on, or chairmanships of the parliamentary delegations or the joint parliamentary committees. With the prospect of increasing emphasis being placed by Parliament on the holding of public hearings by its committees it should be possible for an ambitious chairman or rapporteur of one of Parliament's committees to make a name for himself through the skilful exploitation of public hearings or through initiative reports on major topics of public concern. In the days of the nominated Parliament some members of the Parliament obtained promotion to ministerial rank in their home countries as a result of their work in the Parliament. In the directly elected Parliament there might be fewer chances for members of political promotion at home since with three quarters of the members of the new Parliament having a single mandate only most of them have deliberately opted for a European career rather than a national one. But the possibilities for influencing and helping to shape the policies of the Community which are provided through the work of the Parliament are, in themselves, members' main reward.

Material Conditions

What material benefits do members of the European Parliament receive ? As far as salaries are concerned, each member of the Parliament who is not also a member of his national Parliament receives, from his national authorities the same salary as a member of his national Parliament. The situation of dual mandate members is explained below. Since the salaries of members differ in the case of each country, the financial situation of members of the Parliament is complex. This strange state of affairs is due to the failure of the Council to agree on a single salary level for members, and to its consequent proposal in December 1978, that national salaries should be paid to members, whilst the European Parliament should be responsible for allowances[1]. This decision has given rise to criticism on at least two grounds. First, it has been argued that the principle of "the same wage for the same job" should apply. Second, it has been argued that although the national parliamentary salary is doubtless appropriate and sufficient for parliamentarians working and living in a purely national setting, it is inadequate for members of the European Parliament from countries where the national parliamentary salary is low, especially since they must spend a high proportion of their time working in countries where the cost of living is higher than in their home countries. Thus a British member or an Irish single mandate member with a salary of £10,735 and £IR 10,387 respectively would find it difficult to make ends meet in

1. The question of salaries had previously been examined at the Bremen meeting of the European Council in June 1978 and it appears that the European Council favoured the national parliamentary salary solution. The European Parliament itself had suggested to the Council that an appropriate salary level for all members of the Parliament might be either 40% or 60% of the salary of a Commissioner, which amounts to some £51,600 a year, before Community tax and not including allowances—the President and Vice-Presidents of the Commission being paid more.

Brussels, Luxembourg, or Strasbourg, all three expensive cities, were it not for the daily allowance he receives from Parliament.

The annual salaries paid by member states of the Community to members of the European Parliament are as follows:

Country[1]	National currency	£sterling	Dual mandate member
Belgium	BF 1,390,483	£19,950	One salary only.
Denmark	Kr 137,828	£10,876	National salary will be paid on a daily basis for periods (minimum one week) when leave of absence has been formally granted by the *Folketing*.
France	FF 232,740	£24,376	One salary only.
Germany	DM 90,000	£21,551	One salary only.
Ireland	£IR 10,387	£9,389	Dual mandate members from the Dail will be paid double their Dail salary, £IR 20,774 (£18,777) and from the Senate their Senate salary plus a Dail salary, £IR 16,301 (£14,734).
Italy	Lire 20,972,896	£11,133	One salary only.
Luxembourg	LF 906,366	£13,004	One salary only.
Netherlands	Fls 88,089	£19,273	One salary only.
United Kingdom	£10,735	£10,735	House of Commons one salary only. House of Lords members also entitled to their Lords' expenses allowance.

Financially, the daily allowance provides members of the Parliament with a very useful supplement to their basic salary. A member receives BF 3,500 (£50) for every working day which he attends a European Parliament meeting—including plenary sessions, committee meetings, group meetings, delegations, etc. Out of this daily allowance a member meets his own hotel and subsistence costs.

Although this may appear to be very generous it should be remembered that hotel and restaurant prices are high in the Parliament's three places of work—Brussels, Luxembourg, and Strasbourg—so that the high daily

1. Greek members of the European Parliament are paid Drachmas 1,387,200 (£12,080) a year. They have one salary only.

allowance is necessary, especially since members of the Parliament are expected to do a lot of entertaining. But although real expenses quickly eat up much of the daily allowance, the allowance does go some way to even out the discrepancies between the widely differing salaries received by members.

Apart from the daily allowance members also receive a flat rate allowance of about 23 pence per kilometer for the first 400 kilometers, and 9 pence for every additional kilometer, for travel from halfway between their national capital and their home to the place of the European Parliament's meeting, regardless of the means of transport used.

The daily subsistence allowance received by members of the Parliament is not subject to income tax except in Britain, where Inland Revenue claims that the allowance is a form of salary and insists on taxing it as if it were earned income. On behalf of the British delegation to the former nominated Parliament, Lord Bruce of Donington, Parliament's former rapporteur on the Community budget, who is a chartered accountant by profession, initiated legal action against the British tax authorities to counter this claim. Although the British court decided in favour of the British Inland Revenue, Lord Bruce has obtained a referral from the British appeal court to the European Court of Justice for an opinion.

Over and above their salaries and their subsistence and travel allowances, members of the directly elected Parliament each receive an allowance of 32,000 EUA (roughly £19,200) a year to pay for research and secretarial assistance, two-thirds of this sum being "accountable".

Members of the European Parliament are free to pursue their professional careers in other fields, though it is obviously difficult for those who work in full-time occupations, such as teachers, to combine membership of the Parliament with their other job. For journalists, lawyers and company directors, who can often meet their professional obligations in a more sporadic manner, the problem is not quite so difficult. Members of the Parliament cannot be, at the same time, Community officials, nor may they be, in the case of Britain and certain other member states, national civil servants. As mentioned in Chapter 1, 125 members of the directly elected Parliament are also members of their national parliaments. Although this permits valuable personal links between the European Parliament and national parliaments the dual mandate intensifies the pressures and strains placed on members.

The provision of money, from the Parliament's budget, to provide for research and secretarial assistance for members results from one of the first decisions taken by the Bureau of the directly elected Parliament. Apart from the help given to them by the research assistants and secretaries financed in this way, members are also able to draw on the resources of Parliament's secretariat and the staff of their own political group. The secretariat of the committee or committees of which they are full or substitute members will help them in the preparation of reports or speeches on the subjects dealt with by their committees, and Parliament's research staff is available to carry out additional background research for them. The staff of the political groups complement this assistance, by giving advice concerning the political stance that members of their political group could adopt in discussing each subject in committee or in plenary session. Help from these sources is particularly useful to the majority of members of the European Parliament who are no longer members of national parliaments and who cannot therefore call on the library and research facilities provided by national parliaments.

Before direct elections only Parliament's President, group chairmen, and a handful of other high-ranking members of the Parliament were provided with individual offices in Brussels, Luxembourg and Strasbourg. Now the town of Strasbourg has constructed a new building near the chamber, in which each member of the Parliament will have a separate office. Both in Brussels and in Luxembourg working accommodation will be provided for members, with each member sharing an office with another. As yet it is not clear what office facilities, if any, will be provided in their home countries. Further, it has not yet been decided what allowances, if any, members will receive to cover the costs of their travel on Parliament business in their constituencies, regions or home countries. A decision on this problem is particularly important for British members with large rural constituencies and for other members elected on a regional list to represent a defined geographic area.

The Seat

One of the most aggravating problems in the lives of members of the European Parliament is that Parliament's work is carried out in three different places. The problem of the "seat" of the European Community as a whole is even more complex since the Council and the Commission are based in Brussels, with a major outpost of the Commission in Luxembourg, whilst the headquarters of the Court of Justice, the Court of Auditors and the European Investment Bank are in Luxembourg together with the administrative headquarters of the European Parliament.

In terms of travel, convenience and efficiency the price of having to attend a large number of meetings in three different places is a high one for members of the Parliament.

Even if all these meetings were held in one city the strain of constant travelling would be considerable. But working in three different towns, of which Luxembourg and Strasbourg have much less efficient air connections than Brussels, and without being able to install himself in a permanent flat and office in one place with his papers and his assistant close at hand, the pressure on a member is even greater.

The logical conclusions are simple. First, the Parliament should conduct its work in one place. Second, the three decision-making institutions of the Community—the Council, the Commission and Parliament—should share a single seat or capital. The reasons for this are straightforward. The democratic supervision of the Commission by Parliament cannot be effectively exercised from Luxembourg or from Strasbourg which are respectively 140 and 280 miles away. Effective parliamentary supervision means that members of Parliament must be within a few minutes' walk of Commissioners and their officials. It also means that members should be able to convene Commission officials at a few hours notice to explain Commission policy and their execution. This can only be done in one city, not from Luxembourg or Strasbourg to Brussels.

Second, simply to enable Parliament to carry out its own work efficiently its activities should be concentrated in one place. How can Parliament work efficiently if, during a Strasbourg session, half its staff remain in Luxembourg? In the present situation there are inevitably many occasions when it is difficult for members to get hold of the officials or documents they need to help them with a report, a speech, or a point arising in committee.

Quite apart from the inefficiency of the present arrangements there are the huge costs involved in moving staff, equipment and documents between Luxembourg, Strasbourg and Brussels. The cost to Parliament of its meetings being held in three places amounts to about 15% of its budget. This means that for 1979 this cost was about £12 million.

There is also the problem of contacts with pressure groups, business and unions. The major sectors of industry, commerce and agriculture are represented by transnational pressure groups in Brussels where many large firms and trades unions have established offices. These provide vital contacts for members of Parliament who need to have the latest facts and figures at their disposal, whether these concern carrots or cotton wool. The Community press corps is based in Brussels and it is difficult for Parliament to persuade more than a small proportion of journalists to leave Brussels to attend meetings either in Luxembourg or in Strasbourg. Since parliamentarians need the press this creates a further difficulty. In brief, Parliament cannot conduct its business efficiently so far away from the Council, the Commission and the whole "Euro-structure" of Brussels.

This does not mean that it is necessary to put every single Community body together in one spot. The Court of Justice, the Court of Auditors and the European Investment Bank, together with some of the Commission technical services, work very effectively in Luxembourg. Centralisation for its own sake is not necessary. What is necessary is to put alongside each other, in one town, the three decision-making institutions.

What are the obstacles to centralisation and can they be overcome? It is sometimes proposed that the European Parliament should itself take a decision concerning its own seat, especially in view of the strengthening of its budgetary powers. But Article 216 of the EEC Treaty lays upon "the governments of the Member States" the obligation to choose "the seat of the institutions of the Community". This would include not just the seat of Parliament but that of the institutions as a whole. The present location of the Council and the Commission in Brussels, and that of Parliament's activities in Brussels, Luxembourg and Strasbourg is based on the decision taken by the Six in April 1965 which states "Luxembourg, Brussels and Strasbourg shall remain the provisional places of work of the institutions of the Communities". Thus until a decision is taken under Article 216 all existing arrangements are only provisional. A Council resolution of April 1970 qualified the Council's undertaking not to infringe the autonomy of the European Parliament to establish its own budget by excepting expenditure on staff or on the seat of the institutions. This means that it is difficult, legally, for Parliament to purchase land or pay for the construction of a building in order to establish its own seat.

But if the governments have the exclusive right of decision concerning the seat, under Article 216, they are also obliged, under the Treaty, to take a decision within a reasonable period of time. If it became clear that individual states were preventing a decision being reached concerning the seat the Commission could bring a case against them before the Court of Justice under Article 169 of the EEC Treaty on the grounds of failure to fulfil a Treaty obligation. But it is unlikely that the Commission would wish to provoke the collision course that such an action would produce.

Other decisions have made the legal situation concerning Parliament's places of work even more complicated. After the Six failed to agree on a single seat for the ECSC in July 1952 they decided that the High Authority and the Court of Justice should begin their work in Luxembourg and that the Assembly should hold its first meeting in Strasbourg. In 1958 the Foreign Ministers again failed to agree on a seat but decided that the Commissions of the two new Communities should hold their first meetings in Brussels and that "the Assembly will meet in Strasbourg". This situation was not changed by the Merger Treaty of 1965.

Vested national interests also make it hard to change the *status quo*. Belgium has a strong interest that the 10,000 officials who work for the Commission in Brussels together with the 2,000 officials who work for the Council remain there, together with their families. Many more who work for pressure groups, the press and other bodies connected with or dependent on the Communities also live in Brussels and thousands of visitors pour into Brussels on Community business throughout the year.

Similarly, the French and Luxembourg Governments wish to maintain Community activity in Strasbourg and the Community presence in Luxembourg. They have opposed all proposals aimed at reducing or ending the Community connection with these two cities. Whereas the Grand Ducal Government has referred to Luxembourg's possible role as a capital of the European institutions the French Government has insisted that the European Parliament should continue to meet regularly in Strasbourg and has protested about the use of Luxembourg for the plenary sessions of the Parliament. The French Government's reservations seem to have been concerned not so much with the holding of sittings in Luxembourg *as such* but with these sittings being held *regularly*.

Strasbourg and Luxembourg have constructed new buildings capable of accommodating sessions of the directly elected Parliament. New committee rooms, capable of holding all committees of the directly elected Parliament have been constructed in Brussels.

The legal and political constraints examined above have made it impossible for Parliament to break the deadlock concerning either its own seat or the Community's seat. But the directly elected Parliament, in cooperation with the other Community institutions, might either insist that the governments fulfil their obligation under Article 216 or override the Treaties by taking a unilateral decision. Any governmental decision that placed the three decision-making institutions of the Community together in one city would be bound to involve trade-offs which might mean locating other Community bodies elsewhere. It would also involve the uprooting of large numbers of officials and their families and, also, housing and schooling problems. Whatever seat might be chosen or created the offices of the centralised institutions must be grouped close together to enable easy communication, and there must be good air and rail connections between the Community capital and the capitals of the member states. Brussels already hosts the Council and Commission and has better air links with the outside world than Luxembourg or Strasbourg. If the Parliament were to be located in Brussels, alongside the Council and the Commission, it would have an opportunity to increase, significantly, its influence on the policy-making and day-to-day running of the Community.

6

The Future

Most of those who have been concerned about the future development of the European Parliament have coupled the holding of direct elections with the growth of Parliament's powers. For some years arguments waged as to whether a dramatic increase in Parliament's powers was a pre-condition for the holding of direct elections so that the directly elected Parliament could start its work from a position of increased authority within the Community, or whether direct elections should be held first in which case an increase in Parliament's powers would automatically follow.

The Vedel report[1] came to a sensible conclusion concerning this problem: "The system of the pre-condition because of a logical trap leads to a vicious circle, for if one cannot imagine a Parliament with real powers which does not draw its mandate from direct universal suffrage, it is even more difficult to imagine the election through direct universal suffrage of a Parliament without extended powers. In this way, two equally desirable objectives are making each other's implementation impossible. The only way to break the vicious circle is to refuse to allow one of the two objectives to be dependent on the achievement of the other first. Neither has priority over the other, nor is their simultaneous achievement necessary. If any logical links exist between them, these are expressed in the fact that any progress made towards the achievement of one will be towards the achievement of the other." One of these two objectives has now been achieved. What about the other?

Many proposals have been made in recent years as to ways and means by which Parliament's powers could be increased. In this chapter the author

1. Vedel Committee, *Report on the Enlargement of the Powers of the European Parliament*, Supplement to Bulletin 4, Brussels 1972.

is ruthlessly selective in concentrating on suggestions that seem to him to have at least a reasonable chance of finding acceptance. The ideas examined are not a blueprint for the Parliament of some ideal United Europe. They take the real situation as it exists now as a starting point and are meant to be signposts signalling ways by which advances, however modest, might be made in the immediate and medium-term future.

It is essential to realise, as David Marquand has put it,[1] that: "The Community is a moving train, not a stationary terminus: a process, not a structure. It is not yet a federal state, and perhaps it never will be. Nor, however, is it a mere association of sovereign states. It is an association of sovereign states which was created with the deliberate and explicit intention that it should gradually develop into something different, and which already possesses certain attributes, of great importance to its day-to-day activities, which point the way to something different. More important still, its value to its members depends on its ability to develop into something different—and to do so at a faster pace than that of the last fifteen years. What is needed, then, is a constitution which not only permits, but actively facilitates, further evolution: a set of arrangements which suits the Community's present needs, which gives more weight than is given at present to the centripetal forces in Community politics and less to the centrifugal ones, and which can be adapted without serious difficulty to the new needs which can be expected to appear as and when those centripetal forces push the Community along the path to greater supranationality. No single set of proposals is likely to achieve all of these aims with equal ease and success. But proposals which are not even designed to achieve them at all, at any rate in part, are not likely to be much use. To adapt a phrase of the late Jimmy Maxton, Community constitution-mongers must at least aspire to ride three horses at once. Those who do not would do better to stay out of the ring."

Since Parliament is not an isolated institution but an integral part of the Community as a whole, proposals made concerning its future must be seen, as David Marquand demonstrates, within the wider setting of the growth of the Community as a whole. The extent to which Parliament's competences and functions can be expanded is in many ways limited by the attitude of the member governments. The British and French Parliaments

1. *Parliament for Europe*, Cape, London, 1979.

have adopted legislation to provide that no increase in the European Parliament's powers will be made without formal agreement between the governments and ratification by national parliaments, and the Danish view of the Community will almost certainly result in similar controls in Denmark. With three governments suspicious of moves to achieve a major break-through in the European Parliament's role, there are three ways in which Parliament might, with some chance of success, develop its present competences. The first is to do so by a quiet but continuing process of building on existing functions where no specific governmental permission is necessary; for instance, through the extension of its power of the "last word" over the non-compulsory part of the budget, in direct proportion to the growth of non-compulsory expenditure. Second, through informal inter-institutional agreements, or "gentlemen's agreements", taking the form of an exchange of letters between Parliament and one or more of the other institutions or of a Joint Declaration by Parliament and other institutions. Third, in the case of more significant changes, through Treaty amendment, which involves ratification by national parliaments.

Some discussion of the word "powers" cannot be avoided. In examining Parliament's work, many commentators fall into the trap of using the same word, "powers", to cover at least two very different meanings. A legal meaning of "power" is to be granted the authority or right to carry out certain tasks. Thus, the power of attorney or the power of appointment can be vested in a person or a body by the responsible authorities. Parliament possesses certain limited and defined "powers" of this kind, conferred upon it by the Treaties or by subsequent inter-institutional agreements. But this "power" should not be confused with the "power" to control others or to influence or to force them to carry out certain policies or tasks, derived from military, political or moral authority. Much of the discussion of the "powers" of Parliament is befogged by a confusion between these two meanings of the word. It is perhaps wiser to limit the use of the phrase "powers of the European Parliament" to the exercise of the authority it has derived from the Treaties, as in the budgetary procedure. For the rest, it seems more useful to speak in terms of the "functions" or "competences" of Parliament. Ambiguous use of the phrase "powers of the Parliament" can actually damage Parliament's case, and make it more difficult for it to extend its competences since a blurring of the two meanings of the word tends to lead governments and anti-integrationists to think in terms of a Parliament which wishes to dominate or force the Council or other institutions into accepting its *diktat*, which is out of the question.

In the remainder of this chapter proposals are made concerning ways in which Parliament's institutional role could be made more effective or increased. These proposals treat different aspects of Parliament's work in the same order as in Chapter 3.

Parliament and the Court of Justice

Under the Treaties, the only opportunity that Parliament has of bringing an action before the Court of Justice is that provided by Article 175 of the EEC Treaty in the case of the Council or the Commission infringing the Treaty by "failing to act". Indeed, the nominated Parliament seriously considered taking such action against the Council for failure to enact the Common Transport Policy provisions of the EEC Treaty. Though Parliament did not act in that sense the threat of recourse to the Court by Parliament still hangs over the Council. The Commission is normally regarded as the watchdog or guardian of the Treaties, but in the event of the Commission being nervous about bringing a case against the Council or a Member Government, Parliament should be able to step in and start legal proceedings. This would require Treaty amendment.

Under the Court's rules Parliament may "intervene" in cases in which it has a direct interest and which are before the Court. The nominated Parliament never made use of this provision, but in December 1979 the directly elected Parliament adopted a resolution, accompanying the Ferri report, in which it denounced a Council regulation of June 1979 on isoglucose as null and void on the grounds that Parliament had not given its opinion on the regulation before the Council took its decision. Parliament considered that such consultation was obligatory under Article 43 of the EEC Treaty. In January 1980, Parliament "intervened" in the two isoglucose cases that were brought before the Court against the Council by French and German firms.[1] Parliament should not hesitate to intervene in other cases before the Court when it has a direct interest in doing so. No Treaty amendment would be required.

1. For details of the Court's judgment see Appendix III.

The Future 117

Parliament's Role in Community Legislation

A realistic understanding of Parliament's role in Community legislation is essential. Many "Europeans" if asked what should be the main result of direct elections, would probably reply: the power for Parliament to legislate at the Community level. Indeed, a European Parliament with "legislative powers" is a classical element in the federalist vision. To many the very word "parliament" conjures up the idea of legislation even though the original French word *"parlement"* only means a place in which to speak, discuss or debate. The role of most parliaments in the modern world is not to introduce major legislation but to debate, criticise and amend, and essentially adopt legislation that in general is conceived, introduced and defended by the executive—some national Parliaments can, quite unlike the European Parliament, influence governments not to introduce legislation and can block legislation they dislike by ensuring it is not adopted within the necessary time limits. The right to initiate major legislation has become essentially the prerogative of government. Thus, although the European Council undertook, in December 1974, that: "The competence of the European Assembly will be extended, in particular by granting it certain powers in the Communities' legislative process", these still undefined "legislative powers" are unlikely to go beyond those possessed by national parliaments or to include major powers of initiative. But if it is unlikely that Parliament will replace the Commission as the main initiator of Community policy, there are other ways in which Parliament's legislative role could be strengthened.

As stressed in Chapter 3, by far the greatest weakness in Parliament's role in the law-making process of the Community is that although the Council almost always consults Parliament on Commission legislative proposals, Parliament's opinion or its suggested amendments do not bind the Council.[1] Thus Parliament's main aim with regard to Community legislation should be to get the Council to agree that its opinion should have greater weight and be given a more binding nature.

What form this "binding nature" should take is an open question. The Vedel Committee proposed that in a first stage Parliament should be given a power of veto over certain subjects—in the event of the Council wishing to depart from the joint view of Parliament and the Commission in taking a

1. Except in the budgetary procedure, as explained in Chapter 3.

decision on a Commission proposal—and powers to delay (a "suspensory veto") over a wider range of subjects. In a second stage this suspensory veto would be transformed into the power of "co-decision" between Parliament and the Council. Several years earlier, Mr Scelba, when President of Parliament, made a similar proposal concerning the introduction of a suspensory veto.

Since the Vedel proposals were made, in 1972, the political climate in Europe has not favoured the granting, by the Community governments, of an across-the-board sharing of the decision-making power with the European Parliament, and co-decision still remains a distant goal.[1]

Another proposal, preferred by the author, was made by Parliament's late rapporteur on its powers and competences, Sir Peter Kirk. The author worked closely with, first, Sir Peter Kirk and, following his death, with Lord Reay, who completed his report, in developing and formulating proposals concerning Parliament's competences and its relations with the other institutions. The proposals of Sir Peter Kirk quoted in this chapter thus result from the joint work of Sir Peter and the author. Sir Peter suggested that the conciliation procedure[2] should be extended so as to be used not only in situations in which the Parliament and the Commission, on the one side, disagreed with the Council concerning a Commission proposal with major financial implications, but also concerning Commission proposals in *all* fields. He proposed that a Commission legislative proposal would be sent by the Commission to Parliament which would debate it *before* the Council started to prepare its decision on the proposal. Here it is interesting to note that the Commission already gives a presentation of its proposals for the preliminary draft budget to Parliament's Committee on Budgets before transmitting them to the Council. Following the adoption of Parliament's opinion. the Commission would send its proposal to the Council together with amendments voted by Parliament. The Council would then decide on the Commission's proposal in the light of Parliament's amendments. If the Council could not accept Parliament's amendments, Parliament would hold a second reading. If, then, within a fixed period of time, the Council did not change its preliminary decision—which would not be final until the end of the proposed procedure, unless

---

1. Again, except for the budgetary procedure.
2. For a detailed explanation of this procedure, see Chapter 3.

the Council agreed entirely with Parliament's amendments—the conciliation procedure would operate automatically. This proposal has the advantage of putting the emphasis on the use of the conciliation procedure rather than that of the suspensory veto, and to that extent is more likely to be acceptable to the governments. To be implemented, this proposal would require either an inter-institutional agreement or a Treaty amendment.

In moving in this direction, Parliament has a weapon at its disposal which it has not so far used. The Council is already obliged to inform Parliament why it does not follow Parliament's opinion in taking a decision concerning "Community instruments having financial implications" or "matters of special importance". Parliament has never insisted that the Council fulfil this obligation which is set out in a letter addressed to Mr Scelba, then President of the Parliament, by Mr Harmel, then President of the Council, in March 1970 and in one sent to Mr Scelba by Mr Scheel, then President of the Council, in July 1970.

If the Council is not prepared to agree to at least a modest reform of this kind, it is difficult to see more significant ways in which the promise given by the European Council in December 1974 that the Parliament would be granted "certain powers in the Communities' legislative process", could be fulfilled.

The second proposal concerning Parliament's legislative role is that Parliament should obtain a *limited* degree of legislative initiative, either through some type of "private member's bill" or through obliging the Commission to introduce legislative proposals at Parliament's request. This suggestion aims only at Parliament's complementing the Commission in taking legislative initiatives, since the basic right of initiative should remain with the Commission.

It should not be too hard for Parliament to achieve this aim since the Council might find it difficult to stop the Commission from following Parliament's legislative suggestions if it wished to do so.

The third proposal is that the directly elected Parliament should invite Commissioners to present their legislative proposals during sessions of Parliament, rather like the way in which ministers introduce governmental programmes and legislation in national parliaments. Under existing Treaty rules, it would still be the Council which would seek Parliament's opinion, not the Commission, but there is no reason why Parliament and the Commission should not handle debates on Commission proposals in this way. An idea of this kind would be likely to appeal to the Commission since it would suggest parallels with national governments. If the Commission wished to announce a legislative proposal or new policy urgently, without waiting for the next session of Parliament, it could do so at a committee meeting in Brussels, and, by agreement between the Commission and the committee concerned, the Commissioner's statement could be made at a public meeting of the committee. To ensure that Treaty rules are respected, the Commission could transmit its legislative proposal to the Council, by letter, earlier on the day that the Commissioner made his declaration. This proposal could be brought into effect by an agreement between Parliament and the Commission.

Finally, in line with numerous proposals to this effect, the Council of Ministers should return to the practice of majority voting as laid down in Articles 148 and 149 of the EEC Treaty. Majority voting in the Council is essential if the Community is to function effectively and to free the blockages in the decision-making process, thus cutting down the "decision mountain" and permitting the Community to work efficiently following its enlargement to include the applicant Mediterranean countries. A return to majority voting in the Council would do much to restore the Commission's vitality and prestige and would give both the Commission and Parliament more weight in their dealings with the Council. Only the governments can take the decision to return to Treaty rules, and they can do so whilst maintaining every safeguard for the protection of "vital national interests", but if they do not take this decision it is almost certain that the Community will not be able to cope adequately with the additional problems resulting from the next enlargement. In this context, the European Council, on the proposal of President Giscard d'Estaing, commissioned a Committee of three "Wise Men"—Mr Barend Biesheuvel, Mr Edmund Dell and Mr Robert Marjolin—to report on the institutional working of the Community in the perspective of enlargmeent. Their report was completed in October 1979 and submitted to the European Council.

Parliament and the Budget

First, Parliament should seek to abolish the distinction between "compulsory" and "non-compulsory" expenditure, on the understanding that its

Treaty powers of the "last word" concerning non-compulsory expenditure could be applied by it, also, to compulsory expenditure. Most probably this would require a new budget Treaty.

Second, Parliament should insist that *all* Community revenue and expenditure be set out in the Budget. At present neither the European Development Fund—which covers aid to the Lomé countries—nor the loans of the European Investment Bank are included in the Community budget. This omission is contrary to Article 199 of the EEC Treaty and should be made good. Article 199 states: "All items of revenue and expenditure of the Community . . . shall be included in estimates to be drawn up for each financial year and shall be shown in the budget." This is not merely a question of accountancy. By including the European Development Fund and Bank loans in the budget, these operations would become subject to scrutiny by Parliament and would thus give it some influence concerning spending policies in these two areas. The agreement of the Council would be required for this proposal to be put into effect.

Third, Parliament's new Committee on Financial Control, with the assistance of the Court of Auditors, should, as its first priority, ensure that the real expenditure of the Commission in any one year corresponds to the budget fought out between and adopted by Parliament and the Council. In this respect unjustified transfers by the Commission of expenditure from one heading to another—without Parliament's assent—should be brought to an end, and Parliament should ensure that the increases it has voted to the budget be spent by the Commission within the appropriate budget year. There is little point in Parliament increasing its influence over the formulation of the Community budget if it has no effective say over the way this budget is spent. It is up to Parliament itself to ensure that the Commission responds to its directives concerning budget expenditure.

Fourth, Parliament should insist on extending its right to reject individual non-compulsory headings of the Community budget to include that of being able to reject compulsory items. This would give it an effective power of selective rejection with regard to the budget as opposed to its existing global power, under the Treaties, of being able to reject the budget as a whole. The extension of Parliament's right of rejection would require Treaty amendment.

Fifth, the directly elected Parliament, with a large majority of full-time single-mandate members, should reorganise the way in which it appraises and influences Community expenditure as a whole. Up till now new Commission proposals for acts with financial implications have been examined by Parliament in a necessarily abbreviated way, to fit in with the crowded schedule of members with national obligations. Parliament's Committee on Budgets gives its opinion at an early stage to the committee competent for the substance of the proposal. In giving its opinion the Committee on Budgets will normally be guided, first, by its view of the substantive merits—or otherwise—of the Commission's proposal, and, second, by its general estimation of whether the Commission's proposal is sensible from a budgetary point of view. It has then basically completed its work.

In his report on inter-institutional relations, Sir Peter Kirk pointed out that this procedure does not give Parliament an adequate opportunity to scrutinise the expenditure involved in Commission proposals since the Commission has not yet developed the practice of submitting detailed financial explanations of their proposals to Parliament. Neither does the procedure give Parliament a genuine voice in shaping the policy options open to the Commission, in view of the budgetary resources available.

The report proposed that a more detailed and effective form of scrutiny could be introduced by Parliament following direct elections, when members would have more time available for in-depth work. It suggested that each of Parliament's committees whose competence concerned the work of a Directorate-General of the Commission should establish a sub-committee responsible to the parent committee for examining the budgetary implications of all Commission proposals falling within the competence of that Directorate-General. Thus, each of Parliament's committees could develop its own expertise within its subject area. The task of the budget sub-committees would be twofold: first, they would examine all the budgetary details of proposals for acts with financial implications; second, they could advise their parent committee on the attitude it could take concerning the medium-term development of the Commission's policies within its sector.

In his report on the Draft General Budget of the European Communities for 1974, Mr Rafton Pounder set out detailed indications of the type of detailed budgetary explanations required from the Commission in the financial schedules they should submit to Parliament concerning proposals for acts with financial implications.

The Kirk report considered that, taken together with the establishment of a full Committee on Financial Control and the Court of Auditors, the introduction of this new procedure would constitute an effective "two-pronged 'before and after' control system over the Community budget". It suggested that the budgetary sub-committees should make use of public hearings in their work of examining and costing proposals for acts with financial implications and in considering alternative policy options. When the parent committees were ready to assess the work carried out by their budgetary sub-committees, the Committee on Budgets itself should be brought back into the picture to give a second opinion. This would permit the Committee on Budgets to examine the proposals of Parliament's other committees and to place them in their overall budgetary setting.

Finally, the report considered that the three-year forecast made by the Commission concerning future expenditure should be extended so that, as well as a definite forecast for the following budget year, the Commission should submit firm estimates for years 2 and 3, together with projections for years 4 and 5. If Parliament were to adopt this complete package of budgetary proposals, it would be able to exert real political influence on the shaping of Commission policies in all fields. This would, in effect, enable Parliament to exercise a profound influence on all spheres of Community legislation. To achieve this aim it would be necessary for Parliament itself to reorganise its internal budgetary procedures, though close cooperation would be required from the Commission in providing adequate financial information and ensuring that Commission representatives reacted positively to invitations to appear at hearings organised by budgetary sub-committees.

It has been suggested, recently, that either the Community as a whole, or specifically the European Parliament, should be granted taxing powers since the revenue available to the Community is approaching its limits. Although this proposal seems a logical and sensible way of providing the adequate revenue that will shortly be needed by the Community, it is likely to be strongly opposed by several of the member states as it directly affects a particularly sensitive aspect of national sovereignty. Thus, it would seem more sensible, in the near future, for Parliament to press the governments to raise the ceiling of the Community's 1% slice of VAT to 2% or to press them to take a decision allowing the Commission to develop its limited power to raise money on the international money market, the

"Ortoli facility", into a more general and large-scale way of increasing the Community's revenue.

As far as loans floated by the Commission are concerned, Parliament should insist that this potentially significant new source of Community revenue should be fully budgetised. This would enable Parliament to examine the Commission's loan policy within the context of the budgetary procedure. Further, Parliament should establish ceilings or platforms for the loans raised by the Commission and ensure that the use of such loans corresponds with the purposes for which they are raised.

Parliament should try to ensure that the European Investment Bank, which manages Commission loans, should be the agent of the member states in their European monetary cooperation activities, which are at present handled by the Bank for International Settlements in Switzerland, a non-Community body whose membership includes non-Community countries. To take on this role the European Investment Bank would require a new, wider and appropriate mandate from the member governments.

Supervision of the Commission

First, the European Parliament should acquire the right to sack individual Commissioners. It might do this quite simply by adopting a motion expressing its disapproval of an individual Commissioner with whom it was dissatisfied. It would seem sensible to require such a vote of censure to be passed by two-thirds of all members of Parliament. If the Commission were to accept the result of such a vote of the directly elected Parliament, there would perhaps be no need for Treaty modification. But if the Commission refused to ensure that a Commissioner resigned following such a vote, on the grounds of the "collective responsibility" of the Commission, an amendment to Article 144 of the EEC Treaty would be necessary. If this were necessary, Article 144 of the EEC Treaty should be changed so as to make it impossible for the Member Governments to re-appoint (under Article 158 of the Treaty) the same member or members of the Commission who had resigned.

Second, Parliament should play a role in the appointment of members of the Commission.[1] The original Treaty procedures have already been adapted (without Treaty modification) in practice to permit the incoming President of the Commission, once he has been chosen by the member governments himself, to discuss with the member governments the selection of the Commissioners. This change followed a decision taken by the European Council on a proposal made by Mr Tindemans, the former Belgian Prime Minister, in his report on European Union, and previously suggested by the Vedel Committee. This process should be broadened further to permit the European Parliament to be consulted in the appointment of Commissioners—either through consultations involving Parliament's President or perhaps through a vote of confidence held by Parliament on the new President and all his Commissioners together, following a policy statement made before Parliament by the new Commission. This would resemble the idea of "parliamentary investiture of the President of the Commission" proposed in the Vedel report. The simple agreement of the Member Governments to this proposal should be, in view of the precedent already established, sufficient to implement this idea.

Relations with the Council

First, the European Parliament should try to establish some degree of accountability to itself from the European Council. This might take the form of the Head of Government chairing the European Council making a statement to the European Parliament at its first session following a meeting of the European Council, and replying to questions put to him on its work. This is consonant with a proposal made by Mr Tindemans in his report on European Union that in an annual debate on "the state of the

---

1. Parliament's desire to influence the appointment of the members of the Commission can be traced back to the early days of the ECSC. When the first President of the High Authority, Mr Jean Monnet, declared that he would resign, the Common Assembly adopted a resolution expressing its wish that the member governments should consult with the Assembly before appointing a new President and asking the High Authority to make a policy statement before the Assembly immediately after naming the new President. Both wishes were met. The President of the Common Assembly, Mr Pella, met the Prime Ministers of all the member states for consultations, and the incoming President of the High Authority, Mr Mayer, made a formal policy statement at the first session held by the Assembly following his appointment.

Union" the President of the European Council could make a statement before Parliament. The agreement of the European Council would be necessary for this proposal to be implemented.

Second, Parliament should try to ensure that extra-Treaty proposals and acts of the European Council and the normal Council of Ministers, such as resolutions or action programmes, should follow a procedure in which consultation of the European Parliament would be obligatory—and would make use wherever possible of Article 235 of the EEC Treaty which permits Community action where the Treaty does not provide the necessary powers. The agreement of the European Council and the Council would be necessary for this.

Third, the Council should, at *all* its levels, agree to consider proposals made in Parliament on the inclusion of suggested items on the agenda of their meetings.

Fourth, the Committee of Permanent Representatives, to the extent that it acts as a *Community body*, should be made accountable to the European Parliament. The Chairman and members of COREPER should be requested to explain the views of the permanent representatives and defend their decisions to committees of the Parliament, when invited to do so, particularly those decisions taken under the "A-points" procedure. To apply this reform, the agreement of the Council would be necessary.

The package of proposals set out above shares the philosophy of the Vedel Report, which aimed at achieving some degree of "accountability" from the different layers of the Council to Parliament. It takes as its starting point the comment of the Vedel Committee that although "the absence of any system of Council responsibility to the Parliament is a basic datum of the Treaties . . . the system does not exclude the development and consolidation of a practice of information and control".

Parliament and the Community's External Relations

First, Parliament should insist on the right to be consulted by the Council on the accession to the Community of a new member state under Article 237 of the EEC Treaty. This would require Treaty amendment.

Second, one of the main proposals made in the Kirk report was that the existing procedures under which Parliament is consulted concerning accession, trade and cooperation agreements should be transformed. At present "consultation" of Parliament amounts to hardly more than Parliament's relevant committees being given information about the negotiations, by the Council, under the Luns[1]Westerterp procedure.[1] The report proposed that, before the Council gives the Commission a mandate to negotiate a debate should be held by Parliament, (already possible under an agreement of the Council of 15 October 1973) which would permit the Council to determine the Commission's mandate in the light of Parliament's views. During the course of negotiations Parliament would continue to be informed, either as at present by the Council or, preferably, by the Commission. When negotiations between the Commission and the country concerned came to a close, a distinction should be made between the "initialling" of an agreement, which could be done by the Commission (as negotiator on the side of the Community) and the final "signature" of the agreement by the Council. Between the "initialling" and the "signature" of agreements, a "ratification" stage should be introduced which would allow Parliament to debate the terms negotiated by the Commission for the Community. Only following a vote of approval by Parliament of the terms negotiated would the Council be able to sign the association, trade or cooperation agreement. The need for a parliamentary ratification procedure is particularly great in view of the considerable financial consequences of these agreements. To introduce this procedure Treaty amendment would be required.

Parliament and European Political Cooperation

First, Parliament should seek to obtain a written annual report on European Political Cooperation from the Foreign Ministers, as proposed by Mr Erik Blumenfeld.[2] This would require the agreement of the Foreign Ministers.

Second, Parliament should be able to make suggestions concerning new subjects to be dealt with in European Political Cooperation. This could be done most appropriately by Parliament's Political Affairs Committee in the

1. For a detailed explanation of this procedure, see Chapter 3.
2. In his report on European Political Cooperation of December 1977, Luxembourg, Document 427/77.

framework of the colloquies which it holds with the Foreign Ministers.[1] The agreement of the Foreign Ministers would be necessary.

Internal Procedures

First, Parliament should make use of initiative reports, both to enable it to request the Commission to introduce legislative proposals or action programmes to achieve aims established by Parliament[2] and to widen the area of subject-matter dealt with by the Community.

Second, Parliament should encourage its committees to meet in public *where appropriate* and to hold public hearings on subjects of concern to the European voter. In view of this aim Parliament's budget should make provision for the additional costs of public hearings up to a ceiling beneath which committees could organise these without having to request the specific permission of the Bureau each time they wished to hold a hearing. Parliament's long-term aims in this respect could include the right to "call for persons, papers and records", but national governments are not likely to concede this power to Parliament in the near future.

Third, Parliament's committees, through such means as initiative reports or hearings, should initiate general policy debates on matters which are due to become the subject of Community legislation. This should be done well before legislative proposals are drafted. The Commission and the Council are used to preparing legislation after consultation with pressure groups. If public opinion, not expressed through pressure groups, is to have any say in Community legislation, then the European Parliament should try to discover what such opinion is.

Fourth, Parliament's committees should develop, individually, their own "question time" to the Commission during normal committee meetings—a practice which has already been pioneered by the Legal and Transport Committees. This would permit committees to be informed regularly by the Commission on "their" subjects, and would reduce the pressure on question time in plenary sessions.

Fifth, although questions are tabled in Parliament concerning the

1. This suggestion has been developed in reports for the European Parliament by both Sir Peter Kirk and Mr Blumenfeld.
2. Such as the Klepsch report which called on the Commission to submit an action programme to the Council concerning the procurement of conventional armaments.

policies and activities of the Council and the Commission there is no opportunity for members to table questions relating to the functioning of Parliament itself. This gap should be filled. Since it might be difficult for the President both to preside and to reply to questions at the same time, the Bureau or Quaestors might appoint some kind of "Leader of the House" who would reply to questions of this kind.

Sixth, as argued in Chapter 4, either the membership of the Enlarged Bureau should be adapted to include the Chairmen of Parliament's committees or meetings should be held regularly between the group and Committee Chairmen concerning Parliament's working programme.

Impact of the New Members

The proposals set out above are a small selection of the many ideas that have been floated in recent years concerning the future of the European Parliament, together with some new proposals of the author. The choice of these proposals has been made on a personal and what may seem arbitrary basis, but however imaginative and attractively presented many other suggestions may be, the author is convinced that it is proposals of the kind made in this chapter that are the most realistic ones in terms of their chances of being put into practice within the next ten years. Obviously the proposals which can be implemented by Parliament on its own, without the need to obtain agreement from the other institutions or the member governments—such as the development of public hearings by Parliament's committees—have the greatest chance of being put into effect. Then the suggestions that require a gentleman's agreement or interinstitutional agreement—such as the consultation of Parliament by the European Council and the Council of Ministers concerning resolutions or action programmes—have the next greatest chance of acceptance. Proposals requiring Treaty amendment, such as Parliament's being given the right to ratify accession, trade and cooperation agreements between the Community and third countries, will be more difficult to implement.

But whether or not Parliament succeeds in extending its competences in the ways suggested here, or by other means, within the next few years, is less important than the real influence it can seize and exert in the decision making process of the Community. Constitutional powers are theoretical. There exist parliaments which have, under their national constitutions, wide-ranging powers of legislation and supervision of the executive, but which, in the face of harsh political realities, such as rule by a dictator, have no influence whatsoever. By contrast, the U.S. Congress, whose theoretical powers are more limited than those of the parliaments of many totalitarian states, can wield enormous influence over almost every detail of American policy.

Before direct elections it was difficult for the members of the European Parliament to give their full attention to either the legislative work of the Parliament or to its work of supervising the Commission and trying to establish some political accountability from the Council. They were always looking over their shoulder to Westminster, Bonn or Paris, dashing home from Strasbourg for three-line whips or to deal with crises in their constituency, and thus were unable to give enough time to the job of being a member of the European Parliament. Following direct elections this situation has changed. Out of the 410 members only 125 are also members of national parliaments. This means that most members are able to spend most of their time on their European work. This should give the work of Parliament, both in plenary and committee, greater depth and substance than it has had in the past: in particular, the time-consuming and fastidious work of financial scrutiny should now take on a new dimension. Members will now have more time to give to the preparation of their reports and speeches and the single-mandate members can concentrate on making their political careers in Europe. Finally members of the new elected Parliament are more highly motivated than the majority of their predecessors in the nominated Parliament and identify completely with it. Indeed, it has already become clear that most members of the new Parliament share a profound sense of commitment to their job.

Together with the democratic impulse given to Parliament by the very holding of direct elections, the effect of all this should be to improve the quality of Parliament's work. The greater degree of professionalism, the more detailed preparation of Parliament's reports and debates, the more exacting scrutiny of the Commission's spending, with the development of new parliamentary techniques, such as committee hearings held in public, should enable the European Parliament to wield greater political influence at all levels of the Community over the whole range of Community policies. Parliament may or may not acquire additional "powers" within the next years, but it has every opportunity to make its influence within the Community effective. In short, it makes even more sense for Parliament to work for influence than for a formal extension of its powers.

What better way of influencing Community policy could the new Parliament adopt than by expressing the concern of its electors about major EEC problems ? The concerns of Community voters will differ from country to country and from employers to unionists or from town workers to farmers, but no other institution or body within the Community now can claim, following direct elections, to rival Parliament in voicing the demands, worries and interests of its peoples. Indeed if the European Parliament does not voice these concerns, and if it does not obtain results in doing so, Parliament will miss the great opportunity it now has to justify its claim to be the democratic voice of the Community.

A majority of British voters probably hope that the directly elected Parliament will initiate the reform of the Common Agricultural Policy. English, Irish and Scottish fishermen will be bitterly disappointed if Parliament does not secure changes in the Community's fisheries policy. Car and ball-bearing manufacturers and workers and those in other industries under pressure from relentless Japanese competition will expect the European Parliament to convince the Community to take decisions that will ensure the future of European industry. Bretons, Corsicans, Scotsmen and Welshmen will expect Parliament, through influencing Community regional policy, to help their efforts to obtain a degree of regional autonomy. If Parliament is to exert real political influence on Community policy, it must not lose any opportunity of coming to grips with the thorniest issues of Community politics and, having worked out its own policies, do everything it can to ensure that these lead to practical and effective action.

7
Conclusions

Direct elections have given the citizen of the European Community the right to influence, through his vote, the direction of EEC policy-making. But this right will be of benefit to the European voter only if the members of the European Parliament prove able, collectively and individually, to justify their mandate by exerting effective political pressure on the Council and the Commission. Ideally, members of the European Parliament would hope to be able to do this with the help of formal increases in Parliament's competences, which would also provide them with the means of obtaining a larger role in Community decision-making. But, as has been made clear earlier, the prospects of the member governments and national parliaments agreeing, by amending the Treaty, to enlarge the European Parliament's powers are limited. The alternative is for the directly elected Parliament to increase its influence on policy-making in developing institutional possibilities of a kind that other Community or national institutions would find it hard to block, such as the conciliation procedure (as explained in Chapter 3), public hearings and initiative reports. To gain greater political influence through these and similar means could in the short term be an even more practical and rewarding political priority for the Parliament than its struggle to increase its formal competences and powers, though this struggle is also important and is bound to continue.

The future of the European Parliament is bound up with the future of the Community as a whole. Thus to the extent that the Community succeeds in solving the problem of enlargement to include Greece, Portugal and Spain; agreeing on and applying European solutions to the problems of industrial recession and unemployment; reforming the CAP and fisheries policy; improving the process of decision-making by the Council; and making monetary union work, Parliament will itself enjoy a share of such success. If the Community fails in its attempts to respond to these challenges, the European Parliament will share its failure.

But the main opportunity opened up to the European Parliament as a separate and distinct institution by direct elections is that of breaking out of the confines of its traditional consultative role, in which it has, in the past, mainly been a passive mirror of initiatives taken by the Commission or the Council, and to become, itself, a major creative and formative force in Community policy-making.

Perhaps the most disappointing feature of the Parliament's history has been its tendency to reflect the views of the Commission rather than imposing a philosophy of its own on the legislative proposals submitted to it. The strength of a parliament should lie in the formulation and expression of political ideas concerning proposed policies and subjects of public concern. It is not to be found in the imitation of the technical expertise of the executive, which is inevitably greater than its own. One of the tests by which the work of the directly elected Parliament will be judged is how far it will be able to transform its traditional complaisance concerning Commission proposals into a more critical and political scrutiny of proposed Community legislation, involving, where necessary, attempts to introduce radical changes of substance or shifts of political emphasis in draft Community laws. Precisely because the European Parliament is not, as opposed to the British House of Commons, a rubber stamp for *government* proposals, it can and should develop this role, which awaits it.

One of the main temptations for members of the directly elected Parliament will be to concentrate on refining its means of supervising the work of the Commission at the expense of tackling the more difficult job of gaining a greater degree of political accountability from the Council. The first task will certainly continue to remain a high priority for Parliament, but the nature of the relationship between the Commission and Parliament is already reasonably satisfactory from Parliament's viewpoint. Although on the one hand the Commission is sensitive both to the suggestions made by Parliament concerning its legislative proposals and also to parliamentary supervision of its activity, on the other hand the replies given to parliamentary questions during plenary sessions, debates, and in parliamentary committees are often vague and unhelpful. However, Parliament's relationship with the Council is very much less satisfactory since the

Council uses the prime responsibility of individual ministers to national governments and to national parliaments as a pretext to minimise its political accountability to the European Parliament.

Even when taking its decisions on Commission legislative proposals the Council is not very greatly influenced by Parliament's opinions. Parliament's main aim in strengthening its all-important relationship with the Council, in the near future, must be, first to ensure that the member governments take its opinions seriously into account in taking legislative decisions—explaining why the Council is not prepared to accept Parliament's opinions when it differs from them—and, second, to insist on a much greater degree of accountability to it from the Council at all three of the levels at which the Council operates, COREPER, the normal ministerial Council and the European Council.[1]

Parliament will continue to be frustrated, politically, until it has succeeded in achieving these two major aims. There is some danger that a politically frustrated Parliament, unable to develop a satisfactory relationship with the Council, will work off its resentment by savaging the Commission in debates, and at question time, and possibly, through motions of censure. Unjustified "Commission bashing" will do nothing to improve Parliament's image nor will it help Parliament to achieve its political and institutional aims. Even when the nationalist and regionalist elements that are undoubtedly significant in the directly elected Parliament are taken fully into account, Parliament remains an "integrationist" force. It should, therefore, remain the ally of the other "integrationist" force in the legislative structure of the Community, the Commission, even though it should be a more critical and independent ally than in the past. It is an alliance between Parliament and the Commission which remains the best hope of encouraging the Council to move, however hesitantly and slowly, in the direction of "integration".

Mention of Parliament's image leads to the next point which is the need for Parliament to develop an effective public relations and information policy. The turn-out in the European elections of June 1979 demonstrated the need for the public in Britain, in particular, to be informed about and interested in the European Parliament and its work. It might have been indifference or hostility to the Community which caused such a high

1. And to insist, likewise, on greater accountability from the foreign ministers meeting in political cooperation.

Conclusions   135

proportion of the British electorate to abstain from voting in the European elections in June 1979. But it is also likely that sheer ignorance was an important reason. Since the citizen of the European Community has been given a major new political right, his vote in the European elections, it would seem logical that he should be told about the existence of this right and of its meaning. Members of the directly elected Parliament are concerned about this problem, and it is to be hoped that Parliament will be able to bring an effective public relations and information policy into being well before the next European elections, which are due to be held in 1984, theoretically under a uniform system. If this can be done, Community voters may still choose to stay away from the polls in forthcoming European elections, but at least their abstention will then result from a deliberate choice and not from ignorance.

But more important than any information programme will be the impact of the Parliament and its members on public opinion as a result of their actions. In Britain the European Parliament gets in the news only when British members speak up for British interests. A row over lamb exports or budget contributions is worth more than thousands of glossy brochures. Of course the trouble is that in this way the European Parliament is most publicised when it is at its least European, federal or *"communautaire"*. Nevertheless, Parliament means a place where people talk, and members are elected not to govern but to express the views of the electors. When they do this on burning issues they will be attended to, at least in their home countries, they will reach the members of the European Parliament from other countries, and they *may* reach the electors in other countries. The German voter may be made aware of the inequity of the present budgetary arrangements. The French voter may learn that his government is defying the Court of Justice. And the British voter may learn something of the problems of French sheep farmers and fishermen, and French and Italian wine growers. On the last point pressure could build up to persuade the British Government to lower wine duties.

It is often claimed, virtually as a commonplace, that parliaments and democracy are in a period of decline. If one accepts this, is it possible for the European Parliament, which does not even possess some of the main theoretical attributes of a national parliament, to avoid being overcome by this general decline, in the face of reluctant governments ? Will it be able to justify the mandate given to it by 110 million European voters ? There does exist a reasonable hope that the European Parliament can go against the tide. One of the main reasons for the decline of national parliaments is that policies and decisions adopted by their home governments are increasingly taken in an international context, and in the case of EEC members, a Community one. Thus the European Parliament has an opportunity, which no longer exists for national parliaments, to influence the decisions taken by the nine member governments acting within the Community. Whenever European solutions have to be found for economic, commercial and agricultural problems, the European Parliament has both the chance and the legal right to play a role in the preparation of the Council decisions broadly similar to that previously played by national parliaments when these decisions were taken at a purely national level by individual governments. The European Parliament has not merely the opportunity but also the obligation, under the Treaties, to fulfil this parliamentary role at Community level. In doing so it neither competes with national parliaments nor subtracts from their powers, but complements their work. In carrying out its transnational task it is essential that the directly elected European Parliament should establish and maintain close and friendly relations with the national parliaments of the Nine.

The second reason why the European Parliament might be able, despite the general parliamentary decline, to score a success for representative democracy arises from the political constraints which have limited the scope, initiative and dynamism of the Commission since the confrontation between the Commission, under Professor Hallstein, and the French Government, under General de Gaulle, which led to the "Luxembourg Agreement". In view of the direct mandate given to them by the European electorate the committed and, for the most part, full-time members of the directly elected Parliament will almost certainly wish to give new life to the work of the Community as a whole and possibly even take over the role of "motor" or "dynamo" of the Community that was played by the Commission in the early years. For example, even if the Parliament is not accorded the power to draft and initiate major legislative proposals, this "dynamo" element could find an outlet in Parliament's instructing the Commission to introduce legislation on the basis of specific proposals made to it by Parliament or its committees.

Much has been written about the development of the political groups in the European Parliament in the direction of transnational political parties.

But even after direct elections it appears to the author, at least, that the political groups in the Parliament remain coalitions of members who, however great their commitment both to Parliament and to the European ideal, continue to act politically in the Parliament as members of British, French or German national parties rather than as members of transnational parties. Thus, although the political groups exercise very great influence on the establishment of Parliament's working programme and do much to shape its policies and attitudes, the heterogeneous national, party political, confessional and other elements from which each political group is constituted, have not yet, in the case of any single political group, been fused into a coherent transnational party.[1] Can genuine transnational parties come into being if the European Parliament is the only stage on which they perform? If the national political parties represented in the European Parliament, and their supporting European political federations, are to become transnational parties perhaps it is also necessary for the different Social Democratic, Christian Democratic and Liberal parties operating in each member state to operate, themselves, as transnational parties in their own home capitals? But is the national party dog prepared to be wagged by the tail of a European Parliament political group?

Meanwhile the European Parliament must not be afraid to indulge in nationalistic squabbles and national line-ups over issues like the financing of agricultural surpluses or net national contributions to the Community budget. This might conflict with Parliament's aim of obtaining greater political influence within the Community and the hopes of its members to develop coherent transnational political parties, but it shows Parliament in action on behalf of its electors and their interests, so if these aims do conflict, that simply cannot be helped.

Parliament's opportunity to become a major creative force in Community policy-making has been noted above. How might Parliament use this opportunity? First, however long it may take the member governments to agree to take one or other step towards the goal of "European Union", Parliament should constantly remind them of that aim and should, from time to time, as and when appropriate, make proposals as to the next major

1. To the extent that the European Democratic Group is more coherent, politically, than the other political groups, this is precisely because its membership is almost entirely drawn from one domestic political party in one country, the British Conservative Party.

advance that the Nine could make in that direction. The European Parliament should, also, be the Community institution primarily responsible for suggesting ways and means of transforming the limited *ad hoc* work of the Foreign Ministers within European Political Cooperation into a coherent common European foreign policy which might include the security aspects of foreign policy. Finally, as suggested earlier, the European Parliament should rapidly build on the practice it has recently started to develop of instructing the Commission to introduce legislation on any subject falling within the broad area covered by the Treaties. In working to these ends Parliament could also strive, as a longer term aim, to obtain the agreement of the member governments to the signature of new Treaties extending the work of the Community to include, formally, foreign policy and defence, together with those other activities which, taken together, would constitute "European Union".

Before the European elections of June 1979, although it already mattered that the nominated parliamentarians of the old European Parliament could influence the decisions taken by the Community and hold accountable the executive bureaucracy of Brussels, it mattered in a way remote from the individual Community citizen, in a way that was essentially part of a closed power game between the different Community institutions. Now the effectiveness of the elected European Parliament is central to the Community and its future. Each European Community voter not only has his personal stake in the Community, but has a member or members of the Parliament to speak and act for his interest. In taking the decision to hold European elections the member governments have at last given the Community the opportunity to become the transnational representative democracy intended by those who drafted the Treaties of Paris and Rome. If this remarkable experiment in transnational democracy succeeds, the rule of law and respect for human rights will be strengthened in Europe. But if the European Parliament fails to develop and use political teeth, or if it is ignored or circumscribed by the Council, direct elections could prove a sham and the future of democracy in the European Community could be a mere charade.

Appendices

Appendix I(a)
Officers and Members of the European Parliament[1]

Essential Facts

President: Simone VEIL
Vice-Presidents:

BUREAU:

Marcel Albert VANDEWIELE
Guido GONELLA
Hans KATZER
Pierre PFLIMLIN
Bruno FRIEDRICH
Gérard JAQUET
Pieter DANKERT
Basil de FERRANTI
Mario ZAGARI
Poul MOLLER
Allan R. ROGERS
Danielle DE MARCH

QUAESTORS:

Ludwig FELLERMAIER
Jean HAMILIUS
Patrick Joseph LALOR
Richie RYAN
Anthony H. M. SIMPSON

CHAIRMEN OF THE POLITICAL GROUPS:

Socialist Group (S):
Ernest GLINNE

1. As of 1 February 1981.

The European Parliament

Group of the European People's Party (EPP):
Egon KLEPSCH
European Democratic Group (ED):
Sir James SCOTT-HOPKINS
Communist and Allies Group (COM):
Guido FANTI
Liberal and Democratic Group (L):
Martin BANGEMANN
Group of European Progressive Democrats (EPD):
Christian de la MALENE
Group for the Technical Coordination and Defence of Independent Groups and Members (CG):
The chairmanship rotates, every four months between the three members of the Bureau who are, at present:
Neil BLANEY, Jens Peter BONDE
and Marco PANNELLA

The abbreviations marked in capital letters after the title of each political group, between brackets, are used to identify the political group to which each member of the Parliament belongs, as set out in the second column of the list below, containing essential information concerning the members of the Parliament. In the case of non-attached members of the Parliament the abbreviation (NA) is used.

CHAIRMEN OF THE COMMITTEES:

1. Political Affairs Committee: Mariano RUMOR
2. Committee on Agriculture: Sir Henry PLUMB
3. Committee on Budgets: Erwin LANGE
4. Committee on Economic and Monetary Affairs: Jacques DELORS
5. Committee on Energy and Research: Hanna WALZ
6. Committee on External Economic Relations: Sir Fred CATHERWOOD
7. Legal Affairs Committee: Mauro FERRI
8. Committee on Social Affairs and Employment: Frans van der GUN
9. Committee on Regional Policy and Regional Planning:
Pancrazio DE PASQUALE
10. Committee on Transport: Horst SEEFELD
11. Committee on the Environment, Public Health and Consumer Protection:
Kenneth COLLINS
12. Committee on Youth, Culture, Education, Information and Sport:
Mario PEDINI
13. Committee on Development and Cooperation: Michel PONIATOWSKI
14. Committee on Budgetary Control: Heinrich AIGNER
15. Committee on the Rules of Procedure and Petitions: Kai NYBORG

The names of the committees are preceded by numbers, which, as set out in the third column of the list of members, indicate the committee or committees to which members belong.

Appendix I **143**

MEMBERS

The name of each member is set out in the first column. The abbreviation in the second column shows the political group to which each member belongs. The figure or figures in the third column indicate, as explained above, the committee or committees on which a member sits. The fourth column shows the country of each member and, in the case of a British member, his constituency. The abbreviation in the fifth column indicates the national party to which a member belongs, the titles of the national political parties being set out, country by country, immediately following the list of members. The sixth column shows the place and date of birth of each member. The last column contains the addresses and telephone numbers at which members can be reached.

Name	Group	Com-mittees	Member State	Party	Place and date of birth	Address and telephone
ABENS Victor	S	8	Luxembourg	P.O.S.L.	Vianden 16-10-1912	Hôtel de Ville Vianden 84106
						48 Grand-rue Vianden 84006
ADAM Gordon J.	S	5	United Kingdom Member for Northumbria	Lab.	Carlisle 28-3-1934	Powdene House Pudding Chare Newcastle upon Tyne NE1 1UE Newcastle upon Tyne 29944
						2, Queen's Road Whitley Bay Tyne and Wear NE26 3BJ Whitley Bay 528616
ADONNINO Pietro	EPP	3-15	Italy	D.C.	Roma 6-11-1923	Via Tronto, 20 00198 Roma 06-856113
						Via di Villa Grazioli, 11 00198 Roma 06-8441330
AERSSEN Jochen van	EPP	6	Germany	CDU	Kevelaer 15-4-1941	Elfgenweg 33 4000 Düsseldorf 11 (0211) 594188
						Bundeshaus Zi: 800 HT 5300 Bonn 12 (02221) 165437

Appendix I(a)   **145**

AGNELLI Sig.ra Susanna	L	6	Italy	P.R.I.	Torino 24-4-1922	Via XXIV Maggio, 14 00187 Roma 6787650
AIGNER Heinrich	EPP	3-14	Germany	CSU	Ebrach (Bayern) 25-5-1924	Bundeshaus Zi 1127 NH 5300 Bonn 12 (0228) 163724 Kaiser-Wilhelm-Ring 14 8450 Amberg (Oberpfalz) (09621) 22883 (09621) 23128
ALBER Siegbert	EPP	11-14	Germany	CDU	Hechingen (Hohenzollern) 27-7-1936	Gammertinger Straße 35 7000 Stuttgart 80 (0711) 725445
ALBERS Willem	S	10	Netherlands	P.v.d.A.	Rotterdam 30-11-1920	Weerdslag 186 7206 BZ Zutphen (05750) 23127
ALEMANN Frau Mechthild von	L	5	Germany	FDP	Seebach/Thüringen 29-1-1937	Friedrich-von-Spee-Straße 3 4000 Düsseldorf 31 (0211) 400257
ALMIRANTE Giorgio	NA	6	Italy	M.S.I.-D.N.	Salsomaggiore (Parma) 27-6-1914	Camera dei Deputati 00100 Roma Via Quattro Fontane, 109 00100 Roma 4740382
ANSART Gustave	COM	1	France	P.C.F.	Roubaix 5-3-1923	Fédération du Parti Communiste Français 18 rue Inkermann 59000 Lille

Name	Group	Com-mittees	Member State	Party	Place and date of birth	Address and telephone
ANSQUER Vincent F. M.	EPD	3	France	D.I.F.E.	Treize-Septiers (Vendée) 11-1-1925	16 rue de la Frérie B.P. 4 85130 La Gaubretière 4 Place de Lattre de Tassigny 92300 Levallois-Perret
ANTONIOZZI Dario	EPP	1-6-14	Italy	D.C.	Rieti 11-12-1923	Via Nomentana, 373 00162 Roma 06-837078-8391627 Via Caroprere, 33 87100 Cosenza 0984-36196
ARFE Gaetano	S	12	Italy	P.S.I.	Somma Vesuviana (Napoli) 12-11-1925	Via IV Novembre, 114 00187 Roma 06-6786515 Borgo Paggeria, 22 43100 Parma 0521-24863
ARNDT Rudi	S	3	Germany	SPD	Wiesbaden 1-3-1927	Europa-Büro Fischerfeldstrasse 7-11 6000 Frankfurt/Main (0611) 291096 Mörfelder Landstraße 278 6000 Frankfurt am Main 70 (0611) 6311473
BADUEL GLORIOSO Sig.ra Maria Fabrizia	COM	8	Italy	Ind.Sin.	Perugia 2-7-1927	Via dell'Arte, 91 00144 Roma

Appendix I(a) **147**

Name	Group	#	Country	Party	Birth	Address
BAILLOT Louis	COM	3	France	P.C.F.	Paris 11-5-1924	Comité Central du Parti Communiste Français 2 Place du Colonel Fabien 75940 Paris Cedex 19 238 66 55 14 rue de l'Abreuvoir 75018 Paris 606 50 02
BALFE Richard A.	S	3	United Kingdom Member for London South Inner	Lab.	Mildenhall (Suffolk) 14-5-1944	259 Barry Road Dulwich London SE22 OJT (01) 299 0868
BALFOUR Nel R.	ED	4	United Kingdom Member for Yorkshire North	Cons.	Lima (Peru) 12-8-1944	24 The Little Boltons London SW10 9LP 373.8092
BANGEMANN Martin	L		Germany	FDP	Wanzleben 15-11-1934	Bundeshaus 5300 Bonn 1 (0228) 165 269/71 Sannentalstraße 9 7418 Metzingen (07123) 4717
BARBAGLI Giovanni	EPP	8	Italy	D.C.	Civitella in Val di Chiana (Arezzo) 24-6-1931	Via Lorenzetti, 30 52100 Arezzo 26.790-441617
BARBARELLA Sig.ra Carla	COM	2	Italy	P.C.I.	Magione (Perugia) 4-2-1940	Via delle Botteghe Oscure, 4 00186 Roma (06) 6711 Via dei Giubbonari, 74 00188 Roma 6567101

Name	Group	Com-mittees	Member State	Party	Place and date of birth	Address and telephone
BARBI Paolo	EPP	3	Italy	D.C.	Trieste 23-8-1919	Via Pigna, 6 00186 Roma 06-6790065
						Via Vincenzo Padula, 2 80123 Napoli 081-7695427
BATTERSBY Robert C.	ED	2-14	United Kingdom Member for Humberside	Cons.	Sheffield 14-12-1924	West Cross Rockshaw Road Merstham Surrey RH1 3BZ 649-3783
						28 First Avenue Bridlington N. Humberside 72489
BAUDIS Pierre	EPP	10	France	U.F.E.	Decazeville (Aveyron) 11-5-1916	Mairie de Toulouse 31000 Toulouse 216838
						28 rue Maurice Fonvieille 31000 Toulouse
BEAZLEY Peter	ED	4-5	United Kingdom Member for Bedfordshire	Cons.	Chale (Isle of Wight) 9-6-1922	"Rest Harrow" 14 The Combe Ratton Eastbourne Sussex BN29 9DB 0323-54460

BEREHOUWER Cornelis	L	1-15	Netherlands	V.V.D.	Alkmaar 19-3-1919	Stationsweg 56 (1851 LL) Heiloo (Alkmaar) 072-332791
BERLINGUER Enrico	COM	1	Italy	P.C.I.	Sassari 25-5-1922	Via delle Botteghe Oscure, 4 00186 Roma (06) 6711
BERSANI Giovanni	EPP	13	Italy	D.C.	Bologna 22-7-1914	Via delle Lame, 118 40136 Bologna 266963 237419 Via di Frino, 4 40136 Bologna 344484
BETHELL The Lord	ED	1	United Kingdom Member for London North West	Cons.	London 19-7-1938	73 Sussex Square London W2 2SS
BETTIZA Vincenzo	L	1	Italy	P.L.I.	Spalato (Yugoslavia) 7-6-1927	c/o Il Giornale Nuovo Piazza di Pietra, 26 00186 Roma 6787841 Via Moscova, 40/1 20121 Milano
BEUMER Bouke	EPP	4	Netherlands	C.D.A.	Valkenswaard 21-11-1934	Wilhelminastraat 24a, 8019 An Zwolle (05200) 13171 Oude Middelhorst 9 9751 TK Haren (Gr.) (050) 343181

Appendix I(a) **149**

Name	Group	Com-mittees	Member State	Party	Place and date of birth	Address and telephone
BEYER de RYKE Luc	L	12	Belgium	P.R.L.	Gand 9-9-1933	19a, avenue du Gui 1180 Bruxelles
BISMARCK Philipp von	EPP	4	Germany	CDU	Jarchlin (Pommern) 19-8-1913	374 30 70 Bundeshaus Zimmer 912 NH 5300 Bonn 1 (02228) 163352-163378
BLANEY Neil T.	CG	9	Ireland	Ind.	Rossnakill Co. Donegal 29-10-1922	Leinster House Kildare Street Dublin 2 789911 Ex. 303 485 Howth Rd. Dublin 5 313085
BLUMENFELD Erik Bernhard	EPP	1	Germany	CDU	Hamburg 27-3-1915	Bundeshaus 5300 Bonn 1 (02228) 163860 Chilehaus B III 2000 Hamburg 1 (040) 321381
BOCKLET Reinhold L.	EPP	2	Germany	CSU	Schongau/Obb. 5-4-1943	Graßlfingerstrasse 22a 8031 Gröbenzell (08142) 5523
BØGH Jørgen	CG	6	Denmark	Folkebe-vaegelsen	Frederiksberg 6-6-1917	Kystvej 47 8000 Århus C 06-121674

Appendix I(a) **151**

BONACCINI Aldo	COM	4	Italy	P.C.I.	Napoli 27-6-1920	Via Raffaele Balestra, 44 00152 Roma
BONDE Jens-Peter	CG	3	Denmark	Folkebe- vaegelsen	Åbenrå 27-3-1948	Nørrebrogade 140 III 2200 København N (01) 81 83 15
BONINO Sig.ra Emma	CG	5	Italy	P.R.	Bra (Cunco) 9-3-1948	Camera dei Deputati 00100 Roma 6793286 Via Giulia, 167 00186 Roma 06/6799745
BOOT Mevr. Elise C.A.M.	EPP	9-15	Netherlands	C.D.A.	Rotterdam 2-8-1932	Parkstraat 29 3581 PC Utrecht (030) 32 23 76 Kerkdwarsstraat 5 3581 RG Utrecht (030) 31 77 80
BOSERUP Fru Bodil Kathrine	COM	3-14	Denmark	SF	Thisted 24-6-1921	Damstien 32 2720 Vanløse 01-740402
BOYES Roland	S	8	United Kingdom Member for Durham	Lab.	Huddersfield 12-2-1937	P.O. Box No. 30 Room No. 4/74 County Hall Durham DH1 5UR Durham 49371 12 Spire Hollin Peterlee Co. Durham

TEP - K

152   The European Parliament

Name	Group	Com-mittees	Member State	Party	Place and date of birth	Address and telephone
BRANDT Willy	S	1	Germany	SPD	Lübeck 18-12-1913	Erich-Ollenhauer Haus Ollenhauerstraße 1 5300 Bonn 1 (0228) 5321 Bundeshaus Zimmer 03 Süd 5300 Bonn 1 (0228) 162758
BROK Elmar H.	EPP	9	Germany	CDU	Verl (Kreis Gütersloh) 14-5-1946	Thomas-Mann-Strasse 15 4800 Bielefeld 17
BROOKES Miss Beata Ann	ED	8	United Kingdom Member for North Wales	Cons.	Rhuddlan N. Wales 21-1-1932	Conservative Office 3 Llewelyn Road Colwyn-Bay Clwyd-North Wales Colwyn-Bay 33878 The Cottage Wayside Acres Bodelwyddan near Rhyl Clwyd-North Wales St. Asaph 583189
BUCHAN Mrs Janey O'Neil	S	12	United Kingdom Member for Glasgow (Scotland)	Lab.	Glasgow 30-4-1926	72 Peel Street Glasgow G11 5LR Scotland

Appendix I(a) **153**

BUTTAFUOCO Antonino	NA	10	Italy	M.S.I.-D.N.	Nissoria (Enna) 20-4-1923	Via Zara, 4 94013 Leonforte (Enna) 0935/61737-61621 Via San Giorgio 3 94010 Nissoria (Enna) 0935/69210-69203
CABORN Richard G.	S	4	United Kingdom Member for Sheffield	Lab.	Sheffield 6-10-1943	European Office Cambridge House Division Street Sheffield S14 GF 737947 393802
CAILLAVET Henri-Guy	L	2	France	U.F.E.	Agen 13-2-1914	28 rue Borghèse 92200 Neuilly-sur-Seine 637 43 20
CALVEZ Corentin	L	8	France	U.F.E.	Telgruc-sur-Mer (Finistère) 26-6-1920	27 avenue du Languedoc 78450 Villepreux 056 22 20
CAPANNA Mario	CG	5	Italy	D.P.	Città di Castello (Perugia) 10-1-1945	Via Giovanni Lanza, 3 20121 Milano
CAREIA Umberto	COM	10	Italy	P.C.I.	Tortoli (Nuoro) 9-9-1921	Viale Merello, 53 09100 Cagliari
CARETTONI ROMAGNOLI Sig.ra Tullia	COM	6	Italy	Ind. Sin.	Verona 30-12-1918	Via Boncompagni, 16 00187 Roma (06) 48 53 81

Name	Group	Committees	Member State	Party	Place and date of birth	Address and telephone
CARIGLIA Antonio	S	1	Italy	P.S.D.I.	Vieste (Foggia) 28-3-1924	Via del Leone, 13 00186 Roma 06-67 81 570 06-47 58 940
						Via della Crocetta, 9 51100 Pistoia (0573) 368574
CAROSSINO Angelo	COM	10	Italy	P.C.I.	Genova 21-2-1929	Via Privata Lanfranco, 34/B Casa A/1 17011 Albisola Capo (Savona) (019) 44364
CASSANMAGNAGO CERRETTI Sig.ra Maria Luisa	EPP	1-8	Italy	D.C.	Bergamo 7-4-1929	Via della Mendola, 57 00135 Roma 32 82 154
						Via Emanuele Filiberto, 190 00185 Roma 7577607
CASTELLINA Sig.ra Luciana	CG	13	Italy	P.d.U.P.	Roma 9-8-1929	Camera dei Deputati Palazzo Raggi Via del Corso, 173 00100 Roma 67179591-9492
						Via San Valentino, 32 00197 Roma

Appendix I(a) 155

CASTLE Mrs Barbara A.	S	2	United Kingdom Member for Greater Manchester North	Lab.	Chesterfield 6-10-1910	Hell Corner Farm Ibstone nr. High Wycombe Bucks. HP14 3XX Turville Heath 464 19 G John Spencer Square London N1 01 359 2012
CATHERWOOD Sir Fred	ED	6	United Kingdom Member for Cambridgeshire and Wellingborough	Cons.	County Londonderry 30-1-1925	7 Rose Crescent Trinity Street Cambridge CB2 3LL (0223) 311310 25 Woodville Gardens London W5 2LL Sutton Hall Balsham Cambridgeshire CB1 6DX
CECOVINI Manlio	L	9	Italy	P.L.I.	Trieste 29-1-1914	Fraz. Padriciano, 74 34012 Trieste (040) 226513
CERAVOLO Domenico	COM	8	Italy	P.C.I.	Bovalino Marina (Reggio Calabria) 26-9-1928	Via Buonarroti 5 35027 Noventa Padovana Padova (049) 628335

Name	Group	Com-mittees	Member State	Party	Place and date of birth	Address and telephone
CHAMBEIRON Robert	COM	7-15	France	P.C.F.	Paris 22-5-1915	16 rue Gustave Zédé 75016 Paris 647 7189
CHARZAT Mme Gisèle	S	5	France	P.S.	Paris 17-2-1941	63 rue Lauriston 75116 Paris 55 35 784 Résidence la Verte Vallée Appartement 209 14510 Houlgate
CINCIARI RODANO Sig.ra Maria Lisa	COM	7	Italy	P.C.I.	Roma 21-1-1921	Sezione Scuola — Federazione Romano P.C.I. Via dei Frentani, 2 00185 Roma 06-491272 Via di Porta Latina, 2 00179 Roma 06-75 75 934
CLEMENT Jean-José	EPD		France	D.I.F.E.	François (Martinique) 6-8-1932	33 rue de la Bienfaisance 75008 Paris 562 11 31
CLINTON Mark	EPP	2	Ireland	F.G.	Moynalty Co. Meath 7-2-1915	Inisfail Newcastle Co. Dublin

Appendix I(a) **157**

CLWYD Ms Ann	S	8	United Kingdom Member for Mid and West Wales	Lab.	Denbigh N. Wales 21-3-1937	Room 208 Dáil Eirann Leinster House Kildare Street Dublin 2 1 Lon Werdd St Fagan's Cardiff Wales 0222-593492
COHEN Robert	S	13	Netherlands	P.v.d.A.	Rotterdam 4-3-1930	E. Speeckaertlaan 87 1200 Brussel (02) 771.52.45 Traay 233 Driebergen 03438-3518
COLLA Marcel G. B.	S	3-14	Belgium	S.P.	Deurne 28-9-1943	ter Rivierenlaan 17 2100 Deurne (031) 24 95 24 Bosuil 27 2100 Deurne (031) 24 35 39
COLLESELLI Arnaldo	EPP	2	Italy	D.C.	Colle Santa Lucia (Belluno) 2-9-1918	Via Garibaldi, 45/B 32100 Belluno 0437/23998 privé 0437/25750 bureau 0437/721398 privé Via Asiago, 14 00195 Roma

Name	Group	Com-mittees	Member State	Party	Place and date of birth	Address and telephone
COLLINS Kenneth D.	S	11	United Kingdom Member for Strathclyde East	Lab.	Hamilton 12-8-1939	11 Stuarton Park East Kilbride G74 4LA (03552) 37282
COLLOMB Francisque	EPP	4	France	U.F.E.	St. Rambert en Bugey 19-12-1910	Sénat Palais du Luxembourg 75291 Paris Cedex 06 3291262 59 rue Duquesne 69006 Lyon 24 28 00
COMBE Francis	L	4-11	France	U.F.E.	Gonesse 14-5-1926	17 rue du Clos de la Ferme Bondoufle 91000 Evry 086 06 45 12 avenue Marceau 75008 Paris
COSTANZO Roberto	EPP	9	Italy	D.C.	San Marco dei Cavoti (Benevento) 27-11-1929	Via Nicola Colandra, 25 82100 Benevento 0824/28864 Via XXIV Maggio, 22 82100 Benevento 0824/28696 0824/24369

Appendix I(a)   **159**

COTTRELL Richard J.	ED	10-12	United Kingdom Member for Bristol	Cons.	Wellington (Somerset) 11-7-1943	Combeside Back Lane Croscombe Wells Somerset (0761) 412100
COURCY LING John de	ED	15	United Kingdom Member for Midlands Central	Cons.	Edgbaston 14-10-1933	31 Chapel Street Belgrave Square London SW1 (01) 235 56 55
						Bellehatch Farm Henley on Thames Oxon. RG9 4AW Henley (04912) 3878
COUSTÉ Pierre-Bernard	EPD	5-14	France	D.I.F.E.	Rochefort-sur-Mer 29-6-1920	Assemblée Nationale Palais Bourbon 75355 Paris Services Publics 07 297 73 83
CRAXI Bettino	S		Italy	P.S.I.	Milano 24-2-1934	Via Foppa, 5 20144 Milano
CRESSON Mme Edith	S	2	France	P.S.	Boulogne (Seine) 27-1-1934	5 rue Clément Marot 75008 Paris 3599788
						21 rue Guillemot 86100 Chatellerault
CRONIN (Jerry) Jeremiah	EPD	9	Ireland	F.F.	Currabeha Fermoy Co. Cork 15-9-1925	71 Main Street Mallow Co. Cork

160 The European Parliament

Name	Group	Com-mittees	Member State	Party	Place and date of birth	Address and telephone
CROUX Lambert V. J.	EPP	5	Belgium	C.V.P.-E.V.P.	Bilzen 6-3-1927	Stationsstraat 19 3820 Alken (011) 312 537
CURRY David M.	ED	2-12	United Kingdom Member for Essex North East	Cons.	Burton-on-Trent 13-6-1944	35 Belgrave Square London SW1X 8QN (01) 235-8914 (01) 245-9382
						The Old Maltings Arkesden near Saffron Walden Essex CB11 4HB (079) 985-368
DALSASS Joachim	EPP	2	Italy	S.V.P.	Leifers (Südtirol) 3-12-1926	39040 Petersberg (Bozen) (Südtirol) (0471) 615191
DALZIEL Ian M.	ED	7	United Kingdom Member for Lothians	Cons.	Edinburgh 21-6-1947	21 Greenhill Gardens Edinburgh EH10 4BL (031) 447 3441 (01) 600 4585 (London office) (031) 556 7352
DAMETTE Felix	COM	5	France	P.C.F.	Auchel 2-6-1936	Comité Central du Parti Communiste Français 2 Place du Colonel Fabien 75940 Paris Cedex 19 238 66 55
						CES Politzer 93100 Montreuil 854 78 93

Appendix I(a)

Name				Country	Party	Birth	Address
DAMSEAUX André R. J.-M. M.-A.	L	1		Belgium	P.R.L.	Verviers 5-3-1937	30 rue des Hougnes 4800 Verviers (087) 22 11 67
D'ANGELOSANTE Francescopaolo	COM	7-15		Italy	P.C.I.	Penne 17-9-1922	Via D. Manin, 29 65100 Pescara 71569 Via Regina Elena, 62 65100 Pescara 23124
DANKERT Pieter	S	3-14		Netherlands	P.v.d.A.	Stiens (Leeuwarderadeel) 8-1-1934	Hoogstraat 1 1135 BZ EDAM 02993-71668 c/o Brignol 31 rue St. Jean Bruxelles (2) 5118639
DAVERN Noel Michael	EPD	2		Ireland	F.F.	Tipperary 24-12-1945	Tannersrath Clonmel Co. Tipperary
DE CLERCQ Willy Cl. E. H.	L	6		Belgium	P.V.V.- E.L.D.	Gent 8-7-1927	Baron Cyriel Buyssestraat 12 9000 Gent (091) 22 59 47 (091) 22 80 09
DE GUCHT Karel L. G. E.	L	7		Belgium	P.V.V.- E.L.D.	Overmere 27-1-1954	O. L. Vrouwstraat 35A 9370 Lebbeke (052) 21 82 98 Groenewegel 14 9380 Lebbeke-Wieze (053) 77 82 82

Name	Group	Committees	Member State	Party	Place and date of birth	Address and telephone
DE KEERSMAEKER Paul Ph. M. H.	EPP	10	Belgium	C.V.P.-E.V.P.	Kobbegem 14-7-1929	Broekstraat 4 1703 Kobbegem (ASSE) (02) 4526080 (02) 4529707
DEKKER Mevr. Suzanne	NA	8	Netherlands	D'66	Amsterdam 31-10-1949	Toussaintkade 36 25 13 CK's-Gravenhage 070-45 36 07
DELATTE Charles	L	2	France	U.F.E.	Longeville en Barrois 20-1-1922	Préfecture de Région 53 rue de la Préfecture 21034 Dijon Cédex Chemin de Cromois 21100 Dijon (80) 65.28.98
DEL DUCA Antonio	EPP	12	Italy	D.C.	Casacanditella (Chieti) 4-7-1926	Ospedale civile 66016 Guardiagrele (Chieti) (0871) 82391/82219 Piazza Spirito Santo, 21 65100 Pescara (085) 27607
DELEAU Gustave	EPD	4	France	D.I.F.E.	Bruay en Artois (P.-de-C.) 18-9-1909	50 rue de Crimée 75019 Paris 202 35 15 4 Avenue des Hauts de Fougères Theoule-sur-Mer (Alpes Maritimes) 38 99 92

Appendix I(a) **163**

DELMOTTE Fernand L.	S	9	Belgium	P.S.	Jeumont (France) 24-7-1920	44 Chemin du Foubertsart 7860 Lessines (068) 33 29 89 (068) 33 21 13
DELOROZOY Robert E. A.	L	4	France	U.F.E.	Versailles 24-5-1922	2 Rte des Sablières Choisel 78460 Chevreuse 052 08 87
DELORS Jacques L. J.	S	4	France	P.S.	Paris 20-7-1925	19 Bd de Bercy 75012 Paris 307 88 83 260 93 60
DE MARCH Mme Danielle	COM		France	P.C.F.	Lérouville (Meuse) 6-8-1939	Le Colbert - Entrée B Avenue Colbert 83000 Toulon 1150 A. Chemin de Forgentier 83200 Toulon (94) 92 37 03
DENIS Jacques	COM	13	France	P.C.F.	Metz 25-5-1922	Comité Central du Parti Communiste Français 2 Place du Colonel Fabien 75940 Paris Cedex 19 202 70 10 9 rue Saint Just 94200 Ivry 672 11 73

The European Parliament

Name	Group	Committees	Member State	Party	Place and date of birth	Address and telephone
DE PASQUALE Pancrazio	COM	9	Italy	P.C.I.	Giardini (Messina) 6-8-1925	Via Libertà, 161/b 90100 Palermo (091) 295589
						Via Consolare Pompea, 51 98100 Messina (090) 56021
DESCHAMPS Pierre M. L. L. C.	EPP	6	Belgium	P.S.C.-P.P.E.	Schaerbeek 5.5.1921	Grand' Place 16 7890 Ellezelles (068) 54 22 31
DESMOND Mrs Eileen	S	9	Ireland	Lab.	Kinsale Co. Cork 29-12-1932	Ballinrea Road Carrigaline Co. Cork
De VALERA Miss Síle	EPD	8	Ireland	F.F.	Dublin 17-12-1954	Dáil Éireann Leinster House Dublin 2
						Charton Kerrymount Avenue Foxrock Co. Dublin
DIANA Alfredo	EPP	2	Italy	D.C.	Roma 2-6-1930	c/o Confagricoltura Corso Vittorio Emanuele, 101 00186 Roma 656 4241
DIDÒ Mario	S	8	Italy	P.S.I.	Livry Gargan (Seine et Oise) France 16-11-1926	Via Filippo Civinini, 37 00197 Roma 876941

Appendix I(a)

DILIGENT André F. E.	EPP	1	France	U.F.E.	Roubaix 10-5-1919	C.D.S. 205 Bd Saint Germain 75007 Paris (1) 5447250 64 rue du Moulin d'Ascq 59560 Villeneuve d'Ascq (20) 910717
DONNEZ Georges H.	L	7	France	U.F.E.	Saint Amand les Eaux 20-6-1922	51 Grand Place 59230 Saint Amand les Eaux
DOUFFET Maurice Ch. H.	EPD	10	France	D.I.F.E.	Saint-Maixent l'Ecole (Deux Sèvres) 8-4-1914	SAEMES 42 rue du Louvre 75001 Paris 236 67 91 4 rue Meissonier 75017 Paris 766 50 24
DOURO The Marquess of	ED		United Kingdom Member for Surrey	Cons.	Windsor 19-8-1945	11 Copthall Avenue London EC2R 7LU 01-628-4761
ELLES The Baroness (Diana Louie)	ED	1-15	United Kingdom Member for Thames Valley	Cons.	Bedford 19-7-1921	75 Ashley Gardens London SW1 (01) 828-0175 House of Lords London SW1 (01) 219 3169/3149

166 The European Parliament

Name	Group	Com-mittees	Member State	Party	Place and date of birth	Address and telephone
ENRIGHT Derek A.	S	13	United Kingdom Member for Leeds	Lab.	Thornaby on Tees (Yorkshire) 2-8-1935	The Hollies 112 Carleton Road Pontefract West Yorkshire WF8 3NQ (0977) 70 20 96
ESTGEN Nicolas	EPP	8	Luxembourg	P.C.S.	Dudelange 28-2-1930	1 rue P. Wigreux Howald 48 68 89 3 rue du Curé Luxembourg 28282
ESTIER Claude	S	1	France	P.S.	Paris 8-6-1925	12 rue Cortot 75018 Paris 208-32-93
EWING Mrs Winifred M.	EPD	9	United Kingdom Member for Highlands and Islands	SNP	Glasgow, Scotland 10-7-1929	52 Queen's Drive Glasgow S2 Scotland 041-423-8060 Goodwill Lossiemouth Morayshire Scotland
FANTI Guido	COM	9	Italy	P.C.I.	Bologna 27-5-1925	Camera dei Deputati 00100 Roma 6760

Appendix I(a) **167**

FANTON André	EPD	2	France	D.I.F.E.	Gentilly 31-3-1928	Corso Vittorio Emanuele 147A 00186 Roma 6567777
					10 rue Danton 75006 Paris 3540663
FAURE Edgar	L	9	France	U.F.E.	Béziers 18-8-1908	134 rue de Grenelle 75007 Paris 70546-56 5552179
FAURE Maurice	S	1	France	M.R.G.	Azerat 2-1-1922	Hôtel de Ville 46010 Cahors 6 rue Jean Admirat 46200 Gourdon 370258
						29 Bd Raspail 75007 Paris 222 80 45
FELLERMAIER Ludwig	S		Germany	SPD	Wien 2-7-1930	Bundeshaus 5300 Bonn 1 (0228) 163333/165718 Emsstraße 8 7910 Neu-Ulm (0731) 81471

Name	Group	Com-mittees	Member State	Party	Place and date of birth	Address and telephone
FERGUSSON Adam	ED	1	United Kingdom Member for Strathclyde West	Cons.	Haddington Scotland 10-7-1932	9 Addison Crescent London W14 (01) 603 7900 Ladyburn Maybole Ayrshire (06554) 206 11 Broomlands Street Paisley Renfrewshire (041) 887 8931
FERNANDEZ Guy	COM	4	France	P.C.F.	St. Etienne 29-10-1942	Fédération du Parti Communiste Français 30 rue Michelet 89000 Auxerre 4 Square Laperrine 89000 Auxerre 51 04 00
FERRANTI Basil de	ED	4	United Kingdom Member for Hampshire West	Cons.	Alderley Edge (Cheshire) 2-7-1930	Ferranti Limited Millbank Tower Millbank London SW1P 4QS 01-834-6611 19 Lennox Gardens London SW1X 0DD 01-584-2256

Appendix I(a) **169**

FERRERO Bruno	COM	13-15	Italy	P.C.I.	Belluno 2-6-1943	P.C.I. Via Chiesa della Salute, 47 10100 Torino 251058
						Strada Moncanino, 63 bis 10099 San Mauro (Torino) 8224465
FERRI Mauro	S	7	Italy	P.S.D.I.	Roma 15-3-1920	Via del Casaletto, 265 00151 Roma 530416
FICH Ove	S	3	Denmark	S	Odense 16-3-1949	S.N.T. Christiansborg 1218 København K (01) 113141
						Falkehusene 15 2620 Albertslund (02) 622942
FILIPPI Renzo Eligio	EPP	6-14	Italy	D.C.	Portogruaro (Venezia) 18-9-1935	Via Nino Oxilia, 14 00197 Roma 803452 870143
						Via Schiaparelli, 11 00197 Roma 802167
FISCHBACH Marc M. J. A.	EPP	7-15	Luxembourg	P.C.S.	Luxembourg 22-2-1946	2 rue Nic. Welter Luxembourg 47 35 45
						29 rue de Vianden Luxembourg 44 37 25

Name	Group	Committees	Member State	Party	Place and date of birth	Address and telephone
FLANAGAN Seán	EPD	3-15	Ireland	F.F.	Dublin 26-1-1922	65 St. Lawrence's Road Clontarf Dublin 3 "St. Anthony's" Ballaghaderreen Co. Roscommon
FOCKE Frau Katharina	S	13	Germany	SPD	Bonn 8-10-1922	Bundeshaus Zim HT 210 5300 Bonn 1 (0228) 161 Pferdmengesstraße 34 5000 Köln 51
FORSTER Miss Norvela	ED	4	United Kingdom Member for Birmingham South	Cons.	Gillingham (Kent) 25-7-1931	c/o (I.A.L.) Industrial Aids Ltd. 14 Buckingham Palace Road London SW1W 0QP 01-828-5036 6 Regency House Regency Street London SW1 01-821-5749
FORTH Eric	ED	3	United Kingdom Member for Birmingham North	Cons.	Glasgow 9-9-1944	40a Goldieslie Road Sutton Coldfield West Midlands (021) 354 4842

Appendix I(a) **171**

FOURGADE Marie-Madeleine	EPD	6	France	D.I.F.E.	Marseille 8-11-1909	41 Bd du Montparnasse 75015 Paris 222 52 90 85 quai d'Orsay 75007 Paris 555 29 38
FRANZ Otmar	EPP		Germany	CDV	6-1-1935	Werntgenhof 31 4330 München
FRIEDRICH Bruno	S	1-15	Germany	SPD	Helmbrechts 31-5-1927	Haus Frankenwarte 8700 Würzburg
						Bundeshaus 5300 Bonn 1 (0228) 161
FRIEDRICH Ingo	EPP	4	Germany	CSU	Kutno 24-1-1942	Bühringerstraße 12 8820 Gunzenhausen (09831) 2425
FRISCHMANN Georges Louis	COM	8	France	P.C.F.	Paris 5-8-1919	Comité Central du Parti Communiste Français 2 Place du Colonel Fabien 75940 Paris Cedex 19
FRÜH Isidor W.	EPP	2	Germany	CDU	Sasbach/Baden 13-4-1922	Oberer Kirchberg 14 7957 Schemmerhofen 2 (07356) 615
FUCHS Karl	EPP	5	Germany	CSU	Empertsreut (Landkreis Freyung-Grafenau) 11-9-1920	Waldschmidtstraße 34 8390 Passau (0851) 47281

Name	Group	Com-mittees	Member State	Party	Place and date of birth	Address and telephone
FUILLET Mme Yvette M.	S	11-14	France	P.S.	Marseille 1-3-1923	Appartement n° 20 Le Corbusier 280 Bd Michelet 13008 Marseille (91) 77 21 86 (91) 64 08 00
GABERT Volkmar	S	10-14	Germany	SPD	Dreihunken 11-3-1923	Landwehrstraße 37 8000 München 2 (089) 594212 Franz-Fackler-Straße 39 8000 München 50 (089) 150 30 63
GAIOTTI DE BIASE Sig.ra Paola	EPP	12-15	Italy	D.C.	Napoli 26-8-1927	Via B. Gosio, 33 00191 Roma (06) 392848
GALLAGHER Michael	S	5	United Kingdom Member for Nottingham	Lab.	Seaham Harbour Co. Durham 1-7-1934	Cattle Market House Nottingham Road Mansfield Nottinghamshire NG18 1BW Mansfield (0623) 648 441 The Cliff 31 Woodhouse Road Mansfield Nottinghamshire NG18 2AY Mans 31659

Appendix I(a)

GALLAND Yves A. R.	L	5-15	France	U.F.E.	Paris 8-3-1941	36 rue Sainte Croix de la Bretonnerie 75004 Paris 1 rue de Platre 75004 Paris 272 27 69
GALLUZZI Carlo Alberto	COM	6	Italy	P.C.I.	Firenze 2-12-1919	Via Fabio Quinto Pittore, 31 00138 Roma 3450542
GASPAED Mme Françoise	S	7	France	P.S.	Dreux 6-7-1945	Mairie de Dreux rue de Châteaudun 28107 Dreux 460112 Domaine Saint Louis Bât. F rue des Gaults 28107 Dreux
GATTO Vincenzo	S	2	Italy	P.S.I.	Messina 1-5-1922	Via Umberto Saba Comparto 25 Scala B, int. 3 Roma-Eur Via Bergamo 35 98100 Messina 2926787
GAUTIER Fritz	S	2	Germany	SPD	Norden 7-1-1950	Schlosstrasse 8III 3300 Braunschweig (0531) 18277 Romintenstrasse 17 3300 Braunschweig (0531) 61 18 84

Name	Group	Com-mittees	Member State	Party	Place and date of birth	Address and telephone
GENDEBIEN Paul-Henry E. M. Ch.	NA	10	Belgium	F.D.F.-R.W.	Hastières-par-delà 9-7-1939	18 rue Liégeois 6530 Thuin (071) 59 15 57
GERONIMI François-Marie	EPD		France	D.I.F.E.	Morosaglia (Corse) 20-3-1911	Résidence Vanina 20200 Toga-Bastia Haute Corse Télex: 31 19 78
GEURTSEN Aart	L	7	Netherlands	V.V.D.	Schiedam 17-1-1926	Koningin Julianaweg 118 3155 As Maasland 01899-13178
GHERGO Alberto	EPP	11	Italy	D.C.	Roma 23.2.1915	Via delle Montagne Rocciose, 21 00144 Roma 596353
GIAVAZZI Giovanni	EPP	4	Italy	D.C.	Bergamo 14-4-1920	Via Monte Ortigara 24100 Bergamo (035) 214111 Via Masone, 32 24100 Bergamo (035) 244106
GIUMMARRA Vincenzo	EPP	6	Italy	D.C.	Ragusa 9-5-1923	Via Marchese Ugo, 74 90141 Palermo Via Dante, 111 97100 Ragusa
GLINNE Ernest	S	13	Belgium	P.S.	Forchies-la-Marche 30-3-1931	Parlement européen rue Belliard Bruxelles

Appendix I(a) **175**

de GOEDE Arie	NA	4	Netherlands	D'66	Vlaardingen 21-5-1928	1 Square Salvador Allende 6180 Courcelles (071) 45 30 66
						Brederode 28 2352 JR Leiderdorp 071-890769
GONELLA Guido	EPP	7	Italy	D.C.	Verona 18-9-1905	Senato della Repubblica 00100 Roma 67061
						Via Colli della Farnesina, 98 00194 Roma 3384286
GOPPEL Alfons	EPP	7	Germany	CSU	Regensburg 1-10-1905	Sommerweg 2 8033 Krailling 8574034
GOUTHIER Anselmo	COM	3-14	Italy	P.C.I.	Roreto Chisone (Torino) 19-6-1933	PCI-KPI Piazza Domenicani, 6 39100 Bolzano
						Via Roma 78/13 39100 Bolzano 91 64 34
GREDAL Fru Eva	S	1	Denmark	S	Norresundby 19-2-1927	S.N.T. Christiansborg 1218 København K (01) 11 66 00
						Østbanegade 11 2100 København Ø (01) 260612

Name	Group	Com-mittees	Member State	Party	Place and date of birth	Address and telephone
GREMETZ Maxime François	COM	6	France	P.C.F.	Canchy 3-9-1940	Comité Central du Parti Communiste Français 2 Place du Colonel Fabien 75940 Paris Cedex19 3 Place Dewailly 8000 Amiens
GRIFFITHS Winston J.	S	9	United Kingdom Member for South Wales	Lab.	Grahamstown S. Africa 11-2-1943	Windsor Arcade Chambers Windsor Road Penarth South Glamorgan CF6 1SA (0222) 705500 The Craig John Street Ceen Cribwr Mid Glamorgan CF32 0AB (0656) 740526
van der GUN Frans G.	EPP	8	Netherlands	C.D.A.	Hagestein (Z.H.) 24-11-1918	Prof. Hugo de Vrieslaan 53 3571 GG Utrecht (030) 711033
HAAGERUP Niels Jørgen	L	1	Denmark	V	Nr. Åby 21-10-1925	Dansk Udenrigspolitisk Institut Bremerholm 6 1069 København K Toftegårdsvej 11 3520 Farum (02) 95 07 36
HABSBURG Otto	EPP	1	Germany	CSU	Reichenau 20-11-1912	Hindenburgstraße 15 8134 Pöcking 08157/1379

HÄNSCH Klaus	S	1-6-15	Germany	SPD	Sprottau 15-12-1938	Akazienstraße 5 4000 Düsseldorf 12 (0211) 201978
HAHN Wilhelm F. T.	EPP	12	Germany	CDU	Dorpat 14-5-1909	Im Hofert 3 6900 Heidelberg (06221) 802817 c/o Klaus Bitter Bachstraße 32 5300 Bonn 1
HAMILIUS Jean	L	11-14	Luxembourg	P.D.	Luxembourg 5-2-1927	c/o Fiduciaire Générale de Luxembourg 21 rue Glesener B.P. 1173 Luxembourg 491071 10 Eicherfeld Luxembourg 432119
HAMMERICH Fru Else	CG	1	Denmark	Folke- bevaegelsen	København 7-9-1936	Folkebevaegelsens Parlamentskontor Nørrebrogade 18 b l.tv. 2200 København N Glumsøvej 40 2700 Brønshøj (01) 607535
HARMAR-NICHOLLS The Lord	ED	10	United Kingdom Member for Greater Manchester South	Cons.	Darlaston W. Midlands 1-11-1912	Abbeylands Weston Stafford (0889)270252 (01)2195353

Appendix I(a) **177**

Name	Group	Com-mittees	Member State	Party	Place and date of birth	Address and telephone
HARRIS David A.	ED	9	United Kingdom Member for Cornwall and Plymouth	Cons.	Exeter, Devon 1-11-1937	Little Trehan Farm Trehan Saltash Cornwall PL12 4QN 3720
HASSEL Kai Uwe von	EPP	1	Germany	CDU	Gare-Tanzania 21-4-1913	Bundeshaus 5300 Bonn 1 (0228) 165574 Haus Belmar Fördestraße 11 2392 Glücksburg (Ostsee) (04631) 2517
HELMS Wilhelm	EPP	2-10	Germany	CDU	Bissenhausen 19-12-1923	2832 Twistringen-Bissenhausen 2 (04246) 353
HENCKENS Jaak P. J.	EPP	12	Belgium	C.V.P.-E.V.P.	Sint-Truiden 22-7-1933	Getelaan 54 3300 Tienen (016) 81 32 79
HERKLOTZ Frau Luise	S	2	Germany	SPD	Speyer 20-8-1918	Hasenpfuhlstraße 7 6720 Speyer (06232) 75657
HERMAN Fernand H. J.	EPP	4	Belgium	P.S.C.-P.P.E.	Boirs 23-1-1932	22 rue Philippe le Bon 1040 Bruxelles 2304105
van den HEUVEL Mevr. Ien	S	1	Netherlands	P.v.d.A.	Tiel 7-8-1927	Engelberg 8 3956 VL Leersum 03434-1376

Appendix I(a) **179**

HOFF Frau Magdalene	S	3	Germany	SPD	Hagen 29-12-1940	Zur Höhe 72 A 5800 Hagen (02331) 75661 (02331) 70854
HOFFMANN Mme Jacqueline	COM	12	France	P.C.F.	Béziers (Hérault) 26-12-1943	32 Square Eugénie Cotton 78190 Trappes
HOFFMANN Karl-Heinz	EPP	10	Germany	CDU	Köln 14-2-1928	Theodor-Heuss-Straße 2 7000 Stuttgart 1 (0711) 20971 Hauweg 28 7067 Plüderhausen
HOOPER Miss Gloria D.	ED	11	United Kingdom Member for Liverpool	Cons.	Southampton 25-5-1939	11 Cleveland Row St. James's London SW1 (01) 839-3929
HOPPER William J.	ED	4	United Kingdom Member for Greater Manchester West	Cons.	Glasgow 9-8-1929	23 Great Winchester Street London EC2P 2AX (01) 588 4545
HORD Brian H.	ED	2	United Kingdom Member for London West	Cons.	Hampstead 20-6-1934	Simon House 15 Golden Square London W1R 3AG (01) 734 2222/5057
HOWELL Paul F.	ED	3	United Kingdom Member for Norfolk	Cons.	Kings Lynn (Norfolk) 17-1-1951	Willy's Croft Church Road Wreningham Norwich Norfolk NR16 1BA Fundenhall (050) 841 596

Name	Group	Com-mittees	Member State	Party	Place and date of birth	Address and telephone
HUME John	S	9	United Kingdom Member for Northern Ireland	S.D.L.P.	Derry (N. Ireland) 18-1-1937	6 West End Park Londonderry N. Ireland
HUTTON Alasdair Henry	ED	9-12	United Kingdom Member for South of Scotland	Cons.	London 19-5-1940	7th Floor 121 St. Vincent Street Glasgow G2 5HW Scotland (041) 221 7850 14 Hamilton Drive Glasgow G12 8DR Scotland 041-334226
IPPOLITO Felice	COM	5	Italy	Ind. Sin.	Napoli 16-11-1915	Via del Tritone, 46 00187 Roma 6781713 Via Archimede, 35 00197 Roma 877094 Podere Poltricia n.1. 53040 Cetona (SI) (0578) 23118
IRMER Ulrich	L	6-14	Germany	FDP	Bochum 19-1-1939	Kaufingerstraße 25 8000 München 2 (089) 223387 Tx 05 280 32 act d Konradstraße 10 8000 München 40 (089) 39 78 39

Appendix I(a) **181**

ISRAEL
Gérard	EPD	12	France	D.I.F.E.	Oran (Algérie)
24-11-1928	85 Boulevard Pasteur
75015 Paris
(1) 281 58 49
46120 Lacapelle-Marival
(65) 40 81 29
JACKSON
Christopher M.	ED	1	United Kingdom
Member for
Kent East	Cons.	Norwich
24-5-1935	Medlars
Oak Hill Road
Sevenoaks
Kent
(0732) 56688
JACKSON
Robert Victor	ED	3	United Kingdom
Member for
Upper Thames	Cons.	Johannesburg
(South Africa)
24-9-1946	4 Churton Place
London SW1
(01) 930 9673
JAKOBSEN
Erharc V.	NA		Denmark	CD	Grene
25-2-1917	Folketinget
Christiansborg
1218 København K
(01) 11 66 00
Søvej 27
2880 Bagsvaerd
JALTON
Frédéric	S	3-12	France	P.S.	Abymes
(Guadeloupe)
21-2-1924	137 rue du Mont Cenis
75018 Paris
(1) 252 36 03
Mairie des Abymes
97110 Abymes
Guadeloupe
(590) 825433
JANSSEN van RAAY
James L.	EPP	7-10	Netherlands	C.D.A.	Muntok
(Indonesië)
1-6-1932	Mecklenburglaan 14
3062 BJ Rotterdam
010-146857

Name	Group	Com-mittees	Member State	Party	Place and date of birth	Address and telephone
JAQUET Gérard	S	13-15	France	P.S.	Malakoff (Hauts de Seine) 12-1-1916	2 rue Armand Moisant 75015 Paris 320 60 95
JOHNSON Stanley P.	ED	11	United Kingdom Member for Wight and Hampshire East	Cons.	Penzance 18-8-1940	30 Maida Av. London W2 West Nethercote Winsford Minehead (Somerset) Exford 325
JONKER Sjouke	EPP	6	Netherlands	C.D.A.	's Gravenhage 9-9-1924	Dahlialaan 36 1900 Jezus Eik/Overijse (België) 02-6571907 Aardbeistraat 26 's Gravenhage 070-230879
JOSSELIN Charles	S	9	France	P.S.	Trigavou (Côtes du Nord) 31-3-1938	13 Place du Champ Clos 22100 Dinan Lauriais 22490 Pleslin-Trigavou (96) 27 85 25
JÜRGENS Heinrich	L	2	Germany	FDP	Oeftinghausen 28-7-1924	Oeftinghausen 3 2831 Ehrenburg (Nds.) 04275/371 (0511) 815045

KATZER Hans	EPP		Germany	CDU	Köln 31-1-1919	Bundeshaus 5300 Bonn 12 (0228) 16 31 79 Kastanienallee 7 5000 Köln 51 (0221) 383770
KAVANAGH Liam	S	12	Ireland	Lab.	Wicklow 9-2-1935	Mount Carmel Wicklow Co. Wicklow (0404) 2582
KELLETT-BOWMAN Edward T.	ED	13-14	United Kingdom Member for Lancashire East	Cons.	Leeds 25-2-1931	33d Curzon Street London W1Y 7AE (01) 499 7248 9 Railway View Clitheroe Lancashire BB7 2HA (0200) 25939
KELLETT-BOWMAN Mrs M. Elaine	ED	9	United Kingdom Member for Cumbria	Cons.	St. Anne's (Lancashire) 8-7-1923	33d, Curzon St. London W1Y 7AE (01) 499 7248 42 School House Lane Halton, Lancaster (0524) 811 340
KEY Brian M.	S	10-14	United Kingdom Member for Yorkshire South	Lab.	Darfield Barnsley 20-9-1947	57 Bly Road Darfield Barnsley S73 9DW Yorkshire (0226) 753741

Appendix I(a)

Name	Group	Committees	Member State	Party	Place and date of birth	Address and telephone
KIRK Kent S.	ED	2	Denmark	KF	Esbjerg 26-8-1948	Bellisvaenget 33 Hjerting 6700 Esbjerg (05) 11 60 31 (05) 12 83 34
KLEPSCH Egon Alfred	EPP	1	Germany	CDU	Bodenbach 30-1-1930	Lüderitzstraße 41 5400 Koblenz-Pfaffendorf 753 42
KLINKENBORG Jan	S	10	Germany	SPD	Emden 26-9-1935	Oberbürgermeister der Stadt Emden 2970 Emden (04921) 87323 Uphuser Straße 9a 2970 Emden (04921) 24009
KROUWEL-VLAM Mevr. J. (Annie) B.	S	11-15	Netherlands	P.v.d.A.	Hengelo 29-6-1928	Bronkhorststraat 28 7555 MK Hengelo (074) 919307
KÜHN Heinz	S	13	Germany	SPD	Köln 18-2-1912	Friedrich Ebert-Stiftung 5300 Bonn 1 Godesberger Allee 149 Roteichenweg 5 5000 Köln 80 688338
LALOR (Paddy) Patrick Joseph	EPD	1	Ireland	FF	Dublin 21-7-1926	Main Street Abbeyleix Co. Portlaoise

LANGE Erwin	S	3	Germany	SPD	Essen 10-5-1914	Am Buchenhain 8 4300 Essen 16
LANGES Horst	EPP	3	Germany	CDU	Koblenz 2-12-1928	CDU-Geschäftsstelle Kaiserstraße 24 5500 Trier 48434 Bonhoefferstraße 32 5500 Trier 31659
LECANUET Jean A. F.	EPP	13	France	U.F.E.	Rouen 4-3-1920	282 Bd. Saint-Germain 75007 Paris 41 rue Thiers 76041 Rouen
LEGA Silvio	EPP	3	Italy	D.C.	Leini (Torino) 4-2-1945	Via Raimondo Montecuccoli, 1 10121 Torino 515990 Via Gianfrancesco Re, 15 10146 Torino 790246
LEMMER Gerd Ludwig	EPP	6	Germany	CDU	Remscheid 13-9-1925	c/o Walther AG Waltherstraße 51 5000 Köln 80 (0221) 6785230 Hindemithstraße 28 5630 Remscheid (02191) 72316
LENTZ-CORNETTE Mme Marcelle	EPP		Luxembourg	P.C.S.	Niederkorn 2-3-1927	76 route d'Esch Belvaux 59 45 36

Name	Group	Committees	Member State	Party	Place and date of birth	Address and telephone
LENZ Frau Marlene	EPP	6	Germany	CDU	Berlin 4-7-1932	Burgstrasse 102 5300 Bonn 2
LEONARDI Silvio	COM	4	Italy	P.C.I.	Torino 16-7-1914	Corso Porta Ticinese, 24 20123 Milano 8396228
LE ROUX Mme Sylvie	COM	12	France	P.C.F.	Nice 13-10-1946	Fédération du P.C.F. 87 rue de Glascgow 29200 Brest 80 19 47 52 rue Pierre Riquet 29200 Brest 80 08 84
LEZZI Pietro	S	13	Italy	P.S.I.	Napoli 15-12-1922	Discesa Gaiola, 8 80123 Napoli (081) 7691995
LIGIOS Giosuè	EPP	2	Italy	D.C.	Bitti (Nuoro) 26-12-1928	Piazza Veneto 08100 Nuoro (0784) 33135 Via Gioberti, 11 08100 Nuoro (0784) 31534
LIMA Salvatore	EPP	9	Italy	D.C.	Palermo 23-1-1928	Via Danae, 19 90149 Palermo (Valdesi) 454561

Appendix I(a) **187**

LINDE Erdmann	S	5	Germany	SPD	Dresden 22-2-1943	SPD Europa Büro Harpener Hellweg 152 4630 Bochum 1 (0234) 233897
LINKOHR Rolf	S	5	Germany	SPD	Stuttgart 11-4-1941	Asangstraße 219a 7000 Stuttgart 61 (0711) 324945
de LIPKOWSKI Jean-Noël	EPD	6	France	D.I.F.E.	Paris 25-12-1920	44 rue du Bac 75007 Paris 548 80 16 123 rue de Lille 75007 Paris 550 32 19
LIZIN Mme Anne-Marie A.	S	5	Belgium	P.S.	Huy 5-1-1949	6 Chaussée d'ANDENNE 5202 BEN AHIN 085-230864 (02) 735 73 21
LOMAS Alfred	S	1	United Kingdom Member for London North East	Lab.	Stockport 30-4-1928	342 Hoe Street Walthamstow London E17 (01) 5200756 23 Hatcliffe Close London SE3 (01) 8525433
LOO Charles-Emile	S	10	France	P.S.	Marseille 4-3-1922	Socoma—1 Rue Forbin 13003 Marseille 959107 8bis, Chemin du Souvenir 13007 Marseille 521288

Name	Group	Com-mittees	Member State	Party	Place and date of birth	Address and telephone
LOUWES Hendrik J.	L	6	Netherlands	V.V.D.	Ulrum 3-2-1921	Westpolder 22 9975 WJ Ulrum 05956-1504
LÜCKER Hans August	EPP	13	Germany	CSU	Krümmel/ Rheinland Pfalz 21-2-1915	Bundeshaus 5300 Bonn 1 (0228) 163754 Über der Klause 4 8000 München 90 647098
LUSTER Rudolf	EPP	7-15	Germany	CDU	Berlin-Schöneberg 20-1-1921	Reichstagsgebäude Platz der Republik 1000 Berlin 21 Douglas Straße 11 1000 Berlin 33
LYNGE Finn	S	2	Denmark	Siumut	Godthåb Grønland 22-4-1933	Lille Bakkegaardsvej 1 3060 Espergaerde (02) 23 54 92
MACARIO Luigi	EPP	4	Italy	D.C.	Andezeno (Torino) 6-9-1920	Via Latina, 18 00179 Roma 7580392
McCARTIN John Joseph	EPP	8	Ireland	F.G.	Ballinamore Co. Leitrim 24-4-1939	Leinster House Kildare Street Dublin 2 (01) 78 99 11 Mullyaster Newtowngore Co. Leitrim (049) 34 359

Appendix I(a) **189**

MACCHIOCCHI Sig.ra Maria Antonietta	CG	7	Italy	P.R.	Isola Liri (Frosinone) 23-7-1922	1 rue Bonaparte 75006 Paris (France) 3257919 Via Francesco Crispi, 83 00187 Roma 6792779
MAFFRE-BAUGÉ Emmanuel P. M.	COM	2	France	P.C.F.	Marseillan (Hérault) 12-12-1921	Route de Gignac Belarga 34230 Paulhan 980058
MAHER Thomas Joseph	L	2	Ireland	Ind.	Cashel Co. Tipperary 29-4-1922	Irish Cooperative Organization Society Ltd. 84 Merrion Square Dublin (00353) 1-764783 Castelmoyle Boherlahan Cashel Co. Tipperary Boherlahan 106
MAIJ-WEGGEN Mevr Johanna R. H.	EPP	11	Netherlands	C.D.A.	Emmen 29-12-1943	Pieter Bedijnstraat 38 2202 Vk Noordwijk aan Zee 01719-10471
MAJONICA Ernst	EPP	6	Germany	CDU	Soest 29-10-1920	Am Buschacker 18 5300 Bonn 2 Bornin Argelander Straße 7 5300 Bonn 1 (0228) 218032 Herzog-Johann-Straße 5 4770 Soest 3741

Name	Group	Com-mittees	Member State	Party	Place and date of birth	Address and telephone
MALANGRÉ Kurt	EPP	7-15	Germany	CDU	Aachen 18-9-1934	Knöpgerweg 25 5100 Aachen 72517
MALÈNE Christian de la	EPD	1	France	D.I.F.E.	Nimes 5-12-1920	Hôtel de Ville 75196 Paris R.P. 31 rue Saint Dominique 75007 Paris
MARCHAIS Georges	COM	1	France	P.C.F.	La Hoguette (Calvados) 7-6-1920	Comité Central du Parti Communiste Français 2 Place du Colonel Fabien 75940 Paris Cedex 19 238 66 55
MARSHALL John Leslie	ED		United Kingdom Member for London North	Cons.	London 19-8-1940	2 Birkdale Road London W5 (01) 991 0162
MART René	L		Luxembourg	D.P.	Esch-sur-Alzette 19-11-1925	12 rue de l'Alzette Esch-sur-Alzette 530 49 541 473
MARTIN Maurice	COM	10	France	P.C.F.	Limoges (Haute Vienne) 4-4-1927	Mairie de Carcassonne 11000 Carcassonne 9 rue Paul Vaillant-Couturier "Vignes Rouges" 11000 Carcassonne (68) 25 77 16

Appendix I(a)   **191**

MARTIN Mme Simone M. M.	L	9	France	U.F.E.	Tourcoing 14-4-1943	Thonnance les Moulins 52230 Poissons (25) 95 52 90 Résidence Cigny Val d'Ornel, Entrée 2 Appartement 19 52100 Saint Dizier (25) 05 75 86
MARTINET Gilles	S	6	France	P.S.	Paris 8-8-1916	12 rue Las Cases 75007 Paris 705 18 82 82 Bd. Flandrin 75116 Paris 727 52 54
MEGAHY Thomas	S	7	United Kingdom Member for Yorkshire South West	Lab.	Wishaw (Lanarkshire) 16-7-1929	6 Lady Heton Grove Mirfield West Yorkshire WF14 9DY County Hall Wakefield West Yorkshire 67111 Ext. 2254
MEETENS Meirolf	EPP	11	Germany	CDU	Bönkhausen 4-6-1923	Bönkhausen 3 5768 Sundern 6
MICHEL Victor J. J.	EPP	13	Belgium	P.S.C.- P.P.E.	Limbourg (Dolhein) 20-9-1915	14 rue de la Marjolaine 1120 Bruxelles (02) 216 47 36
MIHR Kar-Heinrich	S	4	Germany	SPD	Gudensberg 22-7-1935	Schwerinerweg 4 3505 Gudensberg (05603) 2830

192 The European Parliament

Name	Group	Com- mittees	Member State	Party	Place and date of birth	Address and telephone
van MINNEN Johan	S	8	Netherlands	P.v.d.A.	Noordwolde 31-10-1932	Avenue de la Sapinière 4 1180 Bruxelles-Uccle (02) 3588328 Straatweg 224 3621 BZ Breukelen 03462-3443
MODIANO Marcello	EPP	7	Italy	D.C.	Salonicco (Grecia) 7-4-1914	Via Milano, 4 34132 Trieste (040) 30047 Camera di Commercio Piazza della Borso 14 34121 Trieste (040) 60445
MØLLER Poul	ED		Denmark	KF	Frederiksberg 13-10-1919	Carl Baggers Allé 6 2920 Charlottenlund (01) 632441
MOORHOUSE James	ED	10	United Kingdom Member for London South	Cons.	Copenhagen (Denmark) 1-1-1924	Hill House 64 Honor Oak Road Forest Hill London SE23 3SH
MOREAU Jacques P.	S	4	France	P.S.	Saint Estèphe (Gironde) 25-8-1933	5 allée de Tourvoie 94260 Fresnes 237 22 97 7 rue du Faubourg Montmartre 75009 Paris 246 94 92

Appendix I(a) **193**

MOREAU Mme Louise	EPP	6	France	U.F.E.	Grenoble (Isère) 29-1-1921	Esfrala 747 Avenue des Pins 06210 Mandelieu la Napoule (93) 479587 66 Avenue Henri Martin 75116 Paris 504 69 57
MORELAND Robert J.	ED	5-10	United Kingdom Member for Staffordshire East	Cons.	Gloucester 21-8-1941	17 Barnwood Road Gloucester (0452) 21867 7 Vauxhall Walk London SE11 (01) 582-2613
MOTCHANE Didier	S	3	France	P.S.	Paris 17-9-1931	c/o M. Autain Député de la Loire Atlantique Assemblée Nationale 101 rue de l'Université Bureau 6343 75007 Paris 5 rue Payenne 75003 Paris
MÜLLER-HERMANN Ernst	EPP	5	Germany	CDU	Königsberg 30-9-1915	Bundeshaus 5300 Bonn 1 (0228) 162919 Rilkeweg 40 2800 Bremem-Oberneuland 33 (0421) 25 94 17

Name	Group	Com-mittees	Member State	Party	Place and date of birth	Address and telephone
MUNTINGH Hemmo J.	S	11	Netherlands	P.v.d.A.	Amsterdam 30-12-1938	Westerweg 11 9079 PD St. Jacobiparochie 05189-673
NARDUCCI Angelo	EPP	13	Italy	D.C.	L'Aquila 17-8-1930	Via del Tritone, 62/B 00187 Roma 6795795 Via dei Massimi 91 00156 Roma Via Feltre, 71 20134 Milano 7788
NEWTON DUNN William Francis	ED	3	United Kingdom Member for Lincolnshire	Cons.	Greywell Hampshire 3-10-1941	42 Lanchester Road London N6 4TA (01) 883 2527 The Old School House 10 Church Lane Navenby Lincoln LN5 0EG
NICOLSON Sir David Lancaster	ED		United Kingdom Member for London Central	Cons.	London 20-9-1922	15 Hill Street London W1X 7FB (01) 491 4366 Howicks Dunsfold Surrey (048) 649 296

Appendix I(a) **195**

NIELSEN Jørgen Brøndlund	L	2-14	Denmark	V	Ålborg 2-8-1939	Folketinget Christiansborg 1218 København K (01) 11 66 00 B.S. Ingemannsvej 4 8230 Aabyhøj
NIELSEN Fru Tove	L	8	Denmark	V	Durup 8-4-1941	Dansk Arbejdsgiverforening Vester Voldgade 113 1503 København V Kokkedalsvej 5 B 2970 Hørsholm
NORD Hans R.	L	3-15	Netherlands	V.V.D.	Den Haag 11-10-1919	15 rue Conrad I Luxembourg 440283
NORMANTON Tom	ED	5	United Kingdom Member for Cheshire East	Cons.	Rochdale 12-3-1917	House of Commons London SW1 (01) 219 3000 Ext. 4190 Bollin Court Macclesfield Road Wilmslow (Cheshire) SK9 2AP 0625 524 930 6 Paultons Street Chelsea London SW3 5DP (01) 352 6842

196 The European Parliament

Name	Group	Com-mittees	Member State	Party	Place and date of birth	Address and telephone
NOTENBOOM Harry A. C. M.	EPP	3-14	Netherlands	C.D.A.	Roosendaal 31-8-1926	Postbus 347 6900 AH Venlo
						Wilhelminapark 20 Venlo (077) 19668
						Hertog Reinoudsingel 73 Venlo (077) 15869
NYBORG Kai	EPD	4-15	Denmark	F.R.P.	Sønderborg 6-4-1922	Parlement Européen rue Belliard Bruxelles
						Bøgevej 18 6950 Ringkøbing (07) 32 36 64
O'CONNELL John Francis	S	11	Ireland	Lab.	Dublin 20-1-1930	24 Merchant's Quay Dublin 8 777286
						64 Inchicore Road Dublin 8 754751
O'DONNELL Tom G.	EPP	9	Ireland	F.G.	Limerick 30-8-1926	37 Thomas Street Limerick
OEHLER Jean A.	S	8	France	P.S.	Krautergersheim (Bas-Rhin) 30-3-1937	28 rue Virgile 67200 Strasbourg (88) 30 51 31

Appendix I(a) **197**

Name	Group	No.	Country	Party	Born	Address
O'HAGAN The Lord	ED	6	United Kingdom Member for Devon	Cons.	London 6-9-1945	Sutton Court Stowey Pensford Bristol Avon BS18 4DN (027) 589 2933 (01) 219 5454 (House of Lords) (076) 122 526 (Secretary)
O'LEARY Michael	S	3-14	Ireland	Lab.	Cork 8-5-1936	Dáil Éireann Leinster House Kildare Street Dublin 2 789911 Ext. 414 47 Wellington Road Ballsbridge Dublin 4
ORLANDI Flavio	S	3-14	Italy	P.S.D.I.	Canino (Viterbo) 12-4-1921	Via Livio Tempesta, 22 00151 Roma (06) 5346683
d'ORMESSON Olivier	EPP	2-14	France	U.F.E.	Biarritz (Pyrénées-Atl) 5-8-1918	Ferme d'Ormesson avenue Olivier d'Ormesson 94490 Ormesson sur Marne 576 95 28 (Mairie) 576 01 36 (Domicile) Château de Lézignan Lézignan la Cèbe 34120 Pezenas 98 12 95

198 The European Parliament

Name	Group	Committees	Member State	Party	Place and date of birth	Address and telephone
PAISLEY Ian R. K.	NA	5	United Kingdom Member for Northern Ireland	DUP	Armagh Northern Ireland 6-4-1926	The Parsonage 17 Cyprus Avenue Belfast BT5 5NT N. Ireland 655694
PAJETTA Giancarlo	COM	13	Italy	P.C.I.	Torino 24-6-1911	Via delle Botteghe Oscure, 4 00186 Roma Via Pio Foa, 8 00152 Roma
PANNELLA Marco	CG	6	Italy	P.R.	Teramo 2-5-1930	Ufficio Studi Gruppo Radicale Centro Calamandrei Corso Rinascimento, 65 00186 Roma 65 45 112 Via Collalto Sabino, 40 00199 Roma 65 62 557
PAPAPIETRO Giovanni	COM	12	Italy	P.C.I.	Bari 9-1-1931	c/o Comitato Regionale del P.C.I. Via Roberto da Bari, 31 70100 Bari (080) 41 40 78 Via Fanelli, 247 70100 Bari (080) 41 40 78

PATTERSON George Benjamin	ED	12-15	United Kingdom Member for Kent West	Cons.	Hemel Hempstead 21-4-1939	11 Buckingham Street Strand London WC2N 6DF (01) 839 1340 Birchenholt Wellingtonia Avenue Crowthorne Berkshire RG11 6AF
PEARCE Andrew	ED	13	United Kingdom Member for Cheshire West	Cons.	Southport 1-12-1937	30 Grange Road West Kirby, Wirral Merseyside L48 4HA (051) 625 1896
PEDINI Mario	EPP	12	Italy	D.C.	Montichiari (Brescia) 27-12-1918	25018 Montichiari (Brescia) (030) 961114 Via Po, 10 00198 Roma 85 16 90
PELIKAN Jiri	S	6	Italy	P.S.I.	Olomouc (Cecoslovacchia) 7-2-1923	Via della Rotonda, 36 00186 Roma 65 42 228
PENDERS Johannes J. M. (Jean)	EPP	1	Netherlands	C.D.A.	Gemert 5-4-1939	Voorburgseweg 11 2264 AC Leidschendam (70) 27 86 91
PERCHERON Daniel	S	5	France	P.S.	Beauvais (Oise) 31-8-1942	Lycée Diderot Avenue Montaigne 62220 Carvin (16-20) 37 01 73

Appendix I(a) **199**

Name	Group	Com-mittees	Member State	Party	Place and date of birth	Address and telephone
PETERS Johannes Wilhelm	S	8	Germany	SPD	Nedem/Krs. Kleve 10-12-1927	Senftenbergstraße 16 4600 Dortmund 14 (0231) 23 03 74
						SPD Bezirksbüro Westliches Westfalen Brüderweg 10-12 4600 Dortmund 1 (0231) 52 77 81
PETERSEN Eggert	S	5	Denmark	S	Bovrup 26-5-1927	Låsbyvej 2 8464 Galten
PETRONIO Francesco	NA	4	Italy	M.S.I.-D.N.	Trieste 21-12-1931	Via Felice Casati, 20 20124 Milano 222 876
						Via Quattro Fontane, 22 00184 Roma 47 59 600
PFENNIG Gero	EPP	3	Germany	CDU	Jüterbog (Brandenburg) 11-2-1945	Reichstagsgebäude Platz der Republik 1000 Berlin 21 (030) 397-2421/2424
						Waldsängerpfad 6 1000 Berlin 38 803 6416
PFLIMLIN Pierre	EPP		France	U.F.E.	Roubaix 5-2-1907	Mairie 9 rue Brûlée 67000 Strasbourg 32 43 40

PICCCLI Flamino	EPP	Italy	D.C.	Kirchbichl (Austria) 28-12-1915	24 avenue de la Paix 67000 Strasbourg
					Democrazia Cristiana Piazza del Gesù, 46 00186 Roma 6775
					Via Massimi, 45 00136 Roma
PININ-FARINA Sergio	L	8	Italy	P.L.I.	Torino 8-9-1926	Unione Industriale Via Fanti, 17 10128 Torino 57 18 436
					Piazzale Duca d'Aosta, 18 10129 Torino 70 32 32
PINTAT Jean-François A.	L	5	France	U.F.E.	Bordeaux 29-7-1923	Mairie de Soulac 33780 Soulac-sur-Mer
					38 rue Michel Ange 75016 Paris 525 78 95
					Villa Symphonie l'Amélie 33780 Soulac-sur-Mer 59 81 47
PIQUET René-Emile	COM	4	France	P.C.F.	Lanthenay-Romorantin 23-10-1932	Comité Central du Parti Communiste Français 2 Place du Colonel Fabien 75940 Paris Cedex 19 238 66 55
					36 rue Pargaminiere 31000 Toulouse

Name	Group	Com-mittees	Member State	Party	Place and date of birth	Address and telephone
PISANI Edgard Edouard	S	5	France	P.S.	Tunis (Tunisie) 9-10-1918	Sénat Palais du Luxembourg 75291 Paris Cedex 06 8-10 rue Joseph-Bara 75006 Paris 354 03 68
PLUMB Sir Henry	ED	2	United Kingdom Member for The Cotswolds	Cons.	Warwickshire 27-3-1925	35 Belgrave Square London SW1X 8QN (01) 235-8914 (01) 245-9382 Southfields Farm Coleshill Birmingham B46 3CJ Warwickshire (0675) 63133
PÖTTERING Hans-Gert	EPP	9	Germany	CDU	Bersenbrück (Niedersachsen) 15-9-1945	Richard-Wagner-Straße 15 5300 Bonn 1 (0228) 658984 Dombogen 3 4558 Bersenbrück (05439) 1581
POIRIER Mme R. Henriette	COM	6	France	P.C.F.	Bordeaux 26-10-36	Fédération du Parti Communiste Français 15/17 rue Furtado 33000 Bordeaux 91 45 06

PONIATOWSKI Michel C.	L	13	France	U.F.E.	Paris 16-5-1922	Bâtiment A no 11 Résidence Pierre Curie 33000 Floirac 86 10 52
						22 Bd Jean Mermoz 92200 Neuilly 745 4530
PRAG Derek	ED	8	United Kingdom Member for Hertfordshire	Cons.	Merthyr Tydfil Glamorgan South Wales 6-8-1923	Euro-Centre Maynard House The Common Hatfield Herts. AL10 0NF (07072) 71860
						Pine Hill 47 New Road Digswell Herts AL6 0AQ (07073) 5686
PRANCHERE Pierre-Benjamin	COM	2	France	P.C.F.	Brive (Corrèze) 1-7-1927	5 rue Marc Eyrolles 19000 Tulle (55) 26 10 38
PRICE Peter N.	ED	5-14	United Kingdom Member for Lancashire West	Cons.	Aberdare 19-2-1942	6 Gelliwastad Road Pontypridd Mid Glamorgan CF37 2BP
PROUT Christopher J.	ED	7	United Kingdom Member for Salop and Stafford	Cons.	London 1-1-1942	90 York Mansions Prince of Wales Drive London SW11 (01) 622 7336

Appendix I(a)   **203**

Name	Group	Committees	Member State	Party	Place and date of birth	Address and telephone
PROVAN James L. C.	ED	2	United Kingdom Member for North East Scotland	Cons.	Glenfarg Perthshire 19-12-1936	Wallacetown Bridge of Earn Perthshire Scotland PH2 8QA (073) 881-2243 Telex: 76606 Provan G
PRUVOT Mme Marie-Jane	L	12	France	U.F.E.	Pont l'Evêque (Calvados) 13-12-1922	B.P. no 13 78570 Andresy 974 58 73
PULETTI Ruggero	S	9	Italy	P.S.D.I.	Umbertide (Perugia) 10-3-1924	Via Marconi, 14 06100 Perugia (075) 66 933 Via Savonarola, 62 06100 Perugia (075) 30 123 Via Nicola Marchese 16 00141 Roma
PURVIS John	ED	5	United Kingdom Member for Mid-Scotland and Fife	Cons.	St. Andrews (Fife) 6-7-1938	Gilmerton House Dunino St. Andrews Fife Scotland KY16 8NB St. Andrews (0334) 73275 home St. Andrews (0334) 75830 office
QUIN Miss Joyce G.	S	2	United Kingdom Member for South Tyne and Wear	Lab.	Tynemouth (Northumberland) 26-11-1944	41 Preston Avenue North Shields Tyne and Wear 596139

RABBETHGE Frau Renate-Charlotte	EPP 13	Germany	CDU	Göttingen 14-10-1930	Haus Borntal 3352 Einbeck (05561) 5067
RADOUX Lucien	S 6	Belgium	P.S.	Bruxelles 18-7-1921	16 avenue des Arts 1040 Bruxelles (02) 2176139 60c avenue de la Toison d'Or (Boîte 6) 1060 Bruxelles (02) 539 1960 (privé) (02) 513 38 00 (Sénat)
REMILLY Eugène L.	EPD 11	France	D.I.F.E.	Ploemeur (Morbihan) 11-2-1925	92 rue Saint Lazare 75009 Paris 522 94 66 Impasse de la Brise 56260 Larmor Plage (Morbihan) 65 50 58
RHYS WILLIAMS Sir Brandon	ED 4	United Kingdom Member for London South East	Cons.	London 14-11-1927	House of Commons London SW1 (01) 219 4068 32 Rawlings Street London SW3 (01) 58 40 636 Miskin Manor Pontyclun

Appendix I(a)

Name	Group	Com-mittees	Member State	Party	Place and date of birth	Address and telephone
RIEGER Helmut Martin	S	6	Germany	SPD	Graz (Österreich) 16-10-1943	Europabüro Arndtstrasse 8 4800 Bielefeld 1 (0521) 64086
						Damaschkestrasse 21 4902 Bad Sulzuflen 1 (05222) 157 35
RINSCHE Günter	EPP	5	Germany	CDU	Hamm 13-7-1930	Feldgarten 15 4700 Hamm 1 02381-52330
RIPA di MEANA Carlo	S	10	Italy	P.S.I.	Marina di Pietrasanta (Lucca) 15-8-1929	Dorsoduro, 73 30123 Venezia 041 28199
ROBERTS Dame Shelagh	ED	10	United Kingdom Member for London South West	Cons.	Port Talbot (South Wales) 13-10-1924	23 Dovehouse Street Chelsea London SW3 6JY 352 37 11
ROGERS Allan R.	S	4-15	United Kingdom Member for South East Wales	Lab.	Gelligaer Glamorgan South Wales 24-10-1932	3A Cooperative Buildings Ystrad Mynach Hengoed S. Wales CF8 7AG (0443) 812395
ROMUALDI Pino	NA	1	Italy	M.S.I.-D.N.	Predappio (Forlì) 24-7-1913	Camera dei Deputati 00100 Roma 67 86 755
ROSSI André	L	3	France	U.F.E.	Menton 16-5-1921	35A Quai de Grenelle 75015 Paris

Appendix I(a) **207**

ROUDY Mme Yvette	S	11	France	P.S.	Pessac (Gironde) 10-4-1929	162 Bd du Montparnasse 75014 Paris 354 42 01 65 Cours de la Liberté 69003 Lyon
RUFFOLO Giorgio	S	4	Italy	P.S.I.	Roma 14-8-1926	c/o Fime Via Valadier, 37/B 00193 Roma (06) 6798030-6798517 Piazza della Libertà, 20 00192 Roma 35 99 444
RUMOR Mariano	EPP	1	Italy	D.C.	Vicenza 16-6-1915	Via Gregoriana, 54 00187 Roma (06) 6798030-6798517 Via Kenia, 58 00144 Roma (06) 59 19 427 Ponte Pusterla, 16 36100 Vicenza (0444) 21106
RYAN Richie	EPP	3-14	Ireland	F.G.	Dublin 27-2-1929	Dáil Éireann Leinster House Kildare Street Dublin 2 (01) 60 41 13

Name	Group	Com-mittees	Member State	Party	Place and date of birth	Address and telephone
SABLÉ Victor	L	13	France	U.F.E.	Fort de France (Martinique) 30-11-1911	Assemblée Nationale Palais Bourbon 75355 Paris Services Publics 07 297 60 00 140 Avenue Victor Hugo 75116 Paris 727 85 17
SÄLZER Bernhard	EPP	5	Germany	CDU	Berlin 4-9-1940	Dieburger Straße 240 6100 Darmstadt (66151) 714240
SALISCH Frau Heinke	S	8	Germany	SPD	Grevenbroich 14-8-1941	Sonntagstrasse 2 7500 Karlsruhe 1 (0721) 33688
SARRE Georges	S	8	France	P.S.	Chenerailles (Creose) 26-11-1935	Hôtel de Ville 75004 Paris (1) 271 37 39 22 rue Edouard Lockroy 75011 Paris (1) 700 43 90
SASSANO Mario	EPP	5	Italy	D.C.	San Martino in Pensilis (Campobasso) 1-10-1923	Viale XXI Aprile, 5 00162 Roma 831 29 94
SAYN-WITTGENSTEIN-BERLEBURG Casimir J. Prinz zu	EPP	4	Germany	CDU	Frankfurt/Main 22-1-1917	Metallgesellschaft A.G. Reuterweg 14 6000 Frankfurt am Main (0611) 1592513

Appendix I(a)   **209**

Name	Group	No.	Country	Party	Place/Date of Birth	Address
SCHALL Wolfgang	EPP	12	Germany	CDU	Konstanz 31-3-1916	c/o BDI 4 rue Ravinstein 1000 Bruxelles Waldweg 53 7772 Uhldingen 2 (07556) 8390
SCHIELER Rudolf F.	S	1	Germany	SPD	Teningen (Baden) 22-5-1928	Stephanienstraße 21 7800 Freiburg
SCHINZEL Dieter P. A.	S	4	Germany	SPD	Berlin 14-11-1942	Klappergasse 10 5100 Aachen (0241) 35171 (0241) 39394 Melatenerstraße 89a 5100 Aachen 84874
SCHLEICHER Frau Ursula	EPP	11	Germany	CSU	Aschaffenburg 15-5-1933	Bundeshaus 5300 Bonn 1 (0228) 163654 Backoffenstraße 6 8750 Aschaffenburg (06021) 92901
SCHMID Gerhard	S	5	Germany	SPD	Straubing 5-5-1946	Büro: Richard Wagner Straße 4 8400 Regensburg (0941) 55553 Innere Passauer Straße 55 8440 Straubing (09421) 6527

Name	Group	Com-mittees	Member State	Party	Place and date of birth	Address and telephone
SCHNITKER Paul	EPP	4	Germany	CDU	Münster 12-1-1927	Handwerkskammer Münster Bismarckallee 1 4400 Münster (0251) 400 35
SCHÖN Karl	S	9	Germany	SPD	Elstra/Sachsen 26-7-1923	Danngasse 3 5413 Bendorf 1/Rhein (02622) 2021 Dreikaiserweg 4 5400 Koblenz (0261) 12641
SCHÖN Konrad	EPP	3	Germany	CDU	Mannheim 7-5-1930	Hohenzollernstraße 13 (Hansa-Haus) 6600 Saarbrücken (0681) 53787
SCHWARTZENBERG Roger-Gérard	S	4	France	M.R.G.	Pau 17-4-1943	3 rue de Rivoli 75004 Paris 272 78 94
SCHWENCKE Olaf	S	12	Germany	SPD	Pinneberg/Holst. 27-1-1936	Wilhelmstraße 17 3070 Nienburg (Weser) (05021) 13636
SCOTT-HOPKINS Sir James	ED	1	United Kingdom Member for Hereford and Worcester	Cons.	London 29-11-1921	Dartmouth House 2 Queen Anne's Gate London SW1N 9AA (01) 222 0411 602 Nelson House Dolphin Square London SW1 (01) 828 66 82

Appendix I(a)   211

Name			Country		Birth	Party	Address
SCRIVENER Mme Christiane	L	3-11	France		Mulhouse (Ht. Rhin) 1-9-1925	U.F.E.	21 Avenue Robert Schuman 92100 Boulogne-sur-Seine 8254411
SEAL Barry H.	S	6	United Kingdom Member for Yorkshire West		Halifax, Yorks. 28-10-1937	Lab.	City Hall Bradford West Yorkshire BD1 1HY 0274–29577 Extn. 7866
SEEFELD Horst	S	10	Germany		Berlin 21-11-1930	SPD	Im Brettspiel 53 7518 Bretten (07252) 1903
SEELER Hans-Joachim	S	6	Germany		Lauenburg/Elbe 9-8-1930	SPD	Kurt-Schumacher-Allee 10 2000 Hamburg 1 (040) 24 92 29 Sonnentauweg 3 2000 Hamburg 71 (040) 6414199
SEGRE Sergio Camillo	COM	1-11	Italy		Torino 15-9-1926	P.C.I.	Via dei Giornalisti, 64 00135 Roma 3454079 Via Michele Lessona, 1 00143 Torino 772085
SEIBEL-EMMERLING Frau Lieselotte	S	11	Germany		Leobschütz (Oberschlesien) 3-2-1932	SPD	Virchowstraße 15a 8500 Nürnberg (0911) 564467
SEITLINGER Jean	EPP	1	France		St. Louis-les-Bitche 16-11-1924	U.F.E.	19 rue de l'Eglise 57200 Sarreguemines (8) 7982200

212 The European Parliament

Name	Group	Com-mittees	Member State	Party	Place and date of birth	Address and telephone
SELIGMAN Madron Richard	ED	5	United Kingdom Member for Sussex West	Cons.	Leatherhead Surrey 10-11-1918	PO Box No 4 Manor Royal Crawley W. Sussex RH10 2QB (0293) 37 4 57 (0293) 27 7 77 Micklepage House Nuthurst near Horsham Sussex (040376) 259
SHERLOCK Alexander	ED	11-13	United Kingdom Member for Essex South West	Cons.	Coventry 14-2-1922	58 Orwell Road Felixstowe Suffolk IP11 7PS 4503
SIEGLERSCHMIDT Hellmut	S	7-15	Germany	SPD	Berlin 17-10-1917	Reichstagsgebäude Scheidemann Straße 1000 Berlin 21 (030) 3972228 (030) 3972229 (030) 3972238 Nibelungenstraße 5A 1000 Berlin 33 (030) 8036886
SIMMONDS Richard J.	ED		United Kingdom Member for Midlands West	Cons.	Maidenhead 2-8-1944	Woodlands Farm Cookham Dean Maidenhead Berkshire SL6 9PJ Marlow 4293 (office) Telex: 848248 rjsmep

Appendix I(a) **213**

SIMONNET Maurice-René	EPP	3-14	France	U.F.E.	Lyon 4-10-1919	2 rue de la Roche 26290 Donzère (Drôme) 16 (75) 98 61 30 C.D.S.— 205 Bd Saint Germain 75007 Paris 16(1)544 72 50
SIMPSON Anthony M. H.	ED		United Kingdom Member for Northamptonshire	Cons.	Leicester 28-10-35	Avenue Michel-Ange 57 1040 Brussels 73 64 219 Bassets Great Glen Leicestershire 053 759 2386
SKOVMAND Sven	CG	2	Denmark	Folkebe- vaegelsen	Frederiksberg 29-9-1936	c/o Jan Mogelbjerg Avisen Samtid 8961 Allingaabro Ravnsmosevej 2 Hedegård 8584 Tranehuse (06) 387444
SPAAK Mme Antoinette M.	NA	11	Belgium	F.D.F.- R.W.	Bruxelles 27-6-1928	Secrétariat de Mme A. M. Spaak c/o Mme Gribomont 127 chaussée de Charleroi 1050 Bruxelles 35 avenue d'Italie 1050 Bruxelles

Note: SIMONNET address also includes:
Dyars
Cookham Dean
Maidenhead
Berkshire
Marlow 3269

Name	Group	Committees	Member State	Party	Place and date of birth	Address and telephone
SPENCER Tom	ED	8	United Kingdom Member for Derbyshire	Cons.	Nottingham 10-4-1948	Heath House 13 Goulton Road Clapton London E5 8HA (01) 985 5839
						1 Sant Lane Doveridge Derbyshire
SPICER James W.	ED	6	United Kingdom Member for Wessex	Cons.	London 4-10-1925	House of Commons London SW1 (01) 219 4195
						Whatley Beaminster Dorset (0308) 86 2337
SPINELLI Altiero	COM	3	Italy	Ind. Sin.	Rome 31-8-1907	Camera dei Deputati 00100 Roma 6786755
						Clivo Rutario, 5 00152 Roma 06 5896 343
SQUARCIALUPI Sig.ra Vera	COM	11	Italy	Ind. Sin.	Pola (Jugoslavia) 5-8-1928	Via Losanna, 16 20154 Milano 3458781

Appendix I(a) **215**

STEWART-CLARK Sir John	ED	1-6	United Kingdom Member for Sussex East	Cons.	West Lothian 17-9-1929	Holmsley House Holtye Common near Cowden Kent 034286-541
SUTRA DE GERMA Georges	S	2	France	P.S.	Béziers 14-1-1930	Campagne Monplézy 23120 Pezenas 98 12 77
TAYLOR John David	ED	8-9	United Kingdom Member for Northern Ireland	U.U.P.	Armagh 24-12-1937	Mullinure Armagh BT61 9EL N. Ireland Armagh 0861-522409
TAYLOR John Mark	ED	3-14	United Kingdom Member for Midlands East	Cons.	Hampton-in-Arden 19-8-1941	2/4 High Street Solihull West Midlands B91 3TB (021) 704 3071 211 St. Bernards Road Solihull West Midlands B92 3TB (021) 707 1076
TINDEMANS Leo	EPP	1	Belgium	C.V.P.- E.V.P.	Zwÿndrecht (bÿ Antwerpen) 16-4-1922	Jan Verbertlei 24 2520 Edegem (02) 219 10 70
TOLMAN Teun	EPP	2	Netherlands	C.D.A.	Oldeholtpade 22-9-1924	Hoofdweg 45 b 8474 Ca Oldeholtpade p. Wolvega 05610-2463

TEP - O

Name	Group	Com-mittees	Member State	Party	Place and date of birth	Address and telephone
TRAVAGLINI Giovanni	EPP	9-10	Italy	D.C.	Napoli 30-10-1924	Via del Tritone, 201 00187 Roma (06) 6797031 Via Tasso, 480 (Parco Matarazzo, pal. 133) 80127 Napoli (081) 650313
TUCKMAN Frederick A.	ED	3	United Kingdom Member for Leicester	Cons.	Magdeburg (Germany) 9-6-1922	6 Cumberland Road London SW13 9LY (01) 7482392 "Bassetts" 3 The Nook Great Glen Leicestershire
TURCAT André	EPD	5.	France	D.I.F.E.	Marseille 23-10-1921	"Les Frères" Auzerille-Tolosane 31320 Castanet (61) 73 57 26
TURNER Amédée E.	ED	7-15	United Kingdom Member for Suffolk	Cons.	London 26-3-1929	1 Essex Court Temple London EC4Y 9AR (01) 583-8290 The Barn Westleton Saxmundham Suffolk Westleton 235

TYRRELL Alan R.	ED	7	United Kingdom Member for London East	Cons.	Bolobo Belgian Congo 27-6-1933	15 Willifield Way London NW11 (01) 4555798 32 rue Ortelius 1040 Bruxelles 230 99 60
VANDEWIELE Marcel Albert	EPP	5	Belgium	C.V.P.- E.V.P.	Sint-Joris-Ten- Distel 10-7-1920	Witte Molenstraat 108 8200 Brugge—St. Michiels (050) 31 83 03
VAN MIERT Karel A. L. H.	S	1	Belgium	S.P.	Oud-Turnhout 17-1-1942	Keizerslaan 13 1000 Brussel (02) 513 82 70 Merelstraat 7 3078 Everberg
VANNECK Hon. Sir Peter B. R.	ED.	11	United Kingdom Member for Cleveland	Cons.	London 7-1-1922	2 Chaloner Street Guisborough Cleveland (0287) 32031 Tx: 587654 Rowe and Pitman City Gate House 39-45 Finsbury Square London EC2 (01) 606 1066 Tx: 8952485
VAYSSADE Mme Marie-Claude	S	7-15	France	P.S.	Pierrepont (Meurthe et Moselle) 8-8-1936	78 rue du Maréchal Oudinot 54000 Nancy (8) 356 16 72

Appendix I(a) **217**

Name	Group	Com-mittees	Member State	Party	Place and date of birth	Address and telephone
VEIL Mme Simone	L		France	U.F.E.	Nice 13-7-1927	32 rue de Babylone 75007 Paris 556 88 06
						11 Place Vauban 75007 Paris
VERGEER Willem J.	EPP	13	Netherlands	C.D.A.	Zeist 28-3-1926	Rubicondreef 34 3561 JC Utrecht (030) 614411 (08866) 2366
VERGÈS Paul	COM	13	France	P.C.F.	Oubone (Thailande) 5-3-1925	87 rue Pasteur 97400 St. Denis de la Réunion (Ile de la Réunion) 21 08 07
VERHAEGEN Joris J. B.	EPP	8	Belgium	C.V.P.- E.V.P.	Hulshout 3-5-1921	Booischotseweg 11 3160 Hulshout (015) 22 23 39
VERNIMMEN Willy	S	2	Belgium	S.P.	Melle 23-12-1930	Astridlaan 1 9500 Geraardsbergen (054) 413228
VERONESI Protogene	COM	5	Italy	P.C.I.	Bologna 19-2-1920	Via Mascarella, 77 40126 Bologna (051) 22 51 67
VERROKEN Joannes J.	EPP	11-15	Belgium	C.V.P.- E.V.P.	Melden 30-1-1917	Edelareberg 8 9700 Oudenaarde (055) 31 16 63
VETTER Heinz Oskar	S	7	Germany	SPD	Bochum-Werne 21-10-1917	Abgeordneten Büro Heinz Oskar Vetter Breite Straße 13 4000 Düsseldorf 1 (0211) 82 52 12

Appendix I(a) **219**

VIÉ Daniel J. E.	EPD	7	France	D.I.F.E.	Nantes 25-4-1925	von-Behring-Platz 4 4330 Mülheim a.d. Ruhr 64 Bd Meusnier de Querlon 44000 Nantes (40) 76 28 49
VIEHOFF Mevr. P. (Phili) J.	S	12	Netherlands	P.v.d.A.	Zwolle 8-6-1924	Zuidlaarderweg 3 9756 CE Glimmen (05906) 2494
VISENTINI Bruno	L	4	Italy	P.R.I.	Treviso 1-8-1914	Piazza di Spagna, 15 00187 Roma 67 89 788 67 94 651
VITALE Giuseppe	COM	2	Italy	P.C.I.	Locri (Reggio Calabria) 26-8-1923	Via Tembien, 41 00199 Roma 83 64 35
						Viale Stazione 88046 Lamezia Terme (Catanzaro) 214 14
VRING Thomas von der	S	9	Germany	SPD	Stuttgart 27-5-1937	Meissener Straße 7 2800 Bremen (0421) 351557
WAGNER Manfred W.	S	4	Germany	SPD	Hassel/Saar 14-1-1934	Finkenweg 30 6604 Saarbrücken-Brebach- Fechingen (06893) 2786 privat (0681) 46611 Büro

Name	Group	Com-mittees	Member State	Party	Place and date of birth	Address and telephone
WALTER Gerd	S	4	Germany	SPD	Lübeck 26-4-1949	Morier Straße 45 2400 Lübeck 1 49 44 07
WALZ Frau Hanna	EPP	5	Germany	CDU	Templin (Uckermark) 28-11-1918	Bundeshaus Zi 1418 NH 5300 Bonn 1 (0228) 163512 Magdeburger Straße 72 6400 Fulda (0661) 75291
WARNER Sir Fred A.	ED	13	United Kingdom Member for Somerset	Cons.	Bournemouth 2-5-1918	33 Moreton Place London SW1 (01) 828 7531 Laverstock Bridport Dorset Broadwindsor 68543
WAWRZIK Kurt	EPP	13	Germany	CDU	Meiningen (Thüringen) 15-2-1929	Am Wildpark 9 6800 Mannheim 31 (0621) 741600
WEBER Frau Beate	S	11	Germany	SPD	Reichenberg 12-12-1943	Sickingenstraße 1 6900 Heidelberg (06221) 33626
WEISS Mme Louise	EPD	12	France	D.I.F.E.	Nice 25-1-1893	15 avenue du Président Wilson 75116 Paris 723 50 65

Name				Country	Party	Birth	Address
WELSH Michael J.	ED	6		United Kingdom Member for Lancashire Central	Cons.	Dovercourt 22-5-1942	Watercrook 181 Town Lane Whittle-le-Woods Nr. Chorley Lancs. PR6 8AG (02572) 76992
VETTIG Klaus H. W.	S	2-14		Germany	SPD	Göttingen 15-8-1940	Rohnsterrassen 6 3400 Göttingen (0551) 58150
WIECZOREK-ZEUL Frau Heidemarie	S	6		Germany	SPD	Frankfurt/Main 21-11-1942	Michelstädter Straße 1 6090 Rüsselsheim (06142) 32868 Europa-Büro SPD Bezirk Hessen-Süd Fischerfeldstrasse 7-11 6000 Frankfurt (0611) 291096 Euro-Bureau Avenue de la Sapinière 4 1180 Bruxelles-Uccle (02) 35 88 328
WOGAU Karl von	EPP	4		Germany	CDU	Freiburg 18-7-1941	Bertholdstraße 4 7844 Neuenburg/Breisgau (07631) 72867
WOLTJER Eisso P.	S	2		Netherlands	P.v.d.A.	Nieuwe Pekela 9-1-1942	Bergkwartier 10 5801 PS Venray 04780-84324

Name	Group	Com-mittees	Member State	Party	Place and date of birth	Address and telephone
WURTZ Francis	COM	11	France	P.C.F.	Strasbourg 3-1-1948	Comité Central du Parti Communiste Français 2 Place du Colonel Fabien 75940 Paris Cedex 19 238 66 55
						33 rue Compans Appt. 189 75019 Paris 200 49 20
ZACCAGNINI Benigno	EPP		Italy	D.C.	Faenza (Ravenna) 17-4-1912	Camera dei Deputati 00100 Roma 6760
						Via di Roma, 30 48100 Ravenna 27222
ZAGARI Mario	S	1	Italy	P.S.I.	Milano 14-9-1913	161 Avenue Winston Churchill Aile Waldorf App. 91 1180 Bruxelles
						Viale della Tecnica, 302 00144 Roma 5920449
ZECCHINO Ortensio	EPP	9	Italy	D.C.	Asmara (Etiopia) 20-4-1943	Via d'Afflitto, 70 83031 Ariano Irpino (Avellino) 871171
						Piazza Bovio, 22 80133 Napoli 314598

Appendix I(a)   223

SECRETARIAT:

Secretary General: Hans Joachim OPITZ
Directorate General I—Sessional and general services:
    Enrico VINCI, Director General
Directorate General II—Committees and interparliamentary delegations:
    Francesco PASETTI BOMBARDELLA,
    Director General
Directorate General III—Information and public relations:
    Raymond LEGRAND-LANE,
    Director General
Directorate General IV—Administration, Personnel and Finance:
    Karl-Heinz NEUNREITHER,
    Director General
Directorate General V—Research and Documentation:
    John P. S. TAYLOR, Director General

Address of the Parliament: European Parliament
                              Centre Européen
                              Plateau du Kirchberg
                              Luxembourg
                              Grand Duchy of Luxembourg
                              Telephone: 43001
                              Telex numbers:
                              3494 EUPARL LU and 2894 EUPARL LU

ABREVIATIONS

Belgium

S.P.	Socialistische Partij
P.S.	Partie socialiste
C.V.P.-E.V.P.	Christelijke Volkspartij (Europese Volkspartij)
P.S.C.-P.P.E.	Parti social-chrétien (Parti Populaire Européen)
F.D.F.-R.W.	Front démocratique des Francophones (Rassemblement Wallon)
P.R.L.	Parti des reformes et de la liberté
P.V.V.-E.L.D.	Partij voor vrijheid en vooruitgang
	(Europese Liberalen en Demokraten)
V.U.	Volksunie

Denmark

CD	Centrum-Demokraterne
	Folkebevaegelsen
FRP	Fremskridtspartiet
KF	Det konservative folkeparti
	Siumut
S	Socialdemokratiet
SF	Socialistisk folkeparti
V	Venstre, Danmarks liberale parti

TEP - P

France

D.I.F.E.	Défence des intérêts de la France en Europe
M.R.G.	Mouvement des Radicaux de Gauche
P.C.F.	Parti communiste français
P.S.	Parti socialiste
U.F.E.	Union pour la France en Europe

Germany

CDU	Christlich Demokratische Union
CSU	Christlich-Soziale Union
FDP	Freie Demokratische Partei
SPD	Sozialdemokratische Partei Deutschlands

Ireland

F.F.	Fianna Fail Party
F.G.	Fine Gael Party
Lab.	Labour Party
Ind.	Independent

Italy

D.C.	Democrazia cristiana
D.P.	Democrazia proletaria
Ind. Sin.	Indipendenti di Sinistra
M.S.I.-D.N.	Movimento sociale italiano—Destra nazionale
P.C.I.	Partito comunista italiano
P.d.U.P.	Partio di unità proletaria per il communismo
P.L.I.	Partito liberale italiano
P.R.	Partito radicale
P.R.I.	Partito repubblicano italiano
P.S.D.I.	Partito socialista democratico italiano
P.S.I.	Partito socialista italiano
S.V.P.	Südtiroler Volkspartei (Partito popolare sudtirolese)

Luxembourg

P.C.S.	Parti chrétien social
P.D.	Parti démocratique
P.O.S.L.	Parti ouvrier socialiste luxembourgeois

Netherlands

C.D.A.	Christen Democratisch Appèl
D'66	Demokraten '66
P.v.d.A.	Partij van de Arbeid
V.V.D.	Volkspartij voor Vrijheid en Democratie

United Kingdom

Cons.	Conservative and Unionist Party
DUP	Democratic Unionist Party
Lab.	Labour Party
SDLP	Social Democratic and Labour Party
SNP	Scottish National Party
UUP	Ulster Unionist Party

Appendix I(b)
Greek Members of the European Parliament[1]

1. The titles of the Greek political parties are set out following the list of Greek members. Until direct elections to the European Parliament are held later in 1981 all Greek members can be reached at the Greek Parliament as well as at the private addresses listed: Vouli Ton Hellinon, Platia Syntagmatos, Athina. Telephone: (1) 3238 434.

Appendix I(b)   227

Name	Group	Committees	Member State	Party	Place and date of birth	Address and telephone
BOURNIAS Leonidas		1	Greece	N.D.	Chios 9-5-1908	Voukourestiou 21 Athina (1) 5225 662
COUTSOCHERAS Yannis	S	12	Greece	PA.SO.K.	Ziria (Patra) 1904	Skoufa 60a Athina 144 (1) 3613 516
DALAKOURAS Georgios		10	Greece	N.D.	Athina 8-7-1938	Har. Trikoupi 1 Pireas 4527 493
DIMOPOULOS Ioannis		3	Greece	N.D.	Vrontou (Pieria) 1935	Patission 4 Athina (1) 3605 901
FOTILAS Assimakis	S	2	Greece	PA.SO.K.	Patra 1932	A. Fotila 19 Patra (61) 332 734 (61) 274 744 (61) 278 370
FRANGOS Dimitrios		8	Greece	N.D.	Athina 6-6-1935	
GEORGIADIS Antonios	S	3	Greece	PA.SO.K.	Agios Isidoros (Rhodes) 11-5-1944	Kerassoudos 5 Athina 611 (1) 7775 989 (1) 8674 758
GONDICAS Konstantinos		7-14	Greece	N.D.	Athina 27-4-1934	Skoufa 64 Athina 134 (1) 3631 782

228 The European Parliament

Name	Group	Com-mittees	Member State	Party	Place and date of birth	Address and telephone
HARALAMBOPOULOS Ioannis	S	1	Greece	PA.SO.K.	Psari (Trifylia)	Agiou Konstantinou 13 Pireas 4125 775
LOULES Konstantinos	COM	9	Greece	K.K.E.	Tyrnavos 18-4-1906	Kapodistriou 16 Grafio Kedrikis Epitropis K.K. Athina (1) 3628 745
MARKOZANIS Spyridon		4	Greece	N.D.	Pireas 1931	Georgiou A' ke Kolokotroni 72 (P.O. Box 196) Pireas 4172 436
NICOLAOU Konstantinos	S	6	Greece	PA.SO.K.	Athina 1933	
PAPAEFSTRATIOU Efstratios		2	Greece	N.D.	Athina 12-2-1935	Mavromihali 3 Athina 143 (1) 3638 192
PEPONIS Anastassios	S	9	Greece	PA.SO.K.	Athina 1924	Stadiou 10 Athina 133 (1) 3222 065 (1) 3222 077
PESMAZOGLU Ioannis		6	Greece	KO.DI.SO.	Chios 1-3-1918	Komma Dimokratikou Socialismou Mavromihali 9 Athina (1) 3619 577 (1) 3601 716

Appendix I(b) **229**

PLASKOVITIS Spyridon	S	7-15	Greece	Corfu 13-6-1917	Rue du Trône 36 Résidence Cabroke Room 41 7th floor Brussels (2) 3125 468
SOUSSOURO-YIANNIS Evanghelos		5	Greece	N.D.	Kavala 1930	Hotel "Evripidis" Evripidou 79 Athinia (1) 3212 650
VARDAKAS Mihail		13	Greece	N.D.	Thessaloniki	Hotel "Palladion" Panepistimiou 54 Athina (1) 3623 291
					Aristotelous 23 Thessaloniki (031) 271 901
VISAS Themistokles		11	Greece	N.D.	Ptolemaida 13-11-1930	Skoufa 60a Athina 144 (1) 3612 560
VLAHOPOULOS Dimitrios		12	Greece	N.D.	Veria 13-8-1931	Platia Raktivan 1 Veria (0331) 228 51
VOYADZIS Georgios		10	Greece	N.D.	Konistra (Evia) 23-12-1913	Voukourestiou 36 Athina (1) 3601 538

Name	Group	Com-mittees	Member State	Party	Place and date of birth	Address and telephone
ZARDINIDIS Nikos		9	Greece	N.D.	Thessaloniki 17-1-1917	V. Olgas 158 Thessaloniki (031) 823163 ⎫ (031) 823165 ⎬ office (031) 825125 ⎭ (031) 411329 ⎫ private (031) 418614 ⎭
ZIDHDIS Ioannis		4	Greece	E.DH.K.	Lindos (Rhodes) 21-7-1913	Enossi Dimokratikou Kedrou Athina 134 (1) 3612 792 (1) 3609 711

Appendix II
Further Reading

Some suggestions for further reading are set out below. These are by no means exhaustive, and are confined to studies the author has found particularly useful and which are available in English.

1. The European Parliament

BIEBER, R. and PALMER, M.: A Community without a capital, *Journal of Common Market Studies*, Oxford, September 1976.
COCKS, Sir B.: The European Parliament, HMSO, London, 1973.
COOMBES, D.: The future of the European Parliament, PSI, London, 1979.
FITZMAURICE, J.: The party groups in the European Parliament, Saxon House, Farnborough, 1975.
FITZMAURICE, J.: The European Parliament, Saxon House, Farnborough, 1978.
FORSYTH, M.: The Parliament of the European Communities, PEP, London, 1964.
HERMAN, V. and LODGE, J.: The European Parliament and the European Community, MacMillan, London, 1978.
JACKSON, R.: The Powers of the European Parliament, Conservative Group for Europe, London, 1977.
JACKSON, R. and FITZMAURICE, J.: The European Parliament—A guide to the European elections, Penguin, London, 1979.
KIRK, Sir P.: Powers of the European Parliament (as submitted to the European Parliament by Lord Reay following Sir Peter's death), Report on interinstitutional relations, Doc. 148/78, Luxembourg, 1978.
MARQUAND, D.: Parliament for Europe, Cape, London, 1979.
PALMER, M.: The role of a directly elected Parliament, *The World Today*, London, April 1977.
PRIDHAM, J. and PRIDHAM, P.: Towards transnational parties in the European Community, PSI, London, 1979.
Secretariat of the European Parliament: Manual of the European Parliament, Luxembourg, 1979.
Secretariat of the Committee on Budgets of the European Parliament: Purse-strings of Europe—the European Parliament and the Community budget, Information Office of the European Parliament, London, 1979.
The Times: The Times Guide to the European Parliament, London, 1979.

VEDEL, G. et al.: Report of the working party examining the enlargement of the powers of the European Parliament, Bulletin of the European Communities, Supplement 4/72, Brussels, 1972.

2. General

BIEBER, R. and PALMER, M.: Power at the top—the EC Council in theory and practice, *The World Today*, London, August, 1975.

BIESHEUVEL, B., DELL, E. and MARJOLIN, R.: Report of the Committee of Three to the European Council on European Institutions, Brussels, October 1979.

CAMPS, M.: Britain and the European Community, 1955-1963, OUP, Oxford, 1964.

CAMPS, M.: European unification in the sixties, OUP, Oxford, 1967.

HENIG, S. (Ed.): Political parties in the European Community, PSI, London, 1979.

KITZINGER, U.: The challenge of the Common Market, Blackwell, Oxford, 1962.

KLEPSCH, E. and NORMANTON, T.: Two-way street: USA-Europe arms procurement, Brassey's, London, 1979.

MORGAN, R.: Western European integration since 1955: the shaping of the European Community, Batsford, London, 1972.

PALMER, M. et al.: European unity—A survey of the European organisations, PEP, London, 1968.

TINDEMANS, L.: European Union, Report to the European Council, Ministry of Foreign Affairs, Brussels, 1976.

WALLACE, H., WALLACE, W. and WEBB, C.: Policy-making in the European Communities, Wiley, London, 1977.

Appendix III
Recent Developments

Following the completion of the main text of this book in August 1980 three major events involving the Parliament have taken place. These are examined below in chronological order. First, there was the judgment of the Court of Justice concerning the isoglucose case referred to on page 116; second, the adoption of the Community budget for 1981; and third, the accession of Greece to the Community.

On 29 October 1980 the Court of Justice took a decision on the isoglucose case. In its judgment the Court stated that the Council regulation in question was void since the Council had taken its decision before Parliament had given its opinion.

The political significance of the Court's decision is that the Council cannot evade its responsibility to consult Parliament before deciding on Commission legislative proposals. The judgment also implies that the Council should give Parliament a reasonable period of time in which to give its opinion and, further, that the question of how far a Council consultation of Parliament is a question of "urgency" is not for the Council to determine on its own without reference to the views of Parliament.

When examining the preliminary draft budget for the Community for 1981 the Council cut back the estimates prepared by the Commission by more than 820 million u.a. The cuts affected mainly the regional policy, social policy, research and energy sectors and distorted the effort to achieve an improved balance in the budget. When the budgetary procedure reached the final stages during the session of December 1980 Parliament had before it, also, the second supplementary draft budget for 1980 which proposed an addition of 100 million u.a. for the social fund and for aid to the victims of the Italian earthquake disaster. Using its powers adroitly Parliament added 266.4 million u.a. to this darft—primarily to help create employment in certain regions and to assist young people. Having made these extra appropriations available, and knowing that the money from the supplementary budget left unspent in 1980 could be spent during 1981, Parliament went on to vote a relatively modest package of additional expenditure for 1981: 24.5 million u.a. for payments to be made in 1981 with a further 30 million u.a. committed for future expenditure—most of which was also destined for disaster aid to Italy.

The Council did not modify these amendments and the President of Parliament duly declared both budgets adopted on 23 December 1980. Although protests concerning Parliament's tactics were made by a number of member governments and although the Belgian, Danish, French and German Governments originally threatened to withhold payment of the extra appropriations voted by Parliament, Parliament holds that the two budgets were voted and adopted in accordance with the Treaties. In the event of one or more governments withholding payment the Court of Justice might be called upon to take a final decision. By exploiting the procedural possibilities open to it under the Treaties Parliament succeeded in improving the overall balance of Community expenditure.

On 1 January 1981 Greece became a full member of the European Community. For the European Parliament there have been a number of significant consequences.

First, twenty-four Greek parliamentarians have become members of the European Parliament, increasing its size from 410 to 434 members. The Greek members have been nominated by the Greek Parliament but, under the terms of the Treaty of Accession, Greece will hold elections to the European Parliament during 1981. The names of, and relevant information concerning, the Greek members of the European Parliament are set out at the end of Appendix I.

Another major consequence of Greek accession is that Greek has become one of the working languages of the Community. As far as the Parliament is concerned this means that all official documents now appear in Greek as well as in the other six languages of the Community and that interpretation from and into Greek is provided both at plenary sessions and at meetings of Parliament's committees. The recruitment of the necessary Greek linguistic and administrative staff is well advanced.

Further consequences of Greek participation in the European Parliament include the enlargment of the membership of Parliament's committees. The Political Affairs Committee, the Committee on Agriculture, the Committee on Budgets, the Committee on Economic and Monetary Affairs, the Committee on Energy and Research, the Committee on External Economic Relations, the Legal Affairs Committee, the Committee on Social Affairs and Employment, the Committee on Regional Policy and Regional Planning, the Transport Committee and the Committee on Development and Cooperation include two additional Greek members each. The Committee on the Environment, Public Health and Consumer Protection, the Committee on Youth, Culture, Education, Information and Sport, the Committee on Budgetary Control and the Committee on Rules and Petitions have increased their size to include one additional Greek member each.

As a result of the increase in the total number of Parliament's members the numbers of members required to constitute different majorities in votes taken by Parliament have changed. Thus, since January 1981 218 votes are required for a simple majority of Parliament, and the presence of 145 members is necessary to ensure a basic quorum. Changes are also involved in the special procedures laid down for votes under the budgetary procedure, motions of censure on the Commission, and the election of Parliament's officers.

It is probable that Parliament will decide to elect a Greek Vice-President and/or Quaestor. Meetings of Parliament's committees and other organs may now be held in Greece as in other member states of the Community.

A particularly important consequence of Greek participation in the Parliament will be the changed balance between the political groups, depending on the final choice made by Greek members of the political group they wish to join. As of 1 February 1981 the seven members of the Panhellenic Socialist Movement (PA.SO.K.) have decided to sit with the Socialist Group as Allies, and the single member of the Greek Communist Party has decided to join the Communist

Group. The fourteen members of New Democracy have decided to sit, for the time-being, and until they decide whether or not to join one or other of Parliament's political groups, as non-attached members as have the single representative of the Democratic Centre Union and the sole representative of the Democratic Socialist Party.

LIBRARY OF DAVIDSON COLLEGE

Books on regular   two weeks. Books
must be presented
A fine is ch